NORSE PAGANSIM & MYTHOLOGY ULTIMATE COLLECTION 3:1

BE TRANSPORTED INTO THE WORLD OF VIKING CULTURE AND HISTORY. DISCOVER THE MAGIC AND MYSTICISM OF RUNES, NORSE COSMOLOGY, THE GODS AND GODDESSES, CREATURES, MONSTERS, HOLIDAYS, RITUALS & RITES OF PASSAGE

EMMA KARLSSON

© **Copyright October 2023 - All rights reserved.**

The content contained within this book may not be reproduced, duplicated, or transmitted without direct written permission from the author or the publisher.

Under no circumstances will any blame or legal responsibility be held against the publisher or author for any damages, reparation, or monetary loss due to the information contained within this book. Either directly or indirectly. You are responsible for your own choices, actions, and results.

Legal Notice:

This book is copyright-protected. This book is only for personal use. You cannot amend, distribute, sell, use, quote, or paraphrase any part or the content within this book without the consent of the author or publisher.

Disclaimer Notice:

Please note the information contained within this document is for educational and entertainment purposes only. All effort has been executed to present accurate, up-to-date, and reliable, complete information. No warranties of any kind are declared or implied. Readers acknowledge that the author is not engaging in the rendering of legal, financial, medical or professional advice. The content within this book has been derived from various sources. Please consult a licensed professional before attempting any techniques outlined in this book. By reading this document, the reader agrees that under no circumstances is the author responsible for any losses, direct or indirect, which are incurred as a result of the use of the information contained within this document, including, but not limited to, — errors, omissions, or inaccuracies.

EMMA KARLSSON

NORSE MAGIC, RUNES & MYTHOLOGY

Unlock the Ancient Power of the Elder Futhark Through Runic Magic, Learn the Arcane Secrets of Norse Paganism, and Deep Dive Into Viking Folklore of Norse Gods, Goddesses, and Mythology

FREE GIFT JUST FOR YOU!

FREE NORSE GOD & GODDESSES CALENDAR
Use this link https://norsepaganwisdom.info/squeeze-page1679502439646 to get it delivered straight to your email!

OR scan the QR code below:

AN INTRODUCTION TO NORSE MAGIC

> "I know that I hung
> on the wind-swept tree
> all nine nights
> with a spear was I wounded
> and given to Odin,
> myself to me,
> on that tree which no one knows
> from which roots it grows."

Odin, The Prose Edda.

Language, Mystery, Magic, and More

The world around is abound with magic and mystery, with everything possessing a deeper reality than meets the eye. A lake where families gather for picnics may as well be used by someone initiated to the ways of witchcraft to scry the future on the surface of the water. The same clouds that are the portents of joy for a farmer can very well be omens of doom for a shaman.

There are deeper realities than ours. Trees speak to each other in the silence of the forest in secret tongues. The dead hold long talks in the solitude of their graves. Old gods, seated on their thrones, hold discourse in holy languages. At every level, even at the subatomic level of quarks and photons, communication takes place in some language or the other.

Language

It remains an alluring concept in multiple disciplines, whether it's the science of linguistics or the study of ancient civilizations by archeologists. Language, despite being the very tool that uncovers truths and bridges distances, retains its certain shares of mysteries.

Such as where did it come from? Did it evolve over the course of thousands of years from the barbaric caws and yaps of cave-people to this sophisticated tool of nuanced diction and grammar, or did it descend upon us as a revelation from some cosmic source?

Is the nature of language one-dimensional, where words are only used to convey your thoughts, or is there something much more profound at work where words, if spoken with the right intent and inflection, can alter the fabric of nature in a phenomenon known as magic?

If so, does each of us preternaturally possess a propensity toward this paranormal power?

Here, I would like you to take a leap of faith with me and believe that, yes, there *is* something much more profound at work, that we *do* possess an innate albeit mostly dormant talent to harness that power, and that, *yes,* language, besides its natural evolution, did descend upon us from a cosmic source.

Suspend your disbelief, kindle the seeker within, and come with me on a journey that shall take us through time and space into a world of magic, paganism, runes, myth, and mystery. It is a world of Norse magic, paganism, runes, rituals, and powerful gods and goddesses.

A Tale of Sacrifice

I would very much like to begin this book by telling you a story.

A story about a blue-eyed wanderer, a bearded traveler wielding a cane that bears resemblance on second glance to a spear. This lone figure, you can tell, is weathered but not beaten. He has seen much, and much has he braved. Two ravens circle him as he walks, and two wolves trail his steps, ever his eager and loyal companions.

Do not make the mistake of assuming that it is some common mortal. He goes by many monikers and titles. The god of war, for one. The lord of all kingship. He has gone to the most extreme lengths to secure the most arcane magic and archaic knowledge.

What made him a god, perhaps, apart from his omnipotent abilities and his omniscience, was his unquenchable thirst for knowledge. A mortal would have called it quits after reaching a certain point, comfortable that he had learned it all, seen it all, done it all, but not Odin.

Philosophers like Plato and Socrates have often remarked that one of the most humbling aspects of learning includes the realization that you, even after knowing all that you know, don't know anything at all. That the vast sea of unknown far outweighs the bottled known you hold in your hands.

Perhaps it was that same philosophical realization embedded deep within Odin, or perhaps it was that he had to deal with primal forces of nature, almost as powerful as the god himself, sometimes intangible and elusive, to attain sacred knowledge.

For instance, he once stole the Mead of Poetry by taking the shape of an eagle, and once he visited a place of no return, the realm of Hel, to learn about the end of the world from a dead seer.

Apart from the big picture stuff, his two ravens were always flying across the Nine Realms to find out everything they could about what was happening in those worlds, and they would report to him daily.

When Odin's paths came to a drastic crossroads in his quest for knowledge, Odin did not hesitate in sacrificing his own eye to acquire the knowledge from Mimir's well.

He kept a watchful eye on the Norns, the beings who controlled fate and wove the past, present, and future of every being, and learned that they knew more about fate and matters of destiny than anyone else in the world. He observed how they wove fate from the Well of Urd at the roots of Yggdrasil. Odin had great regard for fate and knew that it was such a central force of nature that nothing could avert it.

At this point in our story, Odin stands at the precipice of the Well, contemplating the nature of the sacrifice he has to offer to attain some wisdom from this mysterious and secretive well.

After much meditation, it comes to him. He decides to offer himself as a sacrifice by hanging from the branches of Yggdrasil and piercing himself with his spear.

He hangs like this, in unbearable agony, for nine days and nights. To him, this is a very reasonable sacrifice in exchange for the wisdom of the well and the knowledge of the Norns.

The creatures of the Yggdrasil come to him and try to help him. The eagle, who sits at the top, and the squirrel Ratatoskr who climbs up and down the tree both offer him food and water, but Odin, stalwart in his goal, perseveres without aid.

It is at this point that the Well of Urd takes notice and acknowledges the sacrifice, slowly starting to reveal its knowledge. At first, nine songs are taught to him that contain nine words of power.

Odin can stop here. He knows this. But if he stops, the Well would stop too. So, Odin perseveres harder, and by the end of the ninth day, when he's on the verge of death, the Well of Urd accepts his sacrifice and reveals to him…. runes.

These were more than mere alphabets. Each rune was a symbol containing innate magic, and if used in the right manner, these runes were able to weave magic unlike any.

Odin screams with ecstasy and pain as this knowledge is revealed to him and falls from the tree. His sacrifice has not been for naught. After all, he has just learned the greatest source of magic in the entire universe. Runes.

What You Will Learn In This Book

A large part of this book pertains to runes, and another significant part revolves around Norse magic. However, there's so much more to Norse mythology and magic than just runes and rituals. I'd love to get into all of that with you, primarily:

- How the world of Norse Mythology came into being.
- The Nine Realms of Norse Mythology and the beings that reside in them.
- The Norse Pantheon, including the Æsir and Vanir gods.
- The A-List gods of Norse Mythology, such as Odin, Thor, and Freya.
- An introduction to Norse Paganism.
- A divination of runes.
- The fascinating world of Norse Magic.
- Practicing Norse Magic in our daily lives through different rituals such as Blót and Sumbel.

A Little About Me

Norse Mythology, magic, runes, gods, and goddesses have played a crucial role in my life. Growing up in Kungsträdgården, Sweden, the stories of the gods and goddesses served as a whetstone to the proverbial blade of my imagination. I'd spend days upon days dreaming about the gods and goddesses and doing hilarious cosplays, such as dressing up as Freya and tying a makeshift chariot to my cats.

For me, though, these were more than just folkloric stories. These were the tales of my ancestors. My forefathers believed in these deities and performed these rituals. This realization led me down a rabbit hole of discovery through reading and researching every source I could get my hands on to uncover as much as I could about Norse culture.

Although I was raised Christian, I could never connect with the religion and always felt disconcerted by its beliefs, believing that many of them were forced and contrived. This divide between me and divinity made me dig deeper into my past. That's when I discovered that my ancestors were followers of the old Norse religion. The more I learned about their beliefs, the more I felt them align with my own innate beliefs until a moment of clarity came, and it all clicked into place.

After devoting my time to learning about Norse Mythology and culture, I delved deep into modern practices such as Ásatrú, adopting them into my daily life by performing divination and rituals. The fulfillment and satisfaction that I found in reconnecting with the gods and goddesses and the spirits of my ancestors through these profound practices were second to none.

Why You Should Read This Book

And to you, I extend the same invitation that you rediscover the secrets that were once lost. That you learn about runes, magic, rituals, and beliefs that will transform your life, I can provide you with the framework and tools required to make this journey and initiate you to the old Norse ways.

- If at any time you have felt like you don't know where to begin and how to find your footing in this vast universe, I am here to show you where to start.
- If you're craving deeper knowledge about Norse Mythology after coming across the gods and goddesses in modern media such as video games (God of War, Hellblade, Assassin's Creed), movies (Thor), TV shows (Vikings), and books (American Gods), or any other media, it would be my privilege to share a more mystical and deeper perspective on your favorite icons from Norse mythology such as Loki, Odin, and Thor.
- If you're a keen learner of history, cultures, and religions, then we are well met. There's nothing more amazing than coming across fellow nerds who desire a deep dive into this wondrous topic.
- You may be interested in finding out more about Norse Mythology and its associated rites and rituals after you've taken a DNA test and have discovered that you're related to the Vikings and want to know more about your history.
- If you have felt a calling to the old ways through inexplicable signs, dreams, and visions, or if you've felt drawn to the wisdom of the gods and goddesses and are wondering what it all means, then consider this yet another sign, for you're headed in the right direction. Allow me to be a humble guide in your journey and share some

valuable insights with you that may serve to strengthen your connection with your roots and allow you to connect with the gods through divine rituals.
- Lastly, if you're looking for a reliable source of genuine information on Norse Mythology, let's say, for a school project or a dissertation, then you can use my works as a reference to help you.

Through this book, I aim to teach you about the different forms of magic and divination, give you a solid understanding of who the gods and goddesses were and what domains they held power over, how we prayed to them in the past, and how we can do so in our daily lives now, what modern ceremonies and rituals are being followed by pagans all over the world and how they're connected to the gods and goddesses, and most importantly, how rune magic works.

I hope you're as brimming with excitement and intrigue as I am, for we're going to delve into such rich history and explore such fertile territory of runes, magic, and rituals, that by the time you're finished reading this book, you can confidently say that you're an authority on all these matters.

CHAPTER 1
THE NORDIC BIG BANG — BEGINNING OF NORSE MYTHOLOGY

On the Nature of Myths

Every culture of significance comes with its assorted myths and legends. Some of these are more than just stories and are meant to explain how the world works. A Hindu cleric might have noticed that the night sky resembled a flowing river and concluded that the Ganga flowed down on the earth from the cosmos and that the earth was cradled between the horns of a celestial cow. Abrahamic religions fathomed that the world, which came into being all of a sudden, did so because of the word of God. The Greeks held similar beliefs about the world, believing that Gaia and other divine beings such as Eros, Abyss, and Erebus came from the unending Chaos.

Myths, fables, and legends serve another core function by offering a rational (or rational adjacent) explanation to an otherwise chaotic world. While in other instances, they record such events that are so monumental that they deserve a place in the annals of history. These stories about the supernatural or inexplicable weave themselves into the thread of history and form our current understanding of history.

To that end, there are three types of stories that preserve events or describe phenomena, namely myth, legends, and folklore.

Myths

Myths tackle the big picture stuff, asking questions like where did we come from, how the world came into being, and who granted us the ability to create fire or speak in different languages. But more relevantly, myths concern divinity. They try to unravel the mystery of gods and goddesses and lend credence to their existence through stories.

Because of the diverse range of topics that myths cover, they have generally been categorized into three types:

- **Psychological Myths**
- **Historical Myths**
- **Etiological Myths**

Psychological myths detail journeys that start from the known and end in the unknown such as Oedipus's tale, who travels far away to avoid the prediction that he'll end up killing his father. In this new land, he ends up killing a man who was his father and who had similarly abandoned the same land because he, too, wanted to prevent the prophecy from coming true. The psychological nature of this myth contains a moral lesson that it is futile to avoid your fate as decreed by the gods.

Historical myths retell actual events and elevate them by restructuring the narrative in a grandiose manner. The siege of Troy is described in Homer's Iliad in a reframed way, changing the nature of the story from being factual to being a historical myth.

Etiological myths are concerned with explaining how something came to be or why it is the way it is. Origin stories, in other terms. Thunder, for example, according to etiological myths, is the sound of Thor's chariot racing across the sky. In etiological myths, characters tend to serve a purpose that aligns their role with the story's actions or consequences. In Chinese mythology, Nuwa, the goddess, upon growing tired of creating humans over and over again, decided to call it quits and introduce the practice of marriage so that humans could reproduce on their own.

Perhaps one of the best-known etiological myths is the story of Demeter and her daughter, Persephone. Persephone gets kidnapped by the god of the underworld, Hades. Demeter, who was the goddess of grain and harvest, became so sorrowful at being apart from her daughter that all the crops started failing, and people began starving. Zeus ordered Hades to return Persephone to her mother. However, Persephone, having eaten some of the pomegranate seeds from the underworld, has to spend half of the year under the earth but could come back to the earth for the other half.

Besides telling this epic where Demeter's sorrow moved the gods to interfere with Hades to return Persephone, this myth also tries to explain why seasons changed the way they did in Greece back then. When the weather was warm, and the fields were full, Persephone was assumed to be united with her mom. When it was cold and dark, and barren, people assumed that Persephone was biding her time in the underworld and her mom was mourning.

Legends

Legends are a little more grounded when it comes to the subject matter, dealing not with gods and divinity as much as they do with tales of heroes who perform feats of nobility, courage, and bravery. Legends of people like Ragnar Lothbrok, Robin Hood, and King Arthur have an element of fantasy to them where the stories are sometimes inflated in their magnitude as they pass through generations.

Folklore

Folklores are stories that depict beliefs and convictions, especially those that are confined to a particular region. Fairies in England, the Loch Ness monster in Scotland, Draugrs in Scandinavia, and Djinns in Arabia are all examples of folklore. Some of these folkloric tales are rooted in superstition whilst others are contorted versions of the truth. Regardless of their origin, these serve to entertain and educate people with moralistic values often tethered to them.

Norse Mythology embodies all three types of tales. The great fables of Odin and Thor are examples of myths preserved by historians like Snorri Sturluson. Legends of Erik the Red and Ragnar Lothbrok are instances where the mythology doesn't just rely on gods and goddesses but focuses on the mortal side as well. And folklore about mystical creatures like Huldra and Fossegrim shows us that Norse Mythology is rich with its fair share of folk tales.

The pre-Christian religion, beliefs, legends, and myths of the Scandinavian and Icelandic people are the primary source of Norse Mythology, with many of these stories being shared and propagated by the Northern Germanic tribes of the 9th century. Most of these stories were passed down in the form of poems, songs, and ballads until they were compiled in the form of Eddas and medieval texts between the 11th and 18th centuries.

As with all tales that stand the test of time, the very best of them were compiled and preserved in the Poetic and Prose Edda, which are considered two of the chief references of Norse Mythology.

The old gods took measures to make sure their tales survived time, invasion, and missionaries from other religions. The very air of Scandinavia can attest to that. Even if there were no sources left, the names of old towns and cities would remain, many of which are named after Norse deities. And say, if you will, that even those cease to exist, then the runic inscriptions spread throughout Scandinavia will attest to the existence of the gods. Besides runic inscriptions, a lot of imagery still survives from the old days, depicting scenes such as Thor's fishing trip and Odin being devoured by Fenrir. Many figurines from that era have survived, showing Thor, Freyr, and Odin.

So long as there are devout followers of the Old Norse Religion, and so long as there are reliable sources that have resiliently stood the test of time, we do not have to worry about this great culture losing itself to oblivion. Not while there are kindred spirits such as you and me. The great news I have for you is this: We are an ever-growing movement. Every day, more people are finding their ancient roots and reconnecting with Norse Mythology and its practices through modern paganism sects like Ásatrú, Vanatru, Rokkatru, Heathenism, Lokeans, and so much more. Many New Age movements and recent belief systems, such as Wicca, Witchcraft, and Shamanism, have also adopted various aspects of Norse Mythology.

I can assure you we're only going to keep growing.

The more accessible our modern world has become, the more it has allowed people to get their hands on information that was previously obscure or purposefully kept hidden from them. Not so long ago, there was a time when the Christianization of Europe declared all paganistic elements to be blasphemous. Witches were burnt, heretics were hung, and blasphemers were banished. But that was then, and this is now. Now is our time.

With the internet, social media, and online forums, we have found others like us and formed online and IRL communities, communities that have enabled us to rebirth the ancient religion in new forms.

I can only say that we're living in exciting times where we're getting to witness this rebirth in real-time. It's almost cyclical in nature, much like Norse cosmology, where the end is not an end but a new beginning.

So let's begin anew this tale of cosmic creation and discuss the origin of Norse Mythology itself.

The Beginning, Before, and After

Before there was anything, there was the endless space, the gap known as Ginnungagap, which in Old Norse meant gaping abyss. This is where the Norse creation myth begins.

In the North of that gap was a well known as the Hvergelmir. The great World Tree, Yggdrasil, drew water from this well.

As it happened, the north of the Ginnungagap was intensely cold. Whatever water was not consumed by the Yggdrasil fled up north, where it froze and eventually formed the icy world of Niffelheim.

Ginnungagap's south was as hot as its north was cold. As it grew hotter, the fiery region started to form a realm that was the polar opposite of Niffelheim. This came to be known as Muspelheim, the realm of fire and blaze.

Amidst the endless nothing of the cosmos, something started happening that would serve as the prelude to the world as we know it. The heat from Muspelheim slowly started reaching the cold recesses of Niffelheim, eventually thawing some of the ice and causing water droplets to descend to Muspelheim, where when they came into contact with the fire, they caused sparks.

As this process perpetuated, more water fell on the billowing flames and caused steam and mist to emanate and concentrate until finally, it took shape of the first sentient being, Ymir, the giant. Who knows for how long all that flame and mist and steam must have infused until it became cognizant enough and formed a body?

Ymir, otherwise known as the Screamer, was hermaphroditic, reproducing asexually. When this giant slept, more giants birthed from his legs and the warm sweat of his armpits.

But Ymir and his children weren't the only beings to come forth at this early stage. As the frost melted, a cow, Auðumbla, named so because she hummed in abundance, emerged. This cow had a maternal inclination; she nourished Ymir with her milk. As for her own nutrition, she licked the salt atop the icy rocks of Niffelheim. Through her continued licking, the ice started taking shape. Eventually, the ice took the shape of Buri, the first god.

Buri then had a child named Borr. Though, how he did that is shrouded in mystery. Buri also had a daughter named Bestla, whom Borr married. In other lore, Bestla was one of the first Jötnar who were formed from Ymir's sweat.

Borr and Bestla became parents to three sons, Odin, Vili, and Ve.

The three brothers saw the cruelty of Ymir and his children. In some cases, they even experienced it firsthand. Ymir was chaotic, hoarding, and violent. If Ymir was the epitome of unrealized potential and chaos, the brothers were the opposite. They realized their powers, tapped into them, and plotted to kill Ymir.

They succeeded in killing Ymir. It was only after taking the first giant's life that the brothers found themselves thrust into the process of creation.

A note here. What do Ymir and the Ginnungagap depict, if not chaos and the state of rawness before creation? The Ginnungagap was unending and limitless in its potential, but all of that potential was unrealized for the longest time. Similarly, Ymir, rather than seeking an order or choosing to become an active participant in the process of creation, through his nature, opted to be a source of violence and havoc. The gods, as soon as they came into being, realized their potential, sought order, and did what they could to give the chaotic world around them some semblance of form.

After they killed Ymir, rivers of blood flowed from the dead giant's body, flowing away most of Ymir's children. Those who remained became the progenitors of the Jötnar. Ymir's body hung suspended in the center of the Ginnungagap.

The brothers saw the corpse and realized what had to be done. They had to create something out of this humungous dead body. They formed the surface of the world with his body and used his blood to make bodies of water such as rivers and seas. His bones and teeth were erected to create the mountains and fjords. The gods were very resourceful in their creative process, not letting any part of Ymir go to waste.

From his skull, they created the sky dome and used his brains as clouds. Odin and his brothers captured the sparks flying from Muspelheim and placed them in the sky to serve the purpose of stars, the moon, and the sun.

The gods, having experienced chaos, knew the challenge it posed and how the beings of chaos, the Jötnar, could possibly cause turbulence to the lives of those who would live on this new world. As a precautionary measure, they took the eyebrows of the dead giant and built a wall around this land to keep it secure.

They dubbed this world Midgard, calling it so because of Yggdrasil's frame of reference and Midgard's relative position to it.

Once they were satisfied with the world they had created, they began creating the beings who would reside in this world. They took tree branches and carved them in the shape of a man and woman and imbued them with life. The man and woman were named Ask and Embla and were sent forth into Midgard to live and propagate the race of humanity.

Around this time, new worlds also formed. One such world, called Asgard, became the home of Odin and his kin. Jötunnheim became home to the Jötunn. Other beings nestled in other realms, such as the dwarves in Svartalfheim and the elves in Alfheim.

During the process of Midgard's creation, worms kept crawling out of Ymir's rotting body. Eventually, these worms evolved into dwarves. Odin, Vili, and Ve noticed that the sky would fall if it were not held up at all times. To take care of its precarious nature, they designated four dwarves to hold up the sky. Each dwarf was sent in each direction. Nordi to North, Vestri to West, Sundri to South, and Austri to East. The remaining dwarves who were not given such duties made their home in the rocks and caverns of Svartalfheim, where, through the refinement of their craft, they became masters of forgery and smithery, creating such powerful weapons as Mjolnir, Thor's hammer.

We will get to see these worlds, the beings that thrive in them, and how these worlds shape the history, present, and future of Norse mythology. A few of these worlds will also play a key role in Ragnarök.

Norse Mythology In Our Modern World

There's no doubt about it that Norse Mythology is enjoying a very three-dimensional renaissance in our popular culture, from novels like *The Gospel of Loki* becoming bestsellers to video games like *God of War: Ragnarök* stealing the show at The Game Awards 2022. And who can forget the box-office hit *Thor* movies that introduced us to a whimsical version of Norse Mythology as imagined by Marvel?

Modern video games with hyperrealism and photorealism have created jaw-dropping spectacles where playing each game—*God of War, Assassin's Creed: Valhalla, Hellblade*—feels not like playing a childish game but instead going on a digital pilgrimage across these beautifully recreated lands. As Kratos in *God of War*, you journey through the Nine Realms, come face to face with central figures, and play a key role in the events that shaped Norse Mythology. As an Assassin in *Assassin's Creed*, you don the garb of a Viking as you go on expeditions across England, truly putting yourself in the shoes of those fierce warriors. In *Hellblade*, you get to witness the brutal and raw nature of the Vikings and Scandinavia from a Celtic perspective, descending into Helheim itself and coming across Hela.

There's something for everyone's palettes, for if someone wants a more nuanced approach to the tales of old, there's always *Vikings* by History Channel, which shows the mythos for what it truly is—often bleak, unforgiving, and brutal—and instead of myths, focuses on legends and tells the stories of famous Viking figures such as Ragnar Lothbrok and Erik the Red. There is an entire ecosystem of Norse channels on YouTube where people nerd out about the Vikings, the Norse deities, and ancient Nordic practices reimagined and repurposed for the 21st century.

And I do mean three-dimensional. It's not just pop-culture that has been infused with Norse Mythology, providing us spectacles like Neil Gaiman's *American Gods* and mental-health-oriented games like *Hellblade: Senua's Sacrifice*; Norse Mythology has been resuscitated in a religious and cultural form as well. For thousands of people, it's more than just entertainment; it's a way of life. For thousands of others, it's a way to reconnect with their long-lost roots. Paganistic sects with ties to the Old Norse religion have proudly hoisted their colors in different forms, such as Ásatrú, Vanatru, Heathenry, Shamanism, and Wicca.

Those who practice Norse Paganism have delved beyond the superficial adaptations and have truly embraced that lifestyle by performing runic magic, creating altars for worship and invocation, aligning themselves with the Norse beliefs, and celebrating the holidays of the Norse calendar. I aim to provide you with the necessary background information first and then introduce you to the rituals, runes, and rites that will allow you to become a profound partaker in the subtler and deeper aspects of Norse Mythology.

With that in mind, we're going to learn more about the Nine Realms in the upcoming chapter and then learn about the various deities and beings that reside in those realms.

CHAPTER 2
THE NINE REALMS

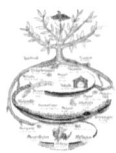

Norse Cosmology has ten important locations that are central to the stories, the adventures of the gods, and the conflict that will eventually cause Ragnarök .

There is a bit of prejudice in historical accounts when writing about the realms as most of the descriptions and stories concern Midgard, it being the home to our race and the only world that we as humans were most familiar with.

These ten locations include:

- Yggdrasil — the World Tree which nestles all the realms.
- Asgard — Realm of the Æsir gods, joined to Midgard through the Bifrost.
- Alfheim — Where the elves dwelled.
- Vanaheim — Realm of the Vanir gods.
- Svartalfheim — Realm of the dwarves.

- Muspelheim — The realm of fire, where Surtr, the fire giant, lived and nourished his forces of chaos.
- Niffelheim — A place of ice, snow, cold, and mist.
- Helheim — A realm where those who died of natural causes, illnesses, and old age went. It's also where Hel, the goddess of the underworld, lives.
- Midgard — Our realm, the realm of human beings.
- Jötunnheim — The land of frost giants, the Jötnar.

Yggdrasil

The great eternal ash tree stands in the center of the universe, its branches stretching out all across the cosmos, cradling the Nine Realms within it. Each Realm has its branch. All life depends upon this tree, as any harm to the Yggdrasil would destroy all realms.

We discussed this tree in the beginning when we read about Odin's journey to divine runes. Yggdrasil is vast, with three giant roots extending deep below. Each root has a well alongside it to nourish it with water and nutrients. The first root is uncannily deep, reaching below Niffelheim, where the realm of Helheim is situated. The first root has a well known as Hvergelmir, also known as the Well of Poison, and yet, this is the same well from where the water rose at the beginning that turned to mist and steam and formed Ymir.

A great dragon by the name of Níðhöggr is trapped under the first root, harming it every moment by chewing on it. On Ragnarök, the dragon will succeed in breaking free from the root and cause havoc hitherto undreamt of.

The second root is in the land of frost giants, besides a well known as Mimir's well, also known as The Well of Wisdom. Mimir drinks from this well and attains wisdom from it. Sometimes, he lets other beings drink from it as well, but at the cost of a heavy sacrifice. When Odin wanted to drink from this well, Mimir asked him to sacrifice something, in response to which Odin tore out his eye and flung it into the water.

The third root is in Asgard and has a well known as the Well of Urd, where the Norns—masters of fate and the personification of destiny and time—reside. The Norns collect water from the well and pour it over Yggdrasil to sustain it. If they stop doing so, the tree will rot.

Yggdrasil has many denizens, such as the mischievous squirrel called Ratatoskr and the elusive eagle who sits atop the tree. The tree has a very protective and paternal role. At Ragnarök, the last two human beings will find shelter inside the tree and will remain within its sanctuary until the end is over, and it's safe to go out.

Asgard

There are few realms in mythologies in general as resplendent as Asgard. Olympus comes to mind, but even Olympus was not as humungous in size as to span an entire cosmic body that the gods called home. For you to understand the sheer scale of Asgard, I'll tell you this: There are dozens of realms within Asgard's walls that are ecosystems of their own such as Valhalla or Fólkvangr, where the Valkyries escort those who died valiantly.

Besides being massive, Asgard is the pinnacle of luxury and magnificence. It is, after all, the land of the Æsir gods. Of the Nine Realms, the only two Realms that have been written prolifically about are Midgard and Asgard.

Odin rules Asgard, holding dominion over other Æsir gods and the brave souls of the martyrs, also known as the einherjar. Complete with castles, throne-rooms, armories, banquet halls, and courtyards, it was a kingdom of plenty, with fortifications barring it from the rest of the world, a magical bridge connecting it to other lands, and vast fields, lush forests, deep rivers, towering mountains, grand fjords, and tumultuous oceans giving it a geographical diversity.

Its halls had hundreds of rooms, its lands were expansive and everywhere in the realm, and the air was vibrant with magic. One of these massive halls with more than five hundred rooms was Valhalla, where the fallen warriors reveled in endless feasts and engaged in sportsmanly displays of fights. Flames roared in fireplaces, and massive boars were roasted for these warriors, also known as the einherjar. They would drink mead and regale each other with tales of their battles on Earth. They'd be reunited with their forefathers in this hall, this hall made of shields and spears.

Another regal location within Asgard was Hliðskjálf, the palace of Odin, where from his throne, he could see into every realm. Other gods had similar halls as well, such as Bilskirnir, Thor's hall, which was said to be one of the grandest halls in Valhalla. Thor had his own land there, too, known as Thrudheim. Freya, another notable goddess, had a field where she'd bring the spirits of the fallen warriors. This field was called Fólkvangr. Baldur, another Æsir god, had a home in Asgard known as Breiðablik, a place so pure and clean that no evil thing could exist within it. Heimdall, a chief god, had a home called Himinbjörg near the border of Asgard near the Bifrost, from where he could watch over all things.

Alfheim

A place of light, beauty, glamour, and radiance, Alfheim was home to the elves. They were described as beings more beautiful than the sun, and their world was a just reflection of its residents.

Alfheim is said to have been ruled by Freyr, the god of fertility, virility, and prosperity. Freyr was originally a Vanir god and was given the realm of Alfheim as a tooth gift, a gift given to infants when they broke their first tooth.

There's a deep relationship between the Vanir gods and nature. While the Æsir gods have more political, physical, and magical strength, the Vanir gods make use of their connection with nature to foster natural growth, fertility, and harmony with all living things. That Freyr was given Alfheim as a gift tells us that Alfheim and its residents must also have been kindred spirits with the Vanir when it came to a respectful relationship with nature.

The Eddas and other surviving texts do not go into great detail about Alfheim, primarily because the elves and Alfheim, as such, do not have much of a narrative role to play in the stories and myths of Norse Mythology. But this has not stopped others to draw inspiration from the

Alfheim elves and their native land, as many authors, especially those of Indo-European literature, reimagined elves and introduced them in their own books. Tolkien comes to mind, with his version of elves and their lands, such as Rivendell, depicting the same resplendence as the source of their inspiration.

The elves who resided in Alfheim were beautiful, intelligent, magical, and had an inclination towards music, arts, and other forms of creativity.

The geographical inspiration for Alfheim was the land between Sweden and Norway between the rivers Gota and Glom, a place that was quite beautiful and bright as compared to the rest of Scandinavia and whose people appeared fairer and more artistic. However, this is just a scholarly claim, and it is not entirely a well-rooted claim at that.

Vanaheim

Home to the Vanir gods, this Realm was a counterpart to Asgard and was the birthplace of Njord, who was the patriarch of the Vanir.

Unfortunately, most of the descriptions in the Eddas are about Midgard and Asgard and shed little light on the other realms, but there are still some scant details mentioned that allow us to learn more about this world.

Even though there isn't much written about Vanaheim or the gods living therein, the Norse people revered the Vanir gods because of their prowess when it came to nature, land, fertility, and holistic magic. In fact, the major war between the Vanir and Æsir took place because of this reason. The Vanir were much more loved by the people and received more sacrifices and offerings as a result.

Even though battle and warfare were the specialties of the Æsir gods, the Vanirs held their own in that war, and eventually, after much bloodshed, the two sides came to a truce. Njord, Freyr, and Freya, three Vanir gods, were sent to live with the Æsir, and Mimir and Hoenir, two Æsir gods, were sent to Vanaheim as part of this barter.

Because of the truce, the gods from both groups were considered equals and would receive an equal amount of honor and sacrifice from the humans.

The underlying reason why the Vanir were, before the war, much more beloved to the humans was because of the powers that fell within their purview. Freya and Freyr were both deities related to the fertility of different types—humans, animals, and crops. Njord was related to the sea, which the Norse people had to rely on for both travel and food. While worshiping the Æsir helped humans in matters such as government, warfare, might, intelligence, and politics, worshipping the Vanir meant prosperity in terms of fertility, peace, happiness, and affluence.

Besides Freya, Freyr, and Njord, some other Vanir deities included Gersemi, Hnoss, Gullveig, and Kvasir.

Lastly, the stark difference between the residents of Vanaheim and Asgard was their perspective on rules. Among the main reasons for the war between the Æsir and Vanir, besides the worship bias, was their opposing view on rules. The Æsir believed that humans should follow strict rules and structure, while the Vanir were more lenient.

One such example of this was the marriage between siblings. While the Æsir completely forbade such an act, the Vanir often married among siblings. Njord was married to his sister. The two had Freya and Freyr. We will discuss more the Æsir and Vanir in the upcoming chapter about the Norse pantheon.

Jötunheimr / Jötunheimar / Jötunnheim

The land of the giants was a cold, desolate, rugged, and mountainous region, with its residents being hostile to outsiders, especially the gods. There was a rivalry between the gods and the giants from the beginning, and the giants remembered this.

Throughout the accounts and Eddas, the giants are described as chaotic beings of violence and malice. This has been mentioned so many times that one cannot help but wonder if the authors were biased in favor of the gods. As Norse mythology has often shown us time and again, there's no such thing as black or white in that world. Evil is not entirely evil, and good is not necessarily good. Loki, often seen as a similar agent of chaos, has redeemed himself many times by doing the right thing. Thor, on the other hand, dubbed good and brave and a friend of humans has sometimes gone out to hunt and kill giants as a sport.

Jötunnheim was the place where the giants took shelter after Ymir was killed, and his blood wiped away most of his offspring. The remaining giants having good reason to hate the gods for killing their ancestors.

The Eddas describe this land as bleak. There is constant darkness looming on the horizon. The forests are deep and dark. The mountains are unconquerable and jagged. There is no fertility here. The giants adapted to this harsh climate by hunting and fishing.

Another important aspect of this land is the river Iving that separates Jötunnheim from Midgard and Asgard. This river never freezes and thus prevents the giants from crossing over to those other realms.

Jötunnheim was also known as Utgard, which translated to "world beyond the fence." Unlike the ordered structure and norms found in Asgard and Midgard, lawlessness and chaos prevailed in Jötunnheim.

Some of the most prominent residents of Jötunnheim include Skadi, Gerd, Jarnsaxa, Bestla, Grid, Rindr, Gunnlod, Hrod, Jord, and Sigyn.

One last interesting bit of trivia about Jötunnheim is that when Thor visits the stronghold of the giant Utgard-Loki, he is told that nothing that Thor will experience on his journey is what it appears to be and that nothing is to be trusted.

Svartalfheim

The dwarves of Norse mythology are very goal-oriented, single-minded, and driven. These characteristics have enabled them to become masters of their smithing craft. The only two times that Svartalfheim is mentioned in the Eddas are related to the craft of the dwarves.

In the first tale, the gods go to the realm to find chains that will be powerful enough to hold a monolithic wolf known as Fenrir. In the second tale, Loki travels to the realm to find Andvari and seize his gold.

The gods rely upon the dwarves in many ways. When Midgard was made, Odin and his brothers sent forth four dwarves in each direction to hold the sky aloft. Because of their craftsmanship, the gods have come to the dwarves time and again for powerful weapons and artifacts. The dwarves made Thor's hammer and Odin's spear. They even built a magic ship for Freyr. The Mead of Poetry is also the creation of the dwarves.

Unlike Jötunnheim, Svartaflheim is not grim. It is dark, sure, and it has many caverns, caves, mines, and forges, but it is not without its share of warmth and homeliness. The dwarves live in the caves, mine in them, and make weapons in them. Call to mind the Mines of Moria from *Lord of the Rings*.

In one of the famous tales written in the Edda, Loki cuts off Thor's wife's hair. Thor seizes Loki and is about to break every bone in his body when Loki says that he's going to make everything all right by traveling to Svartalfheim.

Loki then goes to the realm and seeks out the dwarves. He asks them to make golden hair for Sif. But Loki does not want to stop there. He also commissions them to make an unsinkable ship and a deadly spear.

Loki being Loki, a master of mischief and cunning, finds the two best metalsmiths in the realm and then taunts them that they cannot craft anything as awesome as the items he already possesses. The brothers take the bait and make him a golden-haired boar that glows in the dark and runs through air and water, and can travel faster than any horse. They also make him a golden ring that sprouts eight identical rings every ninth night, and, of course, Mjolnir.

When he returns to Asgard, he gives the golden hair to Sif and the hammer to Thor. One can only suspect that Loki robbed Sif of her original hair for a chance to go to Svartalfheim and get the dwarves to make all these magical artifacts and weapons for him.

Muspelheim

This primeval world of fire was the source and catalyst for creation, along with the other elemental world, Niffelheim. The flames from Muspelheim caused mist and steam to rise after some water from Niffelheim dropped on it, thus creating Ymir and Auðumbla.

This realm will also play a key role in the destruction of the world. Just as the fire from this realm once made Ymir's existence possible, so too will its fires cause the annihilation of the world during Ragnarök .

The fire-giant Surtr will rise from this realm and use his flaming sword to burn the world and kill the gods.

The realm of fire was so remote and dangerous that few seldom ventured there. Besides fiery chasms of flame and magma, there is a vanguard of fire giants commanded by Surtr waiting for his command. When Surtr will rise, he will command his vanguard to go forth and take the fire of Muspelheim with them and destroy the entire world.

Surtr will face off in battle with Freyr. Freyr, who will have given his trusty sword to his servant, will be left relatively compromised and will die in this battle. The last thing the world will know before its death will be Muspelheim's flames.

There is a poetic irony here that Norse mythology starts with ice and flame and ends with ice and flame. It further embeds the notion of the cyclical nature of reality deeper in the belief system of those who follow Norse paganism.

Muspelheim and Niffelheim are considered cosmic constants that control the fate of the world through their continuous existence. After the world will end as a result of Ragnarök, it will begin anew in a similar fashion to how it began once. Because of the chaos it represented and because of its sheer primordiality, it was respected and feared by the Norse people.

Niffelheim

Niffelheim literally means the world of fog. One of the two primeval worlds, this world is the polar opposite of Muspelheim and is host to darkness, cold, mist, ice, and frost. It was because of this realm that Buri, the first of the gods, came into existence after Auðumbla kept licking the ice for her nourishment.

In so many accounts, the world of Niffelheim is often used synonymously with Helheim. There are differences in the accounts, leading to some scholars claiming that both realms were the same and other scholars saying that they were two different lands.

Snorri Sturluson, the author of the Poetic Edda, claimed that most terrible things emerged from Niffelheim, hinting that the world was not just primordial but also a place of evil.

Midgard

Midgard's name suggests that its position was in the center of all the nine realms, cradling it in such a way that the holier worlds of Asgard, Alfheim, and Vanaheim were above it while the drearier lands like Jötunnheim and Hel were below it.

We have already looked at Midgard's creation and the subsequent population at length in the previous chapter.

It is said that the gods feared the offspring of Loki and Angrboða as Odin divined to them that they are going to be the harbingers of Ragnarök. So, as a precautionary measure, the gods separated the siblings. One of these children was the colossal serpent Jörmungandr. The gods flung him into the ocean that surrounded Midgard. Here, the serpent grew and grew until it was humungous enough to envelop the entire world by coiling around it and putting his tail in his mouth.

Thor is often depicted as an ally to Midgard and a friend to its people. He would visit the people often and have a jolly good time.

Upon Ragnarök, the sun and moon will disappear from Midgard's sky, and the earth will start shaking fiercely, causing the trees to topple and the mountains to fall. Jörmungandr will emerge from the water and throw venom in every direction. When he gets out, he'll cause giant waves to drown the realm, eventually destroying it as a result of his battle with Thor.

Helheim

People often mistake the Christian version of Hell for Helheim based on the similar name, but Helheim means "house of Hel" and has no resemblance to the infernal Abrahamic hell.

One of the Nine Realms, this place serves as the afterlife abode for souls who died of old age, natural causes, or disease.

Just as Jörmungandr was thrown to Midgard and Fenrir was chained, Hel, the daughter of Loki, was banished to this realm to avert Ragnarök for as long as possible. Hel is described to be half black and half flesh-colored, showing that she's half dead and half alive. Hel quickly took command of this realm and attained dominion over the souls of the dead.

Hel was not exactly bound in Helheim. She was free to move within her realm as she pleased and even had a home under Yggdrasil's branches. While Helheim didn't exactly have burning pyres of lava pits, it was still a dreadful place because of the cold, fog, and darkness. This was not intentional. It was just the nature of this place. Hel tried to make the people who came here as comfortable as possible, often giving them gifts and lodging in an attempt to provide them some small comfort.

Once a soul traversed to Hel, it could not come back. One of the most popular instances of this is when Baldur, the beloved god of the Æsir, died because of Loki's trickery. Hermod volunteered to go to Hel on Frigg's behalf. Odin lent him his steed, Sleipnir, and even on that steed, it took nine nights for Hermod to travel between the realms. Hermod saw that Baldur was being treated quite honorably in Hel. He asked Hel if he could take him back. Hel said that if everything in the world would weep for him, she'd consider sending him back.

Hermod went back to Asgard and told the gods of this. The gods spread the word throughout the Nine Realms, asking every creature to weep for Baldur. Everyone cried, except for Thokk, an old giantess who said that she had no love for Odin and his kin and she'd rather let Baldur stay in Hel then mourn him. Some sources claim that Thokk was Loki in disguise.

Because the wager was not fulfilled, Baldur had to stay in Hel indefinitely.

Before Ragnarök, Hel will rise from Helheim with her horde of the dead. Jörmungandr will emerge from the sea. Fenrir will break free from his chains. A battle like none other will take place where Loki will command the armies of the dead, eventually causing the end of the world.

Other notable creatures residing within Hel include the dragon Níðhöggr, the guard-dog Garm, and a Völva whom Odin used to receive prophecies of Ragnarök.

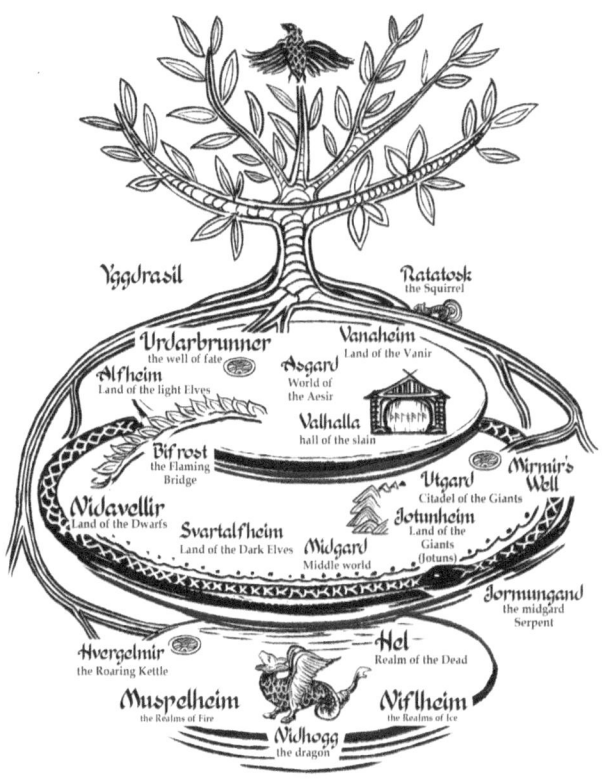

In this chapter, we learned about Norse cosmology, including the World Tree and the Nine Realms. In the upcoming chapter, we will look at the pantheon of Norse Mythology and shed light on the two main clans of gods, the Æsir and the Vanir. After that, we're going to look at their abilities and their distinguishing features. The reason this information is important is that it gives us insight into how different magics, rituals, and rites work concerning different deities.

CHAPTER 3
THE PANTHEON OF NORSE MYTHOLOGY

Before the Eddas and other such volumes were compiled somewhere between the 11th and 18th centuries, the stories that we now know as Norse Mythology were passed down in the form of poetry. Often, these tales were told around the fire, much in a folkloric sense, and just as often, these tales were told to the children by their parents to instill the importance of their culture from an early age.

The old Norse religion and the assorted myths came from the Northern Germanic tribes of the 9th AD. Before Christianity became prevalent through missionary work, the Scandinavian people, including the Icelandic folk, adhered to the old Norse religion. The Norse Mythology we know of today comes from figures and stories derived from multiple sources, including medieval scripts, archeological evidence, and folklore. It is a descendant of the Indo-European religion of the late Neolithic period.

The gods and goddesses they worshipped were divided into two main categories, the Æsir and the Vanir. Most of what we know about these deities comes from Snorri Sturluson's Prose Edda and Poetic Edda.

The Æsir Gods

Descendants of Buri, the first god, the Æsir gods embodied power, warfare, might, politics, and strength. They were known for their physical traits and their military tactics as compared to the Vanir, who had more of a natural disposition. There are more significant differences between the two groups, including their values. While the Æsir are more concerned with how the humans who worship them should be more adherent to rules and order, the Vanir believe that humans should be granted leniency and should do as they please. The Æsir valued strength and battle tactics, while the Vanir valued nature, harmony with one's surroundings, and mysticism.

The term Æsir comes from ansaz, which means beam or pole, or ansuz, which means life or vitality.

They were natives of Asgard and, with their collective governance under Odin, were able to hold dominion over the cosmos for a certain period. Unlike deities from other mythologies, the Æsir were not entirely immortal. They had to consume golden apples from Iðunn's tree to maintain their immortality and their strength. Even according to the lore, the gods were destined to die at Ragnarök, creating a stark difference between Norse gods and gods from other religions.

They are worshipped to this day, especially by neo-paganism sects like Ásatrú, which was built upon the polytheistic foundation of the old Norse religion.

While we're only going through the names of the gods and goddesses for now, we're going to take a deeper look at the A-list of Norse deities in the next chapter. Some of the most prominent Æsir gods include:

Odin

The chief of the Æsir, Odin, was known for his love for knowledge and his quests for wisdom. He had sacrificed so much in his journey to attain the truth. Besides being an ardent pursuer of knowledge, Odin was a god of war and held dominion over battlefields.

Because of his many salient attributes, he is considered the patron deity of poets, slain warriors, kings, and courageous men. He oversees the fallen warriors in Valhalla.

Frigg

Frigg was Odin's wife. She was a clever and attentive goddess by nature, she was the embodiment of regality. Everything that she did reflected her stature. She lived in the marshlands of Fensalir. Frigg was the mother of Baldur, Hod, and Hermod.

Loki

Odin once called Loki his blood brother. Loki is a half-giant and embodies the jötunn chaos within him in almost everything he does. One of the most catastrophic seeds of chaos that he sows is the children from his marriage with the Jötunn Angrboða. The three children, Hel, Jörmungandr, and Fenrir, all play a role in Ragnarök.

Thor

Considered a divine figure to the people of Midgard and hailed as a champion in Asgard, Thor, the god of thunder, was the son of Odin, husband to Sif, and a somewhat loving father to his three children. One of Thor's defining features was his hotheadedness when it came to the giants. He was always picking fights with them, and after he got his hands on his magical hammer, Mjolnir, the fights became a bit one-sided.

Baldur

Baldur was so beautiful that his mother made every living thing take a vow not to hurt him. Loki, being the personification of chaos that he was, decided to find out the one thing that had not taken the vow. Mistletoe. Yes. Mistletoe, of all things. He fashioned arrows out of mistletoe and managed to get Baldur killed, which eventually plunged the world into Fimbulwinter, the prelude to Ragnarök. Loki was soon after imprisoned for his crime.

Tyr

The Norse god of war, treaties, and justice, Tyr was known for binding Fenrir by sacrificing his hand to subdue the giant wolf. Tyr was the son of Odin and, as such, embodied his father's wisdom and valiance. The Romans equated Tyr to their god of war, Mars.

Var

The goddess Var was the goddess of promises, oaths, and agreements between two people. Her realm is concerned with more than just treaties, as she's concerned with punishing oath breakers.

Back in those days, oaths were taken upon items such as swords, rings, and shields. The people were expected to uphold their oaths, and if the said oath was broken, there was a terrible penalty for it.

Gefjun

Gefjun was the goddess of plenty, virginity, prosperity, and agriculture. She was responsible for keeping people's hearts full and for maintaining prosperity within storehouses. That's why her name originated from Gefa, which meant to give. She played a very integral role in agriculture, especially in the act of plowing.

Vor

Vor was a goddess of truth and prophecy. She was wise and ancient, having served as the handmaiden of Frigg ever since the end of the great war between the Æsir and the Vanir. Before that, she was an advisor to Odin.

Vor was originally from Jötunnheim, but after she pledged herself to Frigg, she made Asgard her second home and was known as an honorary Asgardian or Æsir goddess.

Syn

The goddess of refusal and rejection, Syn ensured to bar the way. She was also part of Frigg's entourage. She guarded the doors to Fensalir and would ask trespassers to leave. No one was allowed to loiter around Fensalir. Syn would also turn to violence if trespassers persisted.

Bragi

Bragi was the god of poetry and speech. After hearing about Bragi's skill, Odin assigned him to be Valhalla's bard. Bragi was more verbally inclined and musical as opposed to other gods in the Æsir pantheon. He had a wife, Iðunn, whose apples were the source of the gods' immortality.

In battles, Bragi took on the role of a war poet, inciting his troops to violence and slinging insulting poetry and mockery at the opponents.

Heimdall

The god of vigilance and foresight had the responsibility of being the divine sentry at the Bifrost to ensure that no unwanted being would walk through that bridge and cause any havoc. Heimdall was a fierce warrior, but just as he was fierce, he was also immaculately beautiful, with white skin and golden teeth. His hearing was so honed he could hear the grass blades grow.

Njord

Njord is a particularly strange addition to this group because originally, he was a Vanir, but after the Æsir-Vanir war, he, the patriarch of the Vanir tribe, was sent as part of the treaty to the Asgardians.

Njord was the patron god of the seas and had the most splendid fleet of all the Æsir.

Fulla

The deity of secrets, Fulla, was an asynjur in charge of maintaining Frigg's jewelry. She was also Frigg's confidante. She is said to hold domain over plentitude, but nowhere is her role as a goddess completely defined, putting scholars into a speculative position regarding her.

Hod

The god of darkness is blind and is unfortunate enough to be manipulated by Loki into killing Baldur. Baldur was Hod's brother. Hod was murdered by his half-brother Vali as vengeance for killing Baldur.

Eir

The patron of healing and medicine, Eir would come to your aid if you got injured in battle or even in a minor way. Those who were grievously injured on the battlefield looked to Eir to save them. She shares her name with a Valkyrie.

Vidar

Vidar, one of Odin's sons, is the god of revenge. Born out of Odin's union with the giant Gridr, he served as his father's avenger. The god is said to have been almost as strong as Thor. When given the chance, Vidar proved himself on the battlefield by showing his reckonable strength.

Saga

Some scholars suggest that Saga is just another of Frigg's alter-egos. She shared many characteristics with Frigg and often drank with Odin. She was a goddess known for her prophetic abilities and her wisdom.

Freya

Freya was also a Vanir originally, but after the war treaty, she was sent to Asgard and integrated into the Æsir tribe. She was quite beautiful and had a radiance to her personality, which made her perfect as the goddess of love, fertility, seiðr, and battle.

Freyr

Freya's brother was the god of peace, good weather, sunshine, fertility, and male virility. He was often connoted with a phallic symbol based on his male-sexual propensity.

Vali

Vali was the second god of vengeance, and it is said that he was conceived specifically to kill Hod.

Foresti

The child of Baldur and Nanna, Foresti was a god of justice and mediation. He was able to fix issues between two parties through his levelheadedness. He had his own courthouse where he was able to settle disputes. His axe was a symbol of negotiation.

Sfojn

Sfojn was an asynjur responsible for Freya's messages. She was also the guardian of engagements and betrothals. She was associated with love, caring, affection, and romance.

Lofin

Lofin was the sister of Sjofn and was associated with another facet of romance—forbidden love, unrequited love. She was the supporter of star-crossed lovers and would go on to bless their marriages. Lofin was so vehement in her pursuit of this mission that Odin and Frigg gave her permission to marry the forbidden lovers. Even though these marriages were considered banned, they were deemed valid.

Snotra

The elder sister of Lofin and Sjofn, Snotra was associated with wisdom, cleverness, and wit of all sorts, especially that connected to riddles and puzzles. She was the mother of a legendary sea-king Gautrek.

Hlin

The guardian of mourners, Hlin was also a member of Frigg's entourage and worked directly with the goddess by using Frigg's prophetic abilities to foresee if someone would get some bad luck. She would then intervene and help the people preemptively.

Ullr

Ullr, son of Sif, was a handsome polymath god. His father is not known, and much of what Ullr was all about remains a subject of speculation and mystery. His followers used to call him the Glorious One.

Gna

Gna controlled the wind and speed. She was also part of Frigg's entourage. She rode on a horse that could tread water and fly in the sky. She used to deliver Frigg's messages and would often run errands for the goddess.

Sol

Sol was the personification of the sun, according to some myths. She was the sister of Mani, the personification of the moon.

Bil

Bil and Hjuki represented the different phases of the moon, and because of this, Mani had taken them as his attendants.

The Vanir Gods

If the Æsir were renowned as the gods of warfare, might, and battle-wits, the Vanir, belonging to the second pantheon of Norse mythology, were associated with magic, fertility, zeal and zest, and nature. The Vanir knew a brand of magic called seiðr which could shape the future as well as prophesize it. The Vanir became key players in Norse mythology through their interaction, conflict, and union with the Æsir. The most well-known gods from the Vanir are Njord, Freya, and Freyr.

But what, weren't those gods covered under the Æsir part? Well, yes, but they were originally from Vanaheim.

While the Vanir gods are fewer in number, their stature and their importance were undeniable in Norse society.

Kvasir

Kvasir was considered the god of wisdom, poetry, wit, diplomacy, eloquence, and inspiration. He was born after the gods of both tribes gathered for a treaty and spat in a cauldron to represent their unity. From this mixed spit, Kvasir came into existence.

He was always eager to share his knowledge with others, often traveling to strange lands to find people to divine his wisdom. He was considered almost as wise as Mimir and Odin. He loved to wander, which eventually got him in trouble, as he was found by two dwarven brothers who murdered him and used his blood to form the Mead of Poetry.

Odin then stole the Mead of Poetry from these dwarves and used it often for wisdom and inspiration.

Nerthus

Nerthus was the goddess of abundance, stability, and fertility and was correlated with Earth. She was the sister-wife to Njord and the mother of Freya and Freyr, according to some sources. She was widely worshipped by the early Germanic tribes because of her ties to fertility and nature.

Odr

Some state that Odr is Odin's persona or an aspect of Odin from his dark days. Others claim that Odr was a god of madness and frenzy and was nothing like Odin. Odr was rough, callous, reckless, and vagrant, often leaving his wife Freya alone, causing her to weep and go out in search of him. Odr was the father of Hnoss and Gersemi.

While Odin was considered wise, tactful, and very considerate in his actions, Odr was considered like a loose cannon.

Hnoss and Gersemi

The goddesses of wealth, beauty, treasures, worldly possessions, and desires were sisters. They were Freya's daughters and were said to be indistinguishable from each other. Their names became synonymous with that of treasure, with Norse people calling their treasure hnossir.

Nanna

Nanna was the goddess of fertility and matronliness. She was symbolic of motherhood. She is said to have died from a broken heart after her husband died. Some accounts say she was grief-stricken after her husband Baldur's death, and threw herself into the burning ship with Baldur's body, not wanting to live a life without her husband.

Gullveig

She was the goddess of metals and gold. One can even say that she's the personification of purified gold. She triggered the events of the Æsir and Vanir war. She was burned three times and was born three times after she visited the Æsir. Her poor treatment at their hands is another factor that prompted the war.

The Æsir-Vanir War

Put yourself in the shoes of the Æsir gods for a moment and imagine how they must have felt when they discovered that instead of worshipping them as much as they should, the humans had turned to the Vanir gods and were paying more attention to them. While this was not exactly what triggered the war, as the Æsir were not *this* petty, this was certainly one of the contributors to the rising hostility.

The Æsir knew by now that the Vanir were able to use magic to manipulate nature, see into the future, and grant human beings boons like fertility, harvest, and familial bliss. Even this did not deter the relationships as badly as what later happened.

The goddess Gullveig came to the Æsir, apparently bearing good news. She said that she would teach them magic, including seiðr, and that she would be available here for a few days as a goddess-for-hire.

Initially, the Æsir gods were quite taken with her and were mesmerized by the magic that she was showing them. However, they soon discovered that they were becoming lenient and were resorting to debauchery and lewd behavior as they pursued their selfish desires through Gullveig's magic. In other words, their values of honor, kin, loyalty, and structure were compromised to such an extent that they perceived Gullveig to be an enemy, a spy, or, worst, someone sent to sabotage the Æsir gods.

Once they learned that this goddess had come to them from Vanaheim, it became apparent that their initial suspicion was correct. In their anger, the Æsir gods murdered her by setting her ablaze. But Gullveig rose from her ashes. This further incited the gods, as they were wary of Vanir's magic, and now here, it was being thrown in their faces again. So they set fire to her again. Again, she rose from her ashes. When they burned her a third time, Gullveig somehow made her way back to her realm and told the Vanir gods of what had happened.

This was the kindling that ignited the hostility between the two tribes. The Æsir and Vanir started to hate each other and even became fearful of what the other might do. The more these hostilities grew, the more it seemed imminent that a war might take place.

The Æsir and the Vanir came face to face on the battlefield, a plane that would be used again later for the last battle of Ragnarök. Here, the Æsir leader Odin flung his spear at the Vanir troops. This was a standard Norse ritual. Warriors would fling their spears into the enemy lines to show that the battle had begun.

The Æsir fought mercilessly, using brute force and their awe-inspiring weaponry. Many times in the battle, their strength lent them the upper hand. However, the Vanir used subtler warfare tactics such as magic and deception.

Both tribes realized as they kept fighting that their opponents were not mortal men or chaotic giants; they were gods. They could not keep fighting each other for eternity. Neither could win nor could they lose.

During the war, the Æsir damaged many of the Vanir's lands. The Vanir replied in kind by destroying the protective wall of Asgard.

This fighting ended only when both sides came to a stalemate. They decided to follow the Norse custom of giving each other tributes at the end of the battle. The gods came to an agreement that they'd treat each other as equals and that both sides would swap hostages. They solidified this agreement by spitting in a cauldron. The spit formed Kvasir, often considered a god and often considered a man.

The Æsir gods gave Hoenir and Mimir to the Vanir as a symbol of their new union. These hostages were also given to ensure that the peace would be maintained rather than disrupted again. The Vanir gave their patron god Njord, and his two children, Freyr and Freya, to the Æsir. The three Vanir gods taught the Æsir how to perform seiðr, therefore becoming important gods within the Æsir pantheon as well.

Hoenir and Mimir had terrible luck. Hoenir was elected the leader of the Vanir, while Mimir gave him counsel. However, Mimir would purposefully make Hoenir speak his own thoughts so that the Vanir would see that they had elected a fool for their leader.

But rather than think that Hoenir was idiotic, the gods perceived Mimir to be dumb and that he was not as wise as the Æsir had claimed. They beheaded Mimir and sent him back to the Asgardians. Although this act was hostile enough to restart the war, Odin reanimated Mimir's head so that he'd counsel the Asgardians instead.

Thus, the peace was kept and maintained. Odin gradually took the position of the de facto leader of all the gods. However, worship was decided to be equally split between the gods.

This chapter was a bit exhaustive in terms of subject matter. We discussed both the Æsir and Vanir tribes, their gods and goddesses, and how continuous friction between both tribes led to a great war between them. Moving forth, we will take a detailed look at some of the most popular gods and goddesses and learn about their traits, history, attributes, and mythology.

NORSE PANTHEON FAMILY TREE ILLUSTRATION

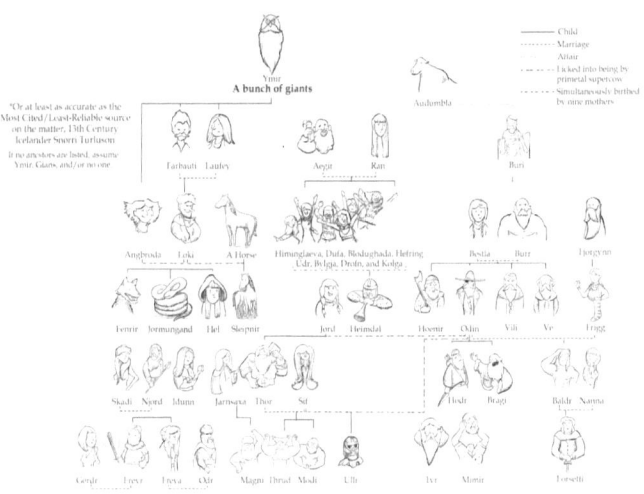

CHAPTER 4
THE A-LIST GODS OF NORSE MYTHOLOGY

Odin

His appearance has inspired the archetypal look of high fantasy wizards like Gandalf. Odin, with his piercing blue eyes, his white beard, and his magnificent spear that looks like a cane, appears every bit the wise, astute, powerful, and mystical god that he is. There is a good reason that Odin is at the top of the Norse hierarchy.

Norse mythology has shown us time and again that if you venture forth on a quest, you will eventually get what you desire and become all the more powerful because of it. This was also a belief rooted deep within the psyche of the Vikings. It was a necessity for them to have faith that their labors and toils will come to fruition because of the nature of their labors and toils. They had to sail across torrential seas to loot and plunder other lands, and quite often, they did not know where exactly they were headed or what kind of opponents they would face there. Or worst, if they'd find any loot there at all or not.

Odin represents the belief system of the Norse people, going on similar quests even though the outcome seemed bleak. One such example is when he sacrificed himself to himself and hung upon the Yggdrasil with his spear piercing him.

Odin was associated with the powers of battle, sorcery, shape-shifting, runic alphabets, healing, death, necromancy, royalty, wisdom, and warfare. He was a majestic god, but his majesty reflected the people who believed in him. There was a ruggedness to how he looked, but that ruggedness lent him character rather than making him look poor.

From atop his tower in his house, Odin can see throughout the Nine Realms.

He was the grandson of Buri and the son of Bestla and Borr.

His two brothers, Vili and Ve, helped him create the world from Ymir's body.

Odin was married to Frigg, with whom he had Baldur and Hod. Odin had other sons from other beings, including Thor. Sometimes, Odin gave in to the temptation of the beautiful giantesses in Jötunnheim. Thor was the result of one such union. Odin had yet another son named Vidar from a giantess called Grid. And another one called Vali from a giantess called Rind.

Like Loki, Odin could shapeshift and turn himself into an animal or a human. This was very vital to him, as it allowed him to wander about the realms without revealing his identity. Odin spoke in riddles and always uttered whatever he had to say in poetic phrases in a voice so soft that anyone who heard him felt that he was telling the truth, even when that was not the case.

Odin had innate control over magic, allowing him just to utter a single word and cause a torrent of fire to appear or to say another word and calm down the sea.

He was well-versed in battle but knew that he had to exercise control, what with him being the strongest and fiercest god out there. He could blind his enemies, imbue them with madness and fear, and render them fearful.

Odin could help his warriors become feral by making them go berserk. The Vikings often prayed to him and sacrificed to him before battles so that they, too, may go berserk.

Due to his wisdom and depth of knowledge, Odin could predict the fate of every human as well as see into their past. He knew about Ragnarök and how there was nothing that anyone could do to prevent it. Despite that, he took many precautionary measures to delay it.

Odin could make people ill just by thinking it and could even kill them with just a thought.

He was fond of his animals. He had two spiritual familiars, often considered an extension of himself, in the form of two ravens, Huginn and Muninn. He'd send them out every day so that they'd bring him news from all over the realms. They'd return in the evening and share what they'd seen by whispering in Odin's ear. Whenever they weren't exploring the worlds, they'd sit by Odin's side on his throne.

Besides the ravens, Odin had two wolves, Geri and Freki, whom he kept feeding from under the table whenever he dined. This was because Odin did not need to drink or eat to sustain himself. All he ever wanted was wine, and that, too, as a luxury, not a necessity.

Loki gifted Odin a magical steed with eight legs named Sleipnir.

Among his possessions was a powerful and magical spear made from Yggdrasil. Odin called this the Gungnir spear, and it had runes etched onto it.

He also had a ring Draupnir, which would sprout eight magical rings every ninth day.

Speaking of days, Wednesday is named after Odin.

Frigg

Frigg plays numerous major roles in Norse mythology. She was more than just Odin's wife and mother to Baldur and Hod. She was a goddess within her right, and at times, her matronly protectiveness made her a formidable opponent even for Odin.

While she was interpreted as a matronly goddess, she held sway over love, fertility, and marriage as well. But this was not entirely what made her stature so high up in the pantheon. The real reason was her gift for prophecy. She guarded this secret so well that she never told anyone what she knew of the future.

Odin knew this but never pestered her about it. He was well aware of her powers and had given her the honor of being the only other deity to sit on his throne. She resided in a marshland named Fensalir. Those who worshipped her often went out to marshlands to be spiritually close to her.

One of Frigg's prominent features was her entourage. She was always followed around by a court of women, of which a select few were her trusted confidantes and messengers. Her attendees included the asynjur of Asgard, who were also considered goddesses but lesser in stature than Frigg. Fulla, Lofn, Gna, and Hlin were some of the famous attendants of Frigg.

With her female attendees, Frigg populated Fensalir. This was considered a more feminine place within Asgard. A sanctuary, if you will.

Just as Odin went to extreme lengths to secure knowledge, Frigg went to equally extreme lengths to ensure the protection of her beautiful son, Baldur. When he was born, he was beloved by all because of his beauty. Frigg worried for him, especially when he started getting dreams in which his life was shown to be in peril.

Frigg went to every single thing in the known universe and asked them to take an oath not to hurt Baldur. Everything obliged, as everything loved Baldur too.

Such fortified was Baldur's protection that the gods often made sport of throwing things at him to watch them swerve in the air to avoid hitting him. Loki disguised himself and went to Frigg to find out how she had made this happen. In doing so, he found out that the only thing that Frigg hadn't gone to for an oath was mistletoe. Loki crafted an arrow from mistletoe and gave it to Baldur's brother, Hod. Hod was blind and was often left out of the throw-things-at-Baldur game because of his blindness.

The first time the blind brother participates in the game was when he shot the mistletoe arrow at Baldur and killed him.

Baldur's death was Frigg's first deep sorrow. Her second sorrow would come at Ragnarök, when her beloved husband, Odin, would die in battle.

Friday is named after Frigg.

Thor

His strength has earned him the title of almighty. Thor's strength and his dexterity over the elements, especially lightning, and thunder, came from his father, Odin, and his mother, the giantess Fjorgyn. His persona is as far apart from the Marvel comics and movies' version of Thor as far apart the authors of those comics in the '60s were from sobriety. Legend has it those authors were tripping on tabs upon tabs of acid and getting high on shrooms when they wrote those comics—and it shows.

The real Thor had red hair and a beard. He was associated with more than just thunder and lightning. He was a god of strength. Oak trees would bend to his command. He was not just an Æsir; he was the protector god of Midgard. While the modern version of Thor—as seen in the comics and movies—has quite the sense of humor and wit, the real Thor was not as smart or wise and was often an easy butt of the joke for many giants.

The giants loved making fun of him. They knew that Thor was ill-tempered and that it'd be very easy to get a rise out of him. Later on, when Thor got on more equal footing with the giants thanks to his magical hammer, Mjolnir, the teasing lessened, although it didn't completely cease. Thor would hit the giants over their heads with his hammer. He wasn't exactly defenseless against the giants. Whenever he was roused, he would make thunder and lightning appear in the sky. The loud grumbles of thunder and the wild flashes of lightning would scare the giants and send them back into their homes.

Thor lived in Asgard in a place called Thrudheim with his wife, Sif. His home had more than 500 rooms and was the known biggest house in Asgard. Thor and Sif had two children, Trud and Modi, and a stepson named Ullr. Thor had a son named Magni with a giantess named Jarnsaxa. The couple also had a servant named Thialfi and a servant-girl named Roskva.

He had two goats that used to pull his chariot. Whenever he would travel to far-off lands, he'd slay the goats and eat their meat. Upon his return, he'd reanimate them with

Mjolnir. Whenever Thor flew across the sky in his chariot, the sound from his wheels became thunder, and the sparks from his wheels became lightning, and both were seen and heard in Midgard.

Thor's magical hammer was one of Brokkr and Eitri's most powerful creations. It could tear down mountains, send out bolts of lightning, and hit any target from a distance. It would then return to Thor's hand on its own. The hammer had resurrecting powers as well. It could shrink and fit inside Thor's shirt if need be.

Thursday was named after Thor.

Baldur

Hailed as the god of light and purity, Baldur was the son of Odin and Frigg. He was extremely beautiful, often compared to the summer sun, and was said to be so pretty that his beauty made the flowers blush when they saw him. He was also quite fair, kind, wise, and gracious.

He had a home in Asgard named Breidablik, which was made of gilded silver. Only those who had a pure heart could enter his home. He also had quite an amazing ship, known as the Hringorni, which was also used as his funeral pyre after he was killed.

His death was a sad affair and was said to plummet the world into Fimbulwinter.

Vidar

Vidar had a terrifying title. The silent god of vengeance is what they called him. He was an Odinson, like Thor and Baldur. The title that he earned originated from the story in the Eddas that stated how he'd avenge his father's death. When Odin would die at the hands of Fenrir, Vidar would go and kill Fenrir. He'd also be one of the few gods who'd survive Ragnarök and would dwell in Idavoll. Vidar wore a thick shoe that he kept constantly mending. This shoe would help him plunge his foot down into Fenrir's mouth and reach down his throat to smash the wolf's heart. Norse shoemakers keep spare scraps of leather from the trimming of their shoes as a veneration of Vidar.

The reason he was known as the silent god of vengeance was rather morbid. Vengeance often forces a man to go silent, and in this silence, he plots his next steps and purifies himself of all other thoughts so he can focus on the vengeance at hand.

In some regards, Vidar was as strong as Thor. I would go so far as to speculate that his silence and his inclination to vengeance had somehow made him stronger, as Thor did not survive Ragnarök, but Vidar did.

Tyr

Tyr was the Norse god of war. He was not only a god of war; he was related to heroic glory, justice, and the formalities of warfare, such as treaties. Because of his enigmatic origins, he is considered to be one of the oldest deities in the Norse pantheon.

Of course, he was later on supplanted by Odin, whom many sources claim was the father of Tyr, while other sources claimed that Tyr was the son of a giant Hymir.

Tyr was depicted as being one-handed due to an act of courage. His limb was bitten off by Fenrir when the gods were trying to subdue the wolf. Because of Tyr's sacrifice, Fenrir was able to be bound until Ragnarök.

Had he not been one-handed, Tyr would have stood a chance against the hordes of Hel on Ragnarök. But due to his disadvantage, he was slain in battle by Garm, the guard dog of Hel.

Tuesday is named after Tyr.

Bragi

Bragi was so well-spoken and eloquent that he was given the title of Bard of Asgard. Because of his lyricism, he was also known as the skaldic god of poetry in Norse mythology.

Bragi was often found in Valhalla, singing to the einherjar and cheering them on with his tunes. But this was not the end of his domain. He would also use his poetry to boost the spirit of his warriors and use malignant verses to dishearten the enemies.

Fittingly enough, the god of eloquence had the youthful goddess of rejuvenation for his wife.

There was more to Bragi than just poetry. He was also the god of music, creativity, and artistic inspiration. He sported a long beard and had runes carved on his tongue.

Idun

Idun was the goddess of eternal youthfulness, or immortality if you will. She had great long hair and fair skin. She possessed golden apples that were the essence of immortality in Asgard. The gods would come to her and eat her fruit to maintain their youth and vigor. This made her a very central figure in Norse mythology, as without her, the gods would have been reduced to mortals.

Loki

Much can be said about the god of mischief with certainty except for one thing—was he truly a god? The Æsir saw him as one of their own even though he was only half Æsir and half Jötunnn. He was the son of Farbauti and Laufey. His mother was an asynja and his father was a giant.

It was very atypical that Loki was an Æsir from his mother's side because, in most circumstances, it was almost always the opposite, such as with Thor. This led Loki to adopt the name Laufeyson. It is speculated that Loki did this because his mother held more stature in Asgard than some giant and also because she was a goddess. Loki wanted everyone to acknowledge that he was the son of a goddess.

He embodied a lot of the chaos that the Jötnar were infamous for. He pursued mischief with such single-mindedness that he came to be synonymous with trickery.

Loki was married to a very loyal wife named Sigyn, who never left his side. From his wife, he had two children named Vali and Narfi. It was his other mistress, a giantess named Angrboða, with whom he had the spawns of chaos itself—Hel, Fenrir, Jörmungandr.

Some sources mistake Loki's penchant for trickery and mischief to be trademarks of evil. Loki wasn't exactly evil. He was not all good, but he wasn't strictly evil either. He was sociopathic, for sure, often resorting to mean feats of cunning to entertain himself at the expense of other gods and goddesses.

It was because of his cunning nature that he was seen as a frightening figure capable of being moody, sly, alluring, strange, and dangerous. He could shapeshift at will and was also well-versed in Seiðr.

Whatever his relationships with the Æsir were—and sometimes a lot of them were troubled—Loki revealed his true nature at Ragnarök when his children attacked Asgard. Loki stood by his children and even commanded their armies to defeat the gods and end the world.

One could say that the reason Loki resorted to such an extreme measure was probably because of how he was treated by the gods. After Baldur's death, Loki, for his many crimes, was chained with the entrails of his son Narfi and tied to three rocks inside a cave. A serpent was placed above him, dripping venom onto him. Only Sigyn remained by his side, sitting with a bowl to catch the venom. Whenever the bowl filled up, she'd go out to empty it. During that time, the venom would drop directly on Loki causing him unbearable pain, making him writhe in agony. Those movements would cause earthquakes. He'd stay chained until Ragnarök.

Perhaps it was this horrendous punishment that permanently pitched Loki against the gods, eventually causing their downfall.

Hel

Hel was the daughter of Loki and the giantess Angrboða. She came to be known as the queen of the realm of the dead after she was banished there. How she was banished, there is an interesting tale in itself. In Helheim, Hel tended to the souls of people who died from old age or illnesses.

Her appearance is described within her relation to Helheim. She is said to be half black and half white, the white half denoting her living self while the black or bluish part denoting her deadened self. Because of the circumstances that she went through and because of her inherent nature as Loki's daughter and the prophesized harbinger of Ragnarök, Hel was considered very cruel, harsh, cold, and threatening.

Odin threw her down into Helheim after he learned that she would be responsible for Ragnarök. Hel did not just resign to her fate. Rather, she crowned herself queen of the dead.

Her realm was surrounded by a large fence. The river Elivagar flowed next to the entrance. The gates of Hel were known as corpse gates. They were located in the Gnipa cave where Garm, the guard dog of Hel, guarded it and howled at the souls who entered.

Within Hel, Níðhöggr was trapped under one of Yggdrasil's roots and was always chewing at it. Whenever Níðhöggr heard the howling of Garm, he'd make his way to the entrance somehow and find the dead people and suck their blood, rendering them pale.

Those rendered pale by Níðhöggr's bloodsucking were then inducted into Hel's legion. Hel would use this army to challenge the gods on Ragnarök.

Within her hall, Hel had everything named after disasters. Her bed was called the sickbed. Her dining table was known as hunger. Her knives were called starvation. The curtains in the hall were called misfortune.

Heimdall

With skin as white as light and golden teeth that shone, Heimdall was a very radiant god. Besides those two attributes, he was tall, handsome, strong, and quite wise. He was tasked with guarding the Bifrost, the bridge that served as the sole entrance into Asgard. Heimdal was the son of Odin and, this is tricky to explain, nine mothers.

He was not very fond of sleeping. He slept less than a bird and was always honing his eyesight and his hearing. He could see as well as the most astute of hawks and could hear so well that he could listen to the sound of wool growing on the back of a sheep.

Heimdall had a place called the Himinbjörg next to the Bifrost. Whenever he was not busy protecting the Bifrost, he was riding around on his horse named Gulltopp. Gulltop was made entirely of gold.

Heimdall made it his habit to roam around humans and consult with them.

He would stand at the Bifrost with his sword, Hofund, by his side. He had an enchanted horn called Gjallarhorn. He'd use this horn at Ragnarök to signal the world's end. The sound of this horn was loud enough to be heard across all Nine Realms.

He would blow it thrice when he'd see the enemies arriving at the plane of Vigrid—the same plain where the Æsir-Vanir war had taken place. Upon hearing his horn, the gods would rush to the plains for that one last epic battle.

Njord

The Vanir god of wind, seafaring, hunting, fishing, and all maritime things, Njord was the chief of Vanir gods up until he was given as part of a treaty with the Asgardians. He was more than just a sea god.

Njord controlled fertility, peace, and wealth as well.

After moving to Asgard, he lived in a house by the sea. This was his favorite place in the entire realm, and he loved to spend his time there, listening to the sounds of the ocean and enjoying the sea wind.

He married a giant named Skadi, who fell in love with him after seeing his feet from underneath a curtain. But their marriage became very rocky after the two could not decide where to live. Skadi was a mountainous being, preferring the hills and mountains. Njord wanted to live by the sea. The two separated from one another soon after this dilemma could not be resolved.

They did have two children, Freya and Freyr.

Freyr

The Vanir, male god of fertility and prosperity was the son of Njord and the brother of Freya. He was associated with rain, harvest, and sunshine. Initially, he used to live in Alfheim as it was given to him as a toothing gift. His pristine nature reflected the nature of Alfheim and its residents, the elves.

The symbols of horses and phalluses were associated with him as he was associated with both. He had a trusty boar, Gullinbursti, and a ship, Skidbladnir, both of which he used to travel wherever he wanted to go. The ship was magical and could be folded into such a tiny size that it could fit inside a pouch.

Once, Freyr secretly ascended to Odin's throne to get a look at the Nine Realms. He saw a woman from there, a woman so beautiful that Freyr thought she was the prettiest thing he'd ever seen. He sent his servant Skirnir to woo the woman on his behalf. The servant was sent to bring the woman to Asgard.

Skirnir was given Freyr's magical sword to defend himself in the land of giants, where Gerd belonged. Gerd said that she wanted some of those magical apples that all the gods in Asgard were eating. When Skirnir said that wasn't possible, she refused the offer.

Skirnir then offered her other alternative gifts, even Odin's ring Draupnir, but Gerd kept refusing.

When Skirnir had exhausted all other options, he threatened her with runes, telling her that he'd curse her with the secret powers of the runes if she didn't come with him. Gerd agreed to marry Freyr because of this threat. She asked Freyr to wait nine days so that he'd yearn even more for her. The two got married, but at a serious cost.

Freyr didn't have his sword by his side anymore. It was given to Skirnir. In the battle of Ragnarök, Freyr would die without his sword in a fight with Surtr.

Freya

Freya was the female deity of sex, lust, eroticism, beauty, sorcery, gold, death, war, and fertility.

Freya knew magic, especially seiðr magic, which everyone coveted in the realms. She taught this magic to Odin and the rest of the Æsir too. Before this, this magic was only practiced by the Vanir. Freya had her own afterlife field for the souls of the bravely departed. This field was called Fólkvangr. It wasn't Odin but Freya who had the first pick of the souls who'd go to her realm. The rest would go to Valhalla.

Freya loved to travel. She had a chariot that was pulled by two cats. Sometimes she wore a cloak made of falcon feathers which allowed her to fly through the skies. Whenever she was not in the mood to fly or use her chariot, she rode her bore, Hildsvini.

Mimir

It was said that Mimir was so wise that his knowledge exceeded even Odin's. Mimir's name means remememberer, which is another indication of his knowledge and wisdom.

After the Æsir-Vanir war, he was beheaded by the Vanir, but Odin resurrected his head by embalming it with herbs and chanting magical songs on it.

Odin brought Mimir back to Asgard, where eventually, Mimir began guarding the Mimisbrunner well.

Odin walked with Mimir's head in his hands for hours and hours, asking him for counsel and advice. Mimir was more respected by Odin than any other god. Odin considered Mimir a friend and a confidante. A peer, almost. The two held intellectual talks that were ripe with knowledge and dripping with wisdom.

Even though they were such close friends, when Odin asked Mimir permission to drink from Mimir's well, Mimir said that he'd only let him drink in exchange for a sacrifice. Odin sacrificed his right eye by throwing it at the bottom of the well. Such was the price of Mimir's wisdom.

After taking a detailed look at some of the A-listers of the Norse pantheon, we're going to discover Norse Paganism and see how we can utilize our thus far theoretical and historical knowledge by putting it to practical use by integrating it in rituals, rites, and venerations of the gods and goddesses. This chapter concluded our theoretical learning of the gods, and goddesses, details about the Nine Realms, and Norse Cosmology. Moving forward, we will understand how runic magic works, how Norse magic in general works, and how we can practice that magic in our daily lives.

CHAPTER 5
NORSE PAGANISM

Characteristics of Norse Paganism

The Old Norse Religion was an organic religion, which is to say that it lacked a structured feel that was characteristic of Abrahamic religions. It didn't come into existence at once, complete with scriptures, commandments, and prayers. There were no central figures such as prophets or messengers to guide the people as a collective toward a religious goal. To that effect, Norse Paganism lacked confining dogmas, restrictive doctrines, and forced creeds. In this particular sense, the Old Norse Religion was rather liberating for its followers, so much so that the term religion does not really fit it all that well. It was more than a religion; it was a way of life and one that was not as high-maintenance or high-demand as Christianity.

Norse Paganism can be traced back to the Bronze and Iron Ages. By the 56th AD, the Roman historian Tacitus noted that the Germanic people whom he had observed followed a polytheistic religion. The religion underwent a gradual evolution, and it wasn't until the Viking Age that Norse Paganism propagated into the rest of the world and became known in a much deeper sense around the world. Norse people moved from Scandinavia and settled across Northern Europe, taking their religion with them.

But as grand as this propagation was, it was rather short-lived in the face of Christianity's missionary work. By the 8th and 12th centuries, Norse Paganism started to dwindle. Christianization took hundreds of years and eventually spread throughout Scandinavia as well, but one can never remove the roots of a culture from its people. Norse Paganism thrived in the form of folklore, stories, and poems among the Scandinavian people, preserving the faith in the long term. After almost a thousand years, although it had not disappeared completely, Norse Paganism came back in the form of neo-paganist movements such as Ásatrú, Vanatru, and Heathenry.

Norse Paganism had certain distinct qualities that set it apart from other religions of that time, especially the monotheistic, structured, and centralized religions such as Christianity. In contrast, Norse Paganism was:

- **Animistic**
- **Pluralistic**
- **Decentralized**
- **Polytheistic**
- **Immanent**
- **Orthopraxical**

Animistic

Followers of the Old Norse Religion believed deeply in the interconnected of things. Everything, whether it was a tree, a squirrel, or the water in a lake, was recognized to have agency. Nothing was more inherently important than anything else. Everything was considered to be equal and was believed to possess a spirit, knowledge, personality, and power. This was not because of some moralistic endeavor or for some holy purpose; Animism was believed to simply exist. Pagans perceived that everything played an important part in life as a participant in the grand interconnectedness of things. That's why they respected everything around them and tried to foster a spiritual relationship with things within the surrounding world.

This belief lent a very three-dimensional nature to every thing and action, taking away the binary "good" and "evil" or "virtue" and "sin" from it. The Norse worldview viewed things not as being either holy or profane but existing as equal. Divinity was considered an inherent part of the world as much as colors, sounds, and matter were. Desire, ambition, vanity, power, jealousy, and trickery were all considered natural feelings and driving forces.

But perhaps the biggest feature of animism was the belief that everything possessed a soul. One should note that the concept of the soul in Norse Paganism is very complex, where souls are multifaceted. Connecting with the spirit of things was a way of life for the Norse folk. They experienced Landvaetter (land spirits) within the land, Husevaetter (house spirits) in living spaces, the Jötunnn in the wilderness, and the Æsir as a manifestation of sacredness.

Animism allowed the Pagans to interact with the world around them in a way that felt most individually engaging to them, allowing them to add a ceremonial component in their everyday life, with each practice sometimes being unique to each individual, setting the premise that there was no one correct way to approach holiness and divinity, but countless. A cleric could attain divinity by worship, and a Viking could attain the same sense of sacredness through battle. A gardener could nurture his garden and send his love to the gods for blessing him with bounties, and an ironsmith could attain the same peace and purpose in making swords and axes. This equality in practice was all thanks to animism.

Rather than create a caste system in society, animism made a place for respect for all professions and endeavors amongst the people, truly allowing them to pursue what they passioned, making them excel in their endeavors, and truly allowing them to feel pride in their work.

Pluralistic

Building upon animism, we have pluralism, which is Norse Paganism's way of explaining how things are connected to each other. While Christianity takes a dualist approach, stating that everything falls into one of two categories (good and evil), and some Sufi sects in Islam follow a monist belief that all life comes from one source (God) and thus everything is in fact, a reflection of God, Norse Paganism entails that things are neither just good or bad nor do they come from just one source. Instead, Norse Paganism adheres to pluralism, which is the belief that all things contain multitudes within them.

Even the concept of soul, when explored through a pluralistic lens, reveals that Norse Paganism believes in a several-part soul. The gods and goddesses are looked upon in a similar fashion, where even the more traditionally malevolent deities such as Loki are not seen as just evil or bad but instead possessing a very complex character that contains a spectrum of traits, some of them good, others not so good, and some others just purely chaotic.

The concept of reward and punishment is a very dualist concept. Do this, that, and the other virtue, and you shall enter heaven. Become depraved in the way of sin, and you shall be spending an eternity in hell. Norse Paganism does not adhere to this belief, at least not in that strict a sense. Yes, those who die with honor in battle do go to Valhalla, and those who have spent a life of depravity and debauchery do indeed get punished in Helheim, but those are not the only two options; rather, they're two of many options of what happens to a person in the afterlife. For example, you can just die a regular death and go to Helheim, where all the departed souls dwell. In Paganism, Helheim is not seen as a place of punishment and torture. It is a realm, just like any other realm.

The pluralistic nature of Paganism gave its followers the freedom to pursue virtue of their own volition rather than be obliged to do virtuous things as a form of currency to gain entry into paradise.

This pluralism extended into their religious practices as well. Those who venerated Odin did so in a very different fashion than those who asked Freya for her bounties. Unlike Sufism or New Age religions, pluralism served as a deep foundation of the creation of the cosmos as well. Rather than just come into existence from one source, the Norse world came from the fire and frost of Muspelheim and Niffelheim, then Midgard came into existence from Ymir's body, and the dwarves and giants and elves similarly went on to inhabit their own realms, truly giving the creation story a pluralistic background.

Decentralized

Where did it come from? Who originated this religion? Was it a single source? No. Norse Paganism was decentralized from the very beginning. There's a very neat explanation for how it came to be.

The first part of the process is called decentralized tribal animism. In this part, small tribal communities start to venerate nature in their distinct ways. These veneration practices and beliefs are very localized to the decentralized tribes. Gradually, these tribes begin to exchange their customs with one another, often discovering in the process that their customs are very similar to each other.

In the second part of the process, decentralized tribal polytheism takes place, where after discussion with adjoining tribes and other people in the vicinity, the religion's nature-based animistic figures start to take shape. For example, Thor took on the role of the god of thunder, and Freya became known as the goddess of fertility. These deities were sometimes recognized in different communities through different names, resulting in the unification of the concept. But even then, the worship and veneration of these deities were very unstructured and folkloric.

Then, the development of decentralized cultus took place. Cultus refers to the parameters of religious practice. Once a civilization is advanced enough to form social classes and divide labor amongst them, the intellectual class thinks about religion and starts to formulate a cultus.

Afterward, the cultus is popularized as a central look of a polytheistic religion, therefore establishing a baseline praxis for that entire religion. In simpler terms, when you think of Norse Paganism and the first thing that comes to your mind are the Æsir and Vanir gods, Valhalla, Vikings, and so forth—that's the popularization of the centralized cultus.

Texts are then written about the cultus, especially if the dominant cultus is intended to propagate and popularize or preserve. Sometimes, these writings serve as scriptures for later followers of the religion.

Doctrines are then established, which lead to the development of transcendent-faith praxis, i.e., the answers to the big questions such as where we came from, where we will go after death, and other grand philosophical questions that revolve around transcendence. Eventually, these philosophies are molded into practices for the followers of the religion.

That being said, Norse Paganism remains just as decentralized today as it was decentralized almost a thousand years ago. It does not have any central scriptures. The

Eddas are historical texts that contain compilations of Icelandic folklore. They are not intended to be followed as scripture.

Polytheistic

Polytheism in Norse Paganism was a result of the decentralized, pluralistic, and animistic nature of the religion. The Norse Pantheon is populated with several gods and goddesses, many of whom we've discussed in detail. As Paganism was never centralized, different gods had different levels of popularity in different regions and times. Someone living by the sea might have venerated Njord more frequently than someone who lived in the mountains and venerated Ullr.

For someone coming from a monotheistic background, the concept might come off as rather jarring and even downright impossible, as many monotheists have provided the argument that if there were more than one god, there would be chaos.

While that's not entirely false—as seen in the numerous stories revolving around Loki—the truth is that having several gods in the Norse Pantheon provided followers of the Old Norse Religion with a rich backstory that had many complex deities instead of just one, allowing them to choose which god they'd like to worship based on the characteristics.

It also makes for interesting lore, where the gods, more or less on an even footing, have risen to challenges against them (such as Ymir and the frost giants) and have also challenged each other in battle, giving the followers a clear idea as to which god excels where and who is the strongest of them all.

One of the redemptive features of polytheism is it allowed the Norse Pagans to realize that the gods were fallible at times, and this created a relatability in the hearts of the followers, knowing that they were fashioned by the gods and thus was also prone to fallibility.

Norse Pagans had a very diverse array of venerating practices, including deity veneration, ancestor veneration, and spirit veneration.

Immanent

Speaking in a religious context, immanence is the opposite of transcendence. Sometimes, religions can be a little bit of both, but in most cases, you will see that religions are either immanent or transcendent.

But what does this mean?

Transcendent religions focus quite literally on transcendence. Abrahamic religions focus on transcending above this realm and into a better hereafter. Being a follower of a transcendent faith gives its followers a "higher purpose" that allows them to attain their desired afterlife by following a set of rules, practices, and worship. The primary goal of transcendent faiths is to elevate one's soul through meditation, enlightenment, devotion, and attaining knowledge.

In Christianity, for example, your actions either bring you closer to God or drive you further away from God. The nobler actions are known as virtues, and the profane ones are called sins. What constitutes sin and what constitutes virtue are detailed in the Bible. Christians adhere to the doctrines and dogmas written in the Bible to attain transcendence.

On the other hand, immanent faiths focus on the quality, fulfillment, actualization, and realization of your current life and the bond that you have with the people, creatures, and the world around you. The practices that encompass immanence are all about your immediate reality, your lived experience, and your well-being.

The goal of the faith here is to improve your present life by providing you with the structure necessary to cultivate harmony with the people and the environment around you. Rather than spend your life doing certain things in a certain way to ensure some rewarding afterlife, immanence requires you to improve your everyday life and to experience the joys of your faith in the things that you do.

It is the prevalent belief in Norse Paganism that you'll automatically join your ancestors in the afterlife (Hel) unless you devote yourself to dying in battle, in which case, you'll get to join the gods in Valhalla. This freedom allows the followers to pursue their goals and ambitions in life without worrying about what kind of afterlife they'll get.

Orthopraxical

The two main schools of religious thought are orthodoxy and orthopraxy. Orthodoxy concerns itself with the right beliefs, while orthopraxy is all about the right actions. Religions often have one of the two beliefs, but in some instances, they may employ both schools of thought. Take Islam and Hinduism, for example. They both employ both practices, where beliefs and faith in the doctrines fulfill the requirement for orthodoxy while actions such as fasting, prayer, pilgrimage, and keeping a karmic balance check the orthopraxy box.

Norse Paganism is an orthopraxical religion. It emphasizes experience, the integrity of practice, the continuation of one's lineage, and sustaining one's legacy rather than prioritizing faith and adherence to certain doctrines.

Orthopraxy provides a very individualized sense of what's right and wrong, meaning that what's right for one individual might not be right for the other. There's no centralized authority to dictate what's entirely right and wrong.

This doesn't mean that Norse Paganism does not have customs. There are customs and traditions carried out by descendants belonging to a certain lineage, but that is because of the orthopraxical nature of the religion rather than the orthodox nature, as maintaining one's legacy is an orthopraxical act.

Norse Beliefs

There are several distinct features of Norse beliefs that will provide you with a deeper understanding of how the Norse Pagans lived their lives and how they interacted with each other. Concepts like morality, hospitality, gifting, and harmony were integral to the functioning of Norse society.

. . .

Morality

In Norse Paganism, morality was not seen as some divine mandate by the gods. It was created very democratically by the people for the people. These moral concepts were concerned with the well-being of one's family, relatives, members of society, and living things in general. When the focus was on the well-being of people as opposed to the glorification of deities alone, traits like loyalty, modesty, self-reliance, hospitality, compassion, courage, wisdom, and kindness were emphasized. It was highlighted in the Hávamál that wealth was considered to be the most fickle of friends while wisdom was said to be the highest of currency, and as opposed to the temporariness of wealth, wisdom was eternal.

Frith

Frith is the experience that you feel when you get a sense of honest welcome from social interactions. Things like compliments, warm greetings, friendliness, drinking together heartily, and camaraderie contribute to the feeling of frith.

Simply put, it was considered to be the most basic love language to exist between people. When you extended someone frith, they felt close to you, and their loyalty was invoked as a result of your hospitable behavior.

Similarly, Norse hospitality was the primary mode through which frith was promoted in their society. When you demonstrated hospitality toward someone, it was a way of showing them respect, love, devotion, and goodwill—all of which were considered to be very important aspects in fostering relationships, whether familial, business-related, or romantic.

Gifting Cycle

The Norse folk were big on gift-giving, believing firmly in the process of reciprocation. They believed that a gift, rather than creating monetary obligation, was a sincere sentiment meant for the well-being of the individual being gifted with something. You could gift someone an item, a favor, your protection, love, your time and energy, space, and even sharing your belongings with them.

The gifting cycle was all about creating outcomes that brought about well-being by fostering harmony between two people. This created a sense of peace, purpose, and happiness throughout the community. The gift-giving cycle was related to wyrd and orlog.

Wyrd and Orlog

Wyrd means destiny. More than that, it represents the living world around you. It is the reality that you live in, the reality that is affected by your actions and their outcomes.

Orlog is the relationship between an action and its outcome. The outcome of your past actions dictates how your present reality is, and the present reality lays the foundations for the outcomes of your future.

Together, wyrd and orlog form the fabric of fate, serving as threads that weave in and out, shaping fates.

Inner-Yard and Outer-Yard

The Norse people had a very distinct boundary between their interior and exterior spaces. The interior spaces referred to their homes, their wall-bound communities, and their villages. Outside, the outer yard was the wilderness with all its mountains, forests, oceans, and wastelands.

Soul

The soul was considered a multi-part entity, with each part being equally important. The four main parts of the soul were hamr, hugr, fylgja, and hamingja.

The hamr was considered your outer appearances, such as your physical form, your personality, and your traits.

The hugr was your mind, will, emotions, and thoughts. Upon one's death, their hugr departed the body.

The fylgja was the essence of a person and could perform astral travel. It could take a certain shape, such as in the case of Odin, whose ravens Hugin and Muninn were his fylgja.

Lastly, **the hamingja** was the potentiality of a person, including their proclivities, inclinations, aspirations, strengths, and weaknesses.

· · ·

Norse Rituals

The Norse Pagans were a celebrative people, finding festivity in each occasion. This was because the world they lived in was very adverse, and harsh, and took a heavy toll on them. The weather was ice-cold in the winter months, severely debilitating their ability to grow crops. Rival tribes would attack each other, claiming the lives of the townsfolk. Wild animals roamed about, posing a constant threat to the people. But despite all these hardships, the people found purpose and joy in their victories, both little and great.

Blót

Blót was a sacrifice practiced to get the goodwill of the gods and goddesses. The rituals were often carried out in large groups by the jarl or local chief. These sacrifices were both a time for people to venerate the gods and for the local chiefs to show off their wealth and prosperity.

Blóts happened four times a year—close to the winter solstice, at the spring equinox, at the summer solstice, and at the autumn equinox. If the people were having bad harvest or other troubles, they'd have additional blóts too.

Sumbel

This was a drinking ritual comprised of toasting, oath-taking, hails, reciting poetry, singing songs, and chanting. Sumbel had rounds during which the horn was passed in a circle, and each person hailed or toasted, then drank and passed the horn along.

The purpose of the sumbel was to invoke powers through words spoken in that holy rite. Oath-taking was a very common aspect of the sumbel, and given the nature of the rite, it was considered especially more meaningful and binding.

A sumbel started with an introduction by whoever was hosting the event. The first round then followed, during which all the gods and goddesses were hailed. In the second round, the ancestors and the great heroes were hailed. In the third round, people made oaths, spoke in a venerating manner, recited poetry, sang songs, and declared things.

As long as it was done in the proper vein, a sumbel could have more than three rounds. It ended with pouring out the remaining drink in the horn, then declaring that the rite is finally over.

Yule

The period between the winter solstice and the blót associated with it was given the title of Yule. It was a celebratory event marked by drinking alcohol, feasting for three days and nights, playing games, and singing. The Yule log was made from a large piece of oak decorated with yew, fir, and holly, and then runes were carved into it. This was to ask the gods for their protection. A piece of the log was preserved by the people to protect their families and to start the first fire of the new year.

Evergreen trees were decorated with clothes, food, runes, carvings, and decorations to invite the tree spirits to return in spring. People dressed up as goats to represent the goats that pulled Thor's wagon across the sky. They'd then go from house to house and perform plays and sing in exchange for food and drink.

Burial

The Norse folk were sent to the afterlife either by cremation or burial. Cremation was quite common among the earliest Vikings, who strongly held to the belief that smoke from the fire would help carry the deceased's spirit to the afterlife. The remains from the cremation were usually buried in an urn.

The burial locations for the dead were quite varied, with some graves being shallow (used for children and women) and others being burial mounds that could hold many bodies in the form of a grave field.

Boats were a symbol of safe passage into the afterlife. That's why boats had such a central role in funeral rites. Even some of the burial mounds were shaped in the form of boats. Vikings and Norsemen who were held in high regard were sometimes buried with their actual boats. Funeral boats were also used to send out the deceased into the sea, after which a flaming arrow was shot to set the boat on fire.

Some rituals were more prevalent than others when it came to burying the dead. The body was draped in fine clothes that were prepared specifically for the funeral. A celebration was held, cherishing the lived life of the deceased in the form of singing songs, drinking alcohol, eating food, and offering tributes. These tributes were known as grave goods and were almost equal to the value of the deceased's status in life. Someone who was a warrior was buried with their swords, axes, and shields.

Wedding

Before the wedding, the bride would remove a gilt circlet from her hair, representing the loss of her virginity. She'd then wear a crown at her wedding. The groom would have to acquire a sword from his ancestor's graves. The groom would carry his sword as a symbol of Thor's hammer. The bride and groom didn't wear particularly special clothes.

The weddings would take place on a Friday as it was Frigg's day, who was the goddess of fertility. The ceremony started by venerating the gods and getting their attention by sacrificing an animal for them. The groom would then give the sword that he'd gotten from his ancestor's grave to the bride so that she'd keep it for their future son. The bride would give her groom a sword, connoting that the job of protecting her was transferred from her father to her husband. Then the two would exchange rings and vows.

What followed was a feast in the hall, where the groom would first help his bride over the threshold by lifting her and then plunge his sword into a pillar. The deeper the sword went, the more luck and prosperity they'd have.

The couple was encouraged to partake in celebratory mead that they'd have to drink for the next month, which is where the concept of honeymoon comes from.

At the end of the feast, the couple would retire to the bed and consummate their love. The next morning, the wife's hair would be tied and covered with a cloth to show that she'd been elevated in her status as a wife. The groom would then provide her with the keys to the house, further cementing that status.

Birth and naming

After a baby was born, it had to undergo a certain ritual before it could be considered a real human being. Before the baby was named, they were not perceived as a real human being. One probable reason for this was so that people could emotionally protect themselves in case of the infant's death, as the mortality rate in infants was extremely high back then.

Once the baby was born, he was placed on the ground. The father came and picked him up and placed him inside his coat. This was done to symbolize that the father had accepted the baby as his. Once the baby was accepted, the father would inspect the child and see if the baby had any physical defects. If the baby were healthy, the father would sprinkle water over the baby. After that, the father would name the child and give him a gift. Gifts included things like rings, weapons, farms, and land deeds. Once this happened, the child was considered a real human being.

• • •

Seiðr

Seiðr was a magic practiced by both the gods and the humans. It was said that this sort of magic was related to influencing fate and interpreting one's destiny. There were wandering wise men and women who would use seiðr to both help and harm others. Its use was considered a bit of a taboo among some people, while others revered it as being a power so holy that Odin and Freya used it. Seiðr was used for clairvoyance and divination. It was a vessel for seeking out hidden things and for uncovering mysteries, both physical and mental. Seiðr could be used to heal the sick, bring about good fortune, and control the weather.

But just as it could be used for good, it could also be used for the opposite. It could be used to curse an individual, make a land barren by blighting it, and induce illness. Someone who practiced seiðr could intentionally tell false futures and send the recipients on a road to chaos and disaster.

Seiðr could even be used to kill people.

Its ambiguous nature was one of the reasons why it was seen as taboo by some.

Runes

Runes were used in the Old Norse Religion to make one's magical incantations permanent. They were carved into things such as wood, bone, stone, and metal so that their effects would last long.

According to the Eddas and the sagas, the runes held magical powers that could assist someone in predicting the future, protection from disasters and misfortune, and imbue things with a magical quality. Additionally, runes were used to write down spells, conjurations, and curses. In the next chapter, we will take a deep dive into runes and find out how they originated, how they worked, and how you can use them in your life.

This was certainly a very packed chapter, containing vital information about the characteristics of Norse Paganism, the beliefs held by the Norse people, and the rites and rituals that they observed. Going forward, we will take some of those rituals and study them in a detailed manner to get some practical understanding of how to be a practicing pagan and how to incorporate those rites in our everyday life, starting with runes.

CHAPTER 6
THE RUNES

Brief History of Runes

The Germanic-speaking people used the runic alphabet for reading and writing from as far back as 150 AD. The Elder Futhark script came into prominence around 700 AD, and the Younger Futhark script, which was a hallmark of the Viking Age, came into prominence around 790—110 AD. Other forms of the script also evolved, including the Anglo-Saxon Futhorc writing system. England had been using runes from the 5th century until the 11th century. Scandinavia, on the other hand, kept using the runes well into the Middle Ages and beyond.

Many runestones were erected throughout Scandinavia, which today serve as a strong connection with the history of the Germanic-speaking people.

Runes were comprised of vertical lines that had branches/twigs jutting out diagonally, upwards, downwards, and in a curved fashion, depending on which rune was being written. They could be written from both right to left and left to right. Each rune represented a phoneme, which was a speech sound, and had a name comprising of a noun that had the same starting sound as the associated rune.

The origins of the runic script date back to 160 AD on the Vimose comb from Denmark. The inscriptions on that rune were so confident, mature, and prolifically used that researchers deduced that such an advanced form of usage must come after hundreds of years of experience in writing in runes. While that gives us a timeline of how old the runes were, how exactly did they come into being?

Archaeological evidence has directed towards Greek and Roman alphabets, considering that unstandardized Greek might have reached the Germanic speakers by way of travelers serving as middlemen.

While those origins are fitting for academic and archaeological purposes, those of the faith believe that Odin gained the knowledge of the runes after sacrificing himself to himself and hanging from Yggdrasil for nine days and nights without food or drink. For the devout, this explanation is far more credible, romantic, and grandiose than, say, stating that the script came into being as a result of Greek and Roman languages.

By 500 AD, the runic script had fanned out across Sweden, Denmark, and Norway, and had spread to outposts in England, Germany, Poland, Russia, and Hungary. Because of this expansion and how different people used them, four main scripts came into being:

- The Elder Futhark
- Younger Futhark
- Anglo-Saxon Futhorc

- Medieval Futhark

There were great variations among the scripts, leading scholars to the conclusion that the Futhark scripts were not used as a definitive script for one language but instead for many different Germanic languages spoken across a vast area. The shapes of these runes differed, as well as their layout, order, medium, and usage depending on the regional, chronological, and social differences. That's why there was never actually a standardized runic alphabet.

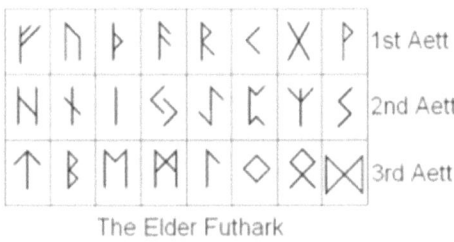

The Elder Futhark

Elder Futhark

This was the earliest classified runic script and was widely used in the Germanic world until 700 AD. 24 characters formed the elder Futhark script, with the first six of the alphabets forming its name 'Futhark'. The runes are grouped into three rows of eight, and each group is called an aett. Each rune was named after things that started with that sound.

While there are examples of written manuscripts in the Younger and Anglo-Saxon Futhark, there aren't any examples when it comes to the Elder Futhark, even though it was used to write Proto-Germanic, Proto-Norse, Proto-English, and Proto-High German. What survives today of the Elder Futhark is barely 400 inscriptions, and even those have shown quite a lot of wear and tear. As of now, they're partly legible. The real number of the inscriptions is unknown, presumed to be lost to time and space. What remains of the Elder Futhark today has been recreated using Younger Futhark and the Gothic and Anglo-Saxon variants.

Some of the inscriptions found were on wood and metal. Other surfaces that had Elder Futhark inscriptions included coins, military equipment, jewelry, combs, brooches, and runestones.

Younger Futhark

After 700 AD, the Elder Futhark was merged and adapted into the Younger Futhark script, mostly reserved for writing Old Norse—the language of the Viking Age. The original 24 characters were replaced and reduced to 16 runes. The 10th century saw the Younger Futhark being widely used all over Scandinavia.

The earlier of the Younger Futhark inscriptions were discovered in Denmark, leading them to being called Danish runes. Another variant came into light in the form of Norwegian-Swedish runes. Yet another variant became prominent, this one being quite minimalistic because it was staveless.

More than 3000 runic inscriptions in the Younger Futhark were discovered from the Viking Age, many telling stories about ownership, inheritance, politics, raiding, religion, magic, travel, literature, and myth.

A lot of the runes were found to be commemorating and celebrating the dead in the form of prayers, obituaries, signatures, and statements saying that the deceased was a good warrior, a noble man, a striving farmer, and so on.

Some of the Younger Futhark runes have signs from the carver on them, signifying that carving runes must have been considered a very specific skill at that time. As Seiðr was considered a very female-oriented task, runes were considered a male-oriented skill.

Anglo-Saxon runes

(5th to 11th centuries)

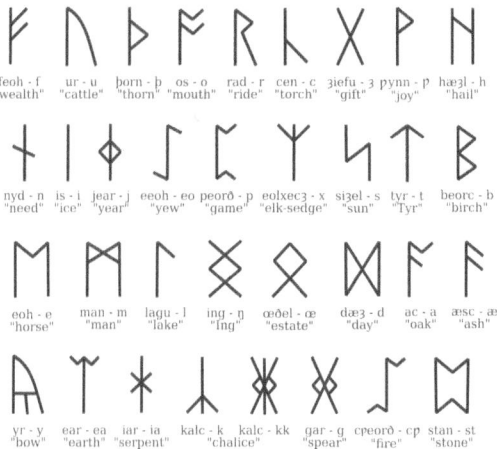

Anglo-Saxon Futhorc

The Anglo-Saxon Futhorc began somewhere around the 5th century in Britain and Frisia. Unlike the Younger Futhark, the Anglo-Saxon Futhorc added runes to the script so that they'd be able to use them in writing old English and old Frisian. Some of the inscriptions that have survived include stone crosses, coins, weapons, and personal items. But the number of these inscriptions is even less than those of the Elder Futhark at just under 200.

Between the 7th and 9th centuries, more of these runes were seen on coins, hinting that the usage went beyond just commemorative; these were practical runes used to denote the value of coins. As Christianity came into the scene in the 7th century, it left its mark on the Anglo-Saxon Futhorc, reforming some of it and competing with it in inscriptions until a time came when Latin was being used side by side with the Futhorc. The Anglo-Saxon runes held their own until the 10th century, after which they were replaced entirely, and their usage came to an abrupt halt.

Medieval Futhark

The Younger Futhark shaped medieval Futhark. Between the 10th and 11th centuries in Scandinavia, this script evolved from the Younger Futhark and was used quite consistently throughout the 13th century. It had the 16 Younger Futhark runes but with some tiny modifications to set them apart from the Younger Futhark.

The Symbols, Meanings, and Usage of Runes

Pop culture, especially video games and high-fantasy franchises, have created this picture of runes as being latently magical and downright mysterious. From *The Elder Scrolls* to games like *Kingdoms of Amalur*, runes have become a staple of Norse-inspired video games and Western RPGs, providing gamers with an extra layer of immersion in the form of this mythical language that is so quintessential of Tolkien-esque concepts of magic and fantasy.

But before they were a fantasy trope, runes were being used by the Germanic and Nordic people a thousand years ago for writing, magic, and divination.

As for what they are, well, the word 'rune' means 'mystery.' Oracles used in the past to help others gain insights into situations or answer questions. In modern paganism, runes have been used to guide you through any issues, help you tackle problems, and show you what can likely happen in the future. They must not be confused with fortune-telling, as runes are riddled with mysticism, and quite rarely do they ever give a straight answer.

Runes offer variables, hints, and suggestions on how to act if a certain probability happens in the future. When you use runic magic or runes for divination, you'll discover that there's a lot of room for interpretation and intuition.

But why? Why is that so? Well, think of it from a logical point of view. The future is not fixed. Thousands, if not millions, of variables affect the future, with the tiniest change in one variable resulting in an entirely different outcome. If the future isn't fixed, then there's no fixed way to tell what exactly is going to happen. But runes can help you cast light on that uncharted territory and allow you to follow the path of the optimum outcome, provided you use their guidance well.

With the guidance of the runes, not only can you anticipate likely possibilities in the future, but also use that knowledge to your advantage and change the outcome.

While there is innate magic in the runes, the general principle that modern paganism follows when working with runes is that when you cast runes, your conscious and subconscious align, allowing you to communicate with the message of the cast runes. It is inferred that the runes that are cast are not random at all but are chosen by your subconscious. That is to say, this is not a definitive explanation for how runes work but one interpretation of modern pagans. Other pagans state that the gods and the Norns themselves decide the order of the cast runes in order to help you. Others state that the runes possess power of their own and have the ability to channelize their magic in runic magic, casting, and divination.

That's why it is so fitting that they are named runes because it remains a mystery as to how they truly work. What matters is that they work, they are potent with magic, and they are one of our best methods to contact the ethereal, the powerful, the fate-weaving, and the holy.

The meanings of the runes are tied to universal forces that change and evolve with time. These forces, elemental in nature, are just as relevant today as they were thousands of years ago. But since these forces have a sentient nature, their manipulation of the runes makes rune reading a very subjective and personal matter.

I would say that rune reading takes a lot of practice. Like any art, the more you hone it, the better you'll get at it. Since it's a religious act and a very magically charged one at that, you must always approach this craft with the respect and honor it deserves. While books, guides, online tutorials, and DIYs can help you practice runes, you should first form a bond with them by studying their meaning, understanding the power they hold, and learning about how they were used in the past and how you can use them in a respectful manner. When using runes, you must always trust your intuition, as divination and oracle reading are very intuition-heavy activities.

Each rune has an associated deity, animal, or entity with whom it is connected. Fehu, for instance, represents cattle.

Thurisaz is associated with the giants. Uruz is a symbol of strength.

While some of the meanings of the runes are decipherable, the greater mystery is still shrouded in mysticism and is very subjective. That's because runes and their meanings evolve and change with time. Everyone interprets them in their own way, with relative meanings. However, the primary aspects of runes that are common throughout include three main characteristics:

- The symbol of the rune and what it represents
- The name and the meaning, along with the sound and the letter value
- The energy, deity, trait, and spirit embodied by the rune

The Elder Futhark—which are the runes that we'll be studying—are sorted into three sets of eight runes known as the aettir. These aettir are respectively known as Freyr's Aett, Heimdall's Aett, and Tyr's Aett. Symbolically, the three aetts represent the three parts of life's cycle. The first set of runes represents finding one's footing in the material world through the accumulation of wealth and an elevation of status. Things like cattle, communication, negotiation, vigor, strength, and business wit are related to the first set. The second set is all about increasing one's growth, maturity, and wisdom. This set holds runes like fate, harvest, abundance, and obstacles one must overcome. The third set of runes is related to developing one's legacy and spirituality. These runes contain birth, intuition, inheritance, and community.

While, yes, some of the meaning of the runes is lost as they once belonged to the Old Norse people and haven't exactly been transcribed into a place, one should not lose hope about this lost legacy as runes have a way of revealing their meaning to the seekers, the searchers, and those who are patient enough to let the runes communicate with them.

Without further ado, let's take a look at the runes and their meaning.

Fehu

Phonetic Value: F

Pronunciation: "FAY-hoo" "FEY-who"

The literal meaning of Fehu is wealth, power, and cattle.

Fehu is symbolic of two branches growing off a tree. It can also be seen as the two horns of a cow. While the literal meaning connotes cattle, cattle itself was a signifier of a family's wealth and power in the past. You could pay off your debts with cattle. If a man was killed unjustly, the blood price would also have to be paid in cattle. If someone did not own their own cattle, the tribe's or clan's cattle were considered to be theirs, provided that they were a person of status. A bard was said to have a blood price equal to that of a king because he was a learned man and a reservoir of tales, beliefs, and anecdotes.

In that sense, cattle were considered a means of exchange, much like we use money today.

If you want to interpret Fehu, know that its appearance signifies the arrival of success and wealth. If the cast shows Fehu, it is considered fated that your hard work will be rewarded soon. While the concept of wealth is ever-changing, given that once cattle were used as currency and nowadays we have so many types of currencies ranging from gold and silver to bitcoin and NFTs, Fehu always signifies an improvement in your business affairs and an increase in your earnings. However, there is a caution attached to the appearance of Fehu. This money does not come scot-free. It has to be applied to things that have some solidity and permanence, for example, real estate or resources whose value will appreciate over time. Fehu also highlights the boost in self-esteem that comes with the attainment of wealth. It is a metric of how one can pursue their dreams and goals with the wealth that they have received. If you see Fehu, it means that your dreams are going to be realized soon through the catalyst of money.

The inverted or reversed meaning of Fehu suggests the loss of wealth or the disadvantages that come with hoarded wealth. Money can corrupt people, sever bonds between friends, cause tension between two parties, and may even destroy one's reputation if said money is spent recklessly. A reversed Fehu can serve as both a warning and foreboding that your wealth might be in danger if you choose to use it in a vile manner. An inverted Fehu can be a warning from the gods to be wary of all the negative aspects that come with wealth. If you were about to embark on a new business venture, an inverted Fehu could be a warning sign, telling you that your venture might not end up the way you thought it would. If it shows up reversed, it could indicate you losing your personal possessions or coming across struggles that cause your self-esteem to dip.

Uruz

Phonetic Value: U

Pronunciation: "OO-rooz"

With its literal meaning being Aurochs, the powerful and extinct ox whose size was between a bison and a mammoth, Uruz is symbolic of power, endurance, wild potential, emotional strength, and vitality. The Vikings used to revere the horns of the Auroch, from which they drank. Another aspect of this rune is its relation to the god Ullr, who was the god of archery, winter, and hunting. In Germanic folklore, Ullr was known as the god of the hunt.

This rune connotes unhindered power. Raw, untamed, physical force. Additionally, this power can be sexual as well, especially when it comes to male sexuality. If this rune shows up for a man, it signifies a change in the man's masculine powers imminently. If it shows up for a woman, it can be a sign that a man will come into her life and affect her either romantically or in a physical (sexual) way.

It wouldn't be uncommon for this rune to show up for athletes, hunters, military personnel, and people who exert their physicality in their fields, such as bodybuilders, MMA fighters, parkour artists, and so on. If Uruz shows up for any of the aforementioned people, it can be a sign that their strength will be reinforced. It can also be a warning sign if they're overexerting themselves, telling them not to abuse their powers to avoid potential injuries.

If you've drawn Uruz, it is telling you that now is not the time for being subtle or passive. It's time to be active and take advantage of the opportunity available to you by being powerful.

An inverted Uruz could be a sign of emotional and physical weakness. Someone around you may be using your energy against you, such as by sapping it from you by making you doubt yourself, sabotaging your plans, or downright degrading you. If it shows up inverted, it's telling you that you have to look out for brutality and violence from others.

Thurisaz

Phonetic Value: Th

Pronunciation: "THUR-ee-sahz"

The literal meaning of this rune is thorn. Why thorn? Well, the frost giants had a son named Loki (you know Loki, big mischief monger, chiefest of calamities, father of Fenrir) who proved to be a thorn in the side of the gods time and again. Thurisaz also means giant, representing the giants and all the danger they represented. You can also look upon Thurisaz as being symbolic of Thor's hammer. It's a very interpretive rune, leaving quite a lot to one's intuitive powers and imagination.

However, this much is certain in its interpretation—the rune warns you to take precautionary measures, to defend yourself against potential thorns that might be lying in your path, and to overcome conflict with your intelligence. If you get this rune in your reading, you should protect yourself by taking the necessary measures. Thurisaz can indicate an ambush from an enemy.

In its representation of a thorn, Thurisaz comes bearing a gift: The wisdom that comes when you're pricked by a thorn for the first time. You will always remember the pain and will be wise enough to avoid thorns whenever you see them in your path again. It's a lesson, a painful one at that, but you have learned it and are now better suited to deal with similar situations in the future. These situations could be harsh outside forces, critical situations in your everyday life, health hazards, some treachery by a foe posing as a friend, or someone opposing you. You have to cultivate discipline and adapt to the change with the realization in mind that things that are fated to happen will happen, and it is only within your power to act bravely and honorably in the face of those things and to endure hardships so that you can get out on the other side.

An inverted Thurisaz means that you're being too obstinate in the face of change. Do not resist, and do not run away from adversity. Think of the long-term instead of just the immediate outcome. You must understand that these hardships are part of life, just as much as a thorn is part of a rose. Do not ignore these problems; otherwise, they will become too big to deal with later on.

Ansuz

Phonetic Value: A

Pronunciation: "AHN-sooz"

Now, this is an important rune, literally meaning god. It represents the breath of Odin. Belonging to the most powerful Norse god, Ansuz is related to wisdom, divinity, culture, creativity, communication, drawing, music, art, inner knowledge, and spiritual growth.

If Ansuz shows up in a draw, be on the lookout for a guiding figure, someone with knowledge and authority, such as a teacher, parent, or employer. This figure can guide you toward a positive life-changing event. You can potentially get a promotion, a raise, or a bonus in your line of work. If you're a creative person, you might be on the verge of your next big project, such as a book or a work of art. If you have been facing a problem for a long time, now might be the time that this problem gets resolved. You will get assistance from someone wise and knowledgeable. This can also hold true in religion. A priest or a spiritual leader may help you untangle some existential crises. Lastly, it can be a symbol of the divine trying to get in touch with you with a message of creation, growth, and guidance.

If this rune shows up inverted, understand that the authority figure who's about to come into your life is going to be a hindrance to your goals. Someone who might be posing as an authoritative figure might be trying to deceive you. Be extra wary of that. The hindrance could very well be within you. Perhaps you're resisting someone's help that you shouldn't resist. Perhaps someone is trying to help you out, but you're being too obstinate and prideful and aren't accepting their help. Whatever wisdom is out there in your immediate circle of contacts, you must accept it and invite it toward you.

Raidho

Phonetic Value: R

Pronunciation: "Rah-EED-ho"

Raidho means journey and riding through a chariot or a wagon. This rune is indicative of the life journey of a person. Raidho signifies that the journey is more important than the stops along the way. One's course in life is decided by the Norns. Raidho reminds us that great events in our life are beyond our control. These include birth, death, winning, losing, suffering, joy, hardships, ease, and everything in between. One must understand that fate is to be respected, not to be controlled. By flowing along fate, one can channel it and become one with it. There is nothing to gain by averting fate. Even the gods knew that. They knew that they weren't able to stop Ragnarök.

When Raidho shows up in a rune reading, it reveals that you're about to embark on a journey, the outcome of which will be in your favor and will result in positive changes in your life. This rune signifies a change in your career with new experiences and insights awaiting you in the future. Raidho wants you to let what's going to happen, happen. All attempts to try to stop the inevitable will result in failure. It can also mean a spiritual journey through which you will become a wiser person. Raidho has a celebratory nature, often revealing reunions with old friends and family members, telling you that if you're feeling lost and down and defeated, worry not, for emotional reinforcements are arriving soon in the form of familiar faces.

An inverted Raidho indicates that the journey you'll embark on will stray you from your primary path. If there's a career change or a business move, it might disrupt your personal relationship and will likely result in a negative outcome. If you had planned something, there will be a delay in those plans. Whatever you intend will be met with challenges and hurdles. However, these challenges, delays, and hurdles will lead you to newer opportunities rather than rob you of existing ones. When a reversed Raidho shows up for a spiritual reading, it indicates the need to push past the agitations, frustrations, and worldly delusions that are holding your spiritual journey back.

Kenaz / Kaunan

Phonetic Value: K

Pronunciation: "KEN-ahz"

Kenaz literally means torch. What that actually stands for is the flame of divine inspiration. With that fire comes creativity, inspiration, vitality, energy, and the banishment of darkness. This rune indicates a rebirth through sacrifice. Creativity through fire. Artists get this rune, especially when seeking a reading about their artistic ventures.

Like a torch, the message of Kenaz is that of a warm welcome. The cold dark has been dispelled. Come into the radiance. Come into the light. Seek shelter here. Rest, if you will. You are in a safe place.

Its interpretation concerns finding solutions to long-standing problems. If you've been struggling with hurdles for a long time, your solution is right around the corner. Kenaz represents that eureka moment that will lead you to discovery. Like flames, sometimes the guidance that Kenaz hints towards will be fiery and intense.

When it shows up reversed, it's a sign of the flame being darkened. A friendship might be ending, a journey may be coming to an end, or a source that you were using for inspiration all this time might be petering out. This must not stop you from achieving your goals. Instead, be patient and bide your time in the trough before you crest again.

Gebo

Phonetic Value: G

Pronunciation: "GHEB-o"

With its literal meaning being generosity through gifting, Gebo represents everything that has to do with the act of giving. It is one of the few runes that cannot be inverted.

It manifests that a gift will be given shortly. Even a marriage proposal or an opportunity to advance your business. Someone is going to come into your life, either romantically or materially, who will change it in a bountiful manner. Sexual union is also one of the meanings of Gebo. If it comes up in a paired reading with Uruz, it may indicate a fleeting encounter. A very intense encounter, at that. It can be cultivated into something more if needed.

Wunjo

Phonetic Value: W

Pronunciation: "WOON-yo"

Wunjo resembles the flag planted on a battlefield after a victory. A victory that results in song, joy, celebration, and rejoicing. That is what Wunjo means. This rune encompasses joy, pleasure, success, comfort, and harmony. It is a call to positive manifestation, stressing the need to take affirming action toward the achievement of a goal.

When Wunjo shows up in a reading, it is telling you to shed your ego and look to a higher purpose and meaning. Align yourself with the universe and become truly mindful of the present so that you can best equip yourself to achieve your goals. Wunjo represented the Law of Attraction before the Law of Attraction was cool. If Wunjo shows up in a reading, especially when you were trapped in a pessimistic and negative space, it is telling you to think positively and adjust your thinking attitude.

An inverted Wunjo says that your journey toward a goal is going to be difficult. It's going to take longer to reach your goal than you expected. However, you don't have to worry, as an inverted Wunjo is an invitation to strive harder rather than retreat. An inverted Wunjo is a sign that the difficulties in your life have severely altered your mentality and that you need to get in touch with your roots and push the reset button on your mindset.

Hagalaz

Phonetic Value: H

Pronunciation: "HA-ga-lahz"

Hagalaz means hailstone. It is the herald of the wrath of nature and the destruction brought about by uncontrollable force. At its core, the rune tells of necessary destruction, a destruction seen in Ragnarök. It was needed to bring about the rebirth of a new world.

This is one of the few runes that cannot be pulled inverted.

When Hagalaz appears, it is an indication that one should prepare for the future and ditch all thoughts of the past. Often, the past holds us back and has a psychological hold on us in the form of emotional blocks and trauma that can debilitate us. Where it represents destruction, Hagalaz also represents rebirth. Let the past go, is what the rune says, and embrace the emotional destruction that shatters you and then makes you anew again so that you can grow in the future.

It is a heavy concept but put it into a simpler analogy, and it will be easier to understand. Someone goes through a terrible breakup or gets fired from their coveted job, or a loved one passes away. All these things have happened to many of us at some point in our lives. While it is right to grieve and become sad at loss, it is pertinent that once that grief has been processed, one must move on, get over that ex, look for a new career opportunity, spend time with one's living relatives and cherish them, and so forth.

Nauthiz / Naudhiz

Phonetic Value: N

Pronunciation: "NOWD-heez"

Nauthiz symbolizes necessity. It is a rune about endurance, willpower, and the factors that sometimes demand endurance and willpower; trouble and constraint.

Imagine, if you will, a worker who has been necessary personnel at a factory for thirty years. He has learned all the tricks of the trade, knows his way around the machinery, and is extremely adept in his craft. One day, he arrives at the factory and sees that a robot has replaced the job that he has been doing for so many years. He is rendered obsolete. What does this man do in the face of such an unconquerable difficulty?

That is what Nauthiz is all about—a chance for someone who has fallen short to step back and take into account what needs to be done. It is a test of one's endurance and willpower. Does that factory worker simply succumb to his obsolete fate, or does he adapt and start his own small business, one that caters to the refinement of handcraft rather than the heartlessness of machine-made things? He relearns, he finds another way, he perseveres, and most importantly, he reevaluates.

That is the interpretation of Nauthiz as well. If faced with setbacks, turn to the route of introspection and growth.

While some claim that Nauthiz cannot be reversed as it is a symmetrical shape, others state that a reversed Nauthiz can indicate the need for even more restraint than before in the face of overindulgence. Rather than material, focus on the spiritual. Learn to let things go and take stock of what is truly needed and what is purely excessive. Understand the difference between the two.

Isa / Isaza / Isaz

Phonetic Value: I

Pronunciation: "EE-sa"

Isa means ice. A simple rune, Isa can be considered the opposite of Kenaz. Where Kenaz was fire, Isa represents the stillness and purity that is characteristic of ice. While the fire is kinetic and instills movement, ice is potential and requires stillness.

It is one of the runes that cannot be reversed.

If Isa shows up in a reading, it wants you to meditate and recharge before you take action. Now is your time to rest. Be still. Once the metaphorical ice thaws, your direction will become clear. Beneath the cold and still and lifeless layer of ice lies a world waiting to bloom. All it is waiting for is the right season. Thus, so too should you wait as well. Do not abandon your goals nor lose sight of the things that you have to achieve. Just take a brief break from them while you meditate and improve your inner self.

Jera

Phonetic Value: J (J in Germanic languages)/ Y (like the "y" in year)

Pronunciation: "YARE-a"

Yet another irreversible rune, Jera means harvest, a time of plenty, summer, completion, reaping, and reward. It represents the natural cycle of the year, especially the turning over of a new cycle. The longest nights are about to come to an end, harkening the time to reap the reward of prior hardships.

It is a representation of change, a positive change at that. If Jera shows up in a reading, understand that reward is on its way. You have toiled, suffered, undergone hardships, and braved harsh weather. Now, you may retire, take a sabbatical, or even go on a vacation.

Jera is the rune of material gain. Gebo is the rune of spiritual gain. If both runes show up in a reading, it's a sign that you're going to get both happiness in relationships and monetarily. While there will be time to work hard again, and surely you will, right now, Jera's appearance suggests that you slow down and celebrate all that you have accomplished.

Eihwaz

Phonetic Value: Y

Pronunciation: "AY-wahz"

Eihwaz means the Yew Tree. Moreover, it represents life and death, enlightenment, balance, renewal, and, most importantly, the World Tree.

The Yew Tree stands in a snowy field. Brave in the face of all the lifelessness around it. Ever it remains so supple and strong; ever it stays green. Its red berries supply nourishment to those who are struggling to survive in that harsh environment. Its grace and majesty are a sign of its refusal to succumb to the opposition all around it. Yew trees have had a very significant role in the occult, and even in Christianity, they represented immortality which was why they were planted in churchyards. The wood from this tree made the best bows and could kill enemies from a long range.

When Eihwaz shows up in a reading, it's telling you that change is in the air. This will be a necessary and major change that will forever change things for you. Going to college, getting married, retiring, getting a new job, changing your profession, having a baby—all these changes are huge changes that require you to brace for what's coming.

There may be different sorts of changes that can happen either one at a time or at once—material, physical, mental, and spiritual. Let these changes serve as the vehicle that takes you from one point in your life to another. Keep yourself steady, focused, and driven through this process. Think of the Yew Tree and how it remains steadfast. You need to embody that in your life.

Eihwaz is also sometimes a sign that there's going to be a problem in your life that you have to sort out in advance before it becomes something grave.

This rune cannot be reversed.

Perthro

Phonetic Value: P

Pronunciation: "PER-thro"

The literal meaning of Perthro is dice-cup. Now, what does the dice cup signify? Fate. Chance. Mystery. Secrets.

You cannot always know all the possibilities for a solution. Sometimes, no matter how hard you'll try, the future will remain shrouded in mystery until such a time when the dice is cast. What does a player do when playing a game of chance when a dice cup is involved? A player constantly remains vigilant of all the moves that his opponents have made and keeps an eye on the board, knowing that while the outcome of the dice is not changeable, the other variables on the board are very well controllable. Thus, be on the lookout for signs that the universe might be sending toward you. Someone close to you might be keeping secrets from you.

When Perthro appears inverted, it's a sign that someone will reveal an unwanted secret to you soon. Sometimes, it indicates that you'll be free of a burdening secret that was otherwise causing you mental and physical harm.

Algiz

Phonetic Value: Z

Pronunciation: "AL-geez" / "el-hahz"

Algiz depicts elk's antlers, a person with his arms upraised, or even Heimdall, who holds his sword in one hand and his horn in the other. The literal meaning of this rune is defense, sanctuary, and protection.

When interpreting Algiz in a reading, one must note that context is extremely important. While the rune does symbolize protection, this protection can either be proactive or reactive. It could be telling you that you're safe from a threat as you have already taken protective measures. That's why the context is important here because if protective measures are not taken, Algiz is a sign that you need to ward yourself against a present threat.

The defense that Algiz represents is also a spiritual defense. You have to draw upon your inner emotions and create a safe space mentally and spiritually to protect yourself from the overwhelming spiritual and mental dangers around you. Use this time to seek solitude and meditate to ascend your spirit into the echelons of divinity to protect yourself from the undivine.

An inverted Algiz is called Ihwar. Ihwar is a warning rune, telling you that you've been lax in your defenses and danger is nearer than you thought. It beckons you to take up arms immediately. Your defenses were down, and others saw this as an opportunity to attack you. All is not lost, though. If you'll listen to the inverted Algiz, you'll still manage to defend yourself.

Sowilo

Phonetic Value: S

Pronunciation: "So-WEE-lo"

Sowilo is the rune symbolizing the sun, therefore signifying health, vitality, wholeness, and good energy. Fertility follows this rune, along with positivity, happiness, and good fortune.

If you draw this rune in a reading, you'll get success and lots of it. It won't be a success in just one aspect of your life; you'll find permanent success that does not depend on the weather, unlike Jera. An example of permanent success is overcoming a serious illness for good or hitting it big in business. It's something that will help sustain you till the end of your days.

Sowilo can never be inverted.

Tiwaz

Phonetic Value: T

Pronunciation: "TEE-wahz"

Tiwaz references Tyr, the legendary God who lost his hand to Fenrir. His victory against Fenrir came at a great personal sacrifice. However, this sacrifice ensured that his people were protected, even though this meant that Tyr was rendered useless in his trade. As harsh as what happened to Tyr was, Tiwaz is a positive rune, hinting towards justice, leadership logic, masculinity, responsibility, loyalty, and sacrifice.

If this rune shows up in a reading and you were looking for a spiritual breakthrough, know that it is on the way. You'll finally be able to perceive things from an elevated perspective. If you were looking for material gain, know that there's going to be an uphill climb. You will have to give it all to your management, leadership, and dexterity if you intend to succeed in whatever venture you're engaged in right now.

Sometimes, success comes at a price. A painful price, at that. This rune can foretell danger—danger in the form of an injury or personal loss. Sometimes, this rune can foretell something grave about to happen to one's family, company, friends, or team.

An inverted Tiwaz suggests that progress through the application of force is not the wisest route in this situation. Find another way, a less aggressive route, something that tends to focus on the brain more than the brawn. A reversed Tiwaz may indicate that you're facing a lack of motivation. Maybe you're being cowardly towards a matter that requires bravery. Perhaps you're feeling overwhelmed in the face of the challenge that lies ahead of you. Again, slow down, reevaluate, and tackle the matter differently. Do not let your ego get in the way.

Berkana /Berkano

Phonetic Value: B

Pronunciation: "BER-kah-na"/ "BER-kah-no"

Berkana is a feminine rune containing a lot of feminine power within its interpretation and meaning. Its literal meaning is that of a birch tree, a symbol of fertility in Norse paganism. Additionally, the shape of this rune is symbolic of the female form. Berkana represents the bond between a goddess and her creation and between a child and their mother. It's a powerful, nurturing, protecting, and supportive indication when this rune appears.

Just as Uruz contains within itself the male mysteries, all the feminine mysteries are contained within the Berkana rune.

When Berkana appears in a reading, it can represent pregnancy and the start of a person's new life. A business venture can be a fertile one, as boded by this rune. When Berkana shows up, it is the herald of good beginnings, whether in marital life, business, or in a spiritual direction. Berkana represents healing as well.

If it shows up inverted, it's hinting towards the person being stubborn and obstinate in the face of growth, stating that the person has to accept the rites of passage of life and has to grow, flow, and evolve if they intend to succeed.

Ehwaz

Phonetic Value: E

Pronunciation: "EH-wahz"

Ehwaz means horse and represents movement, progress, teamwork, trust, loyalty, and travel.

It motions toward forward movement and expending energy into traveling. If it shows up in a reading, it's a telling sign that you need to put in steady effort into attaining a goal. You may need to travel to attain this goal as well. Perhaps your business venture will take on a long-distance form, and you'll either have to communicate over long distances or travel to oversee the business.

If you're in a joint venture, focus on teamwork, communication, trust, and consistency to drive your venture home.

A reversed Ehwaz is suggestive of blocked movement and an inability to act. Your solution for such inaction is to evaluate the situation and gauge whether action or passivity is needed. An inverted Ehwaz also connotes failure to communicate in time. Lastly, this reversed rune represents a lack of trust on your part. Surprisingly, the rune here states that you were right all along to withhold trust from a certain person.

Mannaz

Phonetic Value: M

Pronunciation: "MAN-naz"

Mannaz means man or humankind at large. This is the rune of individuality, cooperation between people, kindling friendship, humanity, and helping others.

This rune is relationship-oriented, reminding us that bonding is at the heart of humanity and that we are all connected through the nature of our being human.

When Mannaz appears in a reading, it's referring to strengthening your relationship with others and thinking of your community as a whole. You will be assisted by others in a task that you need help with and will find that there's a lot of camaraderie and brotherhood in the people around you should you ask for their help.

A reversed Mannaz warns you that you have isolated yourself too much from others and have become disconnected from people, resulting in all the negativities that are going on in your life. Your feelings of depression, sadness, low energy, and dejectedness are arising from the fact that you've disconnected yourself from people. You have to reconnect with the right people, but not before healing yourself and taking the time to reorient yourself.

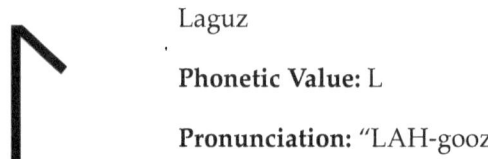

Laguz

Phonetic Value: L

Pronunciation: "LAH-gooz"

Laguz means water, specifically, lakes, the ocean, and seas. It represents the endless possibilities and nourishment that come with water. A ship riding the waves of the sea may end up on a new continent, leading its passengers to discover virgin lands, lands rife with possibility. It's a rune of femininity, intuition, cleansing, and unconsciousness.

This rune reminds us that it's important to have a deep understanding of ourselves. Be like water. Go with the flow. Let yourself loose. Follow your instincts. Become in tune with your feelings. That's what Laguz represents. The universe is trying to get in touch with you, revealing things that were hidden before.

A reversed Laguz indicates obstinateness, a lack of movement, and flowlessness. Are you inadvertently stopping your personal growth? Well, it's time to meditate and cultivate that growth rather than hinder it. Pursue the creative endeavors that truly fulfill you rather than indulge in those activities that are blocking your creative outlets.

Ingwaz / Ingaz

Phonetic Value: Ng

Pronunciation: "ING-wahz" / "eeng-wahz"

Meaning "seed," Ingwaz is a rune regarding reward, growth, awareness, success, and creation. More importantly, it is a rune about the earth, agriculture, and nature. It is one of the alternate names for Freyr, the god of fertility and agriculture.

This rune represents the earth and our relationship with it. It appears when someone is supposed to spend more time with nature. When Ingwaz shows up in a reading, it's telling you to pay attention to outdoor activities like gardening, sports, hiking, and swimming. Why? Because they're good for your body and mind. They're going to improve your health and, in doing so, grant you a sound mind. This personal growth is often overlooked by those who are so busy in their daily lives. Ingwaz wants you to reconnect with nature.

This rune cannot be reversed.

Dagaz

Phonetic Value: D

Pronunciation: "DAH-gahz"

Dagaz represents dawn. It is the rune of transformation, signaling the arrival of the day after a long night. It is a positive rune, signifying clarity, the triumph of good over evil, and light.

When you face challenges in your life, Dagaz's appearance states that you will overcome them with optimism and a positive outlook. This rune is a reminder of the cyclical nature of everything—night and day, life and death, rise and fall. There is an awakening hidden within the meaning of this rune. You are going to come across new possibilities and discover new worlds if you decide to align your mentality positively. This rune truly embodies the adage, "it's darkest before dawn." If you've been stuck in a rut, feeling hopeless, seeing no end to your troubles, Dagaz comes as a welcoming sign that all your troubles are going to come to an end, leaving you with new possibilities and unexpected adventures.

One cannot reverse this rune, either.

Othala

Phonetic Value: O

Pronunciation: "OH-tha-la"

This rune means property, particularly one's home, land, or estate.

This is the rune of the ancient clan lands. Historically, houses and estates have a strong spiritual link with their owner. A person is as much part of their house as the bricks and walls that make it. You build this place to live in, then populate it with memories and actions, giving it new life, every room a separate organ, and you, at the center of it all, running from room to room, living, thriving, alive, and making the house come alive with your spirit. That's why places become haunted, to begin with. The owner might not be there, but within those walls, memory is stored.

Othala is a manifestation of generational accumulation. A father builds a house that the son lives in, and so forth. In that manner, this rune is about nobility, heritage, family, history, honor, hard work, and pride. It's a rune depicting spiritual power, especially ancestral spiritual power that lingers long after the ancestor has departed from this realm.

If you draw this rune, it's telling you that you have to reconnect with your family and get in touch with your roots. You need their emotional support just as much as they need yours. When this rune turns up, you should expect wealth, prosperity, property, and land positively. Additionally, it might be a sign that you have to go back and visit the home of your ancestors and get in touch with the country of one's forebears.

Similarly, a reversed Othala suggests that there's a clash or a rift in the family that has to be immediately resolved cautiously and positively. It can be a sign that you're unable to accept family as a source of happiness in your life. In the worst case, it can be a sign that you're going to lose wealth and land.

How To Cast Runes and Read Them

Rune casting is an excellent way to hone your intuition and access your inner self, the self that is in touch with divinity. This secret self holds the key to divination. You can start by experimenting with different layout styles. Traditionally, runes were cast in multiples of 3 or odd numbers. 5 rune layouts are used commonly as well, along with some 7 and 9-rune layouts too. There's one that has 24 runes which is done at the start of each year to forecast what the year holds. Like Tarot, runes have many layout options you can experiment with, using the ones that suit you best.

At the most basic level, you can use a 1 rune pull for a simple yes and no sort of answer. The 3 runes casting is very similar to the traditional Tarot spreads, with each rune standing for past, present, future, or situation, action, and outcome.

Runes were originally cast by looking at the sky and throwing the runes on a special piece of cloth, then reading the upright landed runes.

The second most common way to read runes is to hold the rune pouch in your non-dominant hand and then think about the question that you want to be answered. Pull the runes out with your dominant hand and place them in your desired layout shape.

You can try out the following layout ideas, after which you'll be adept enough to try your own layouts:

3
action you must take in the face of challange

2
Challenges you may face

1
Overall Circumstance

The 3-Rune Layout

An ideal spread for beginners, the three-rune spread allows you to do a basic reading by removing three random runes from the pouch and putting them in front of you. The first rune should be on the right, the second in the middle, and the third on the left. The first one represents your overall circumstance. The second rune represents the challenges you may face, and the third one represents the action you must take in the face of the challenges.

Positives that might
influence the question

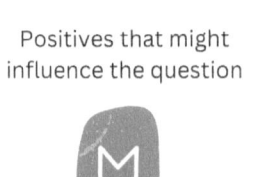

The problems that might influence the question

The Immediate answer to the question

The future influences of the question

Basic influences that impact the question

The 5-Rune Layout

Lay these runes in a cross. The rune at the bottom represents the basic influences that impact the question, while the rune on the far left indicates the problems that might influence the question. The top rune shows the positives that may influence the question, while the rune on the far right shows the immediate answer to the question. The only remaining rune is the one in the middle, which shows the future influences of the question.

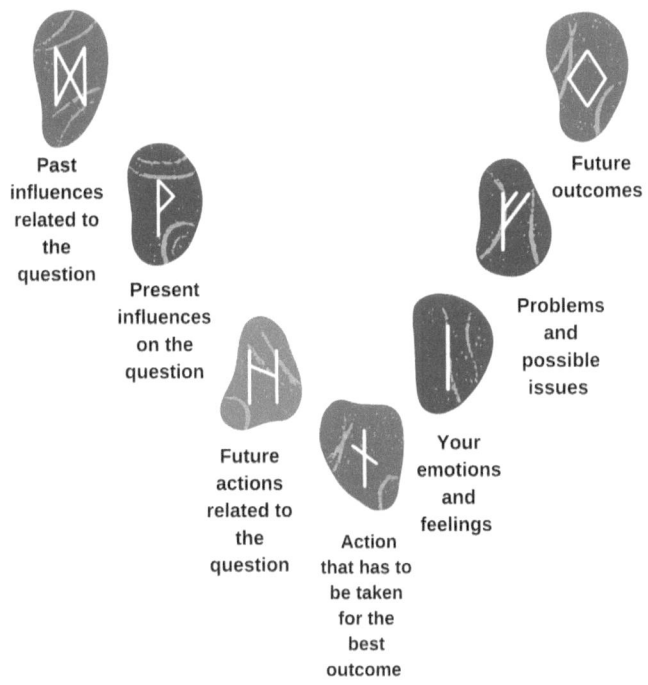

The 7-Rune Layout

This layout is laid in a V shape. The top left rune states past influences related to the question. The rune at the second from the top left shows the present influences on the question. The third rune from the top left states the future actions related to the question. The rune at the center bottom shows the action that has to be taken for the best outcome related to the question. The rune to the right of the center bottom shows your emotions and feelings related to the question. The rune second from the top right shows problems and possible issues related to the question. The top right rune shows future outcomes related to the question.

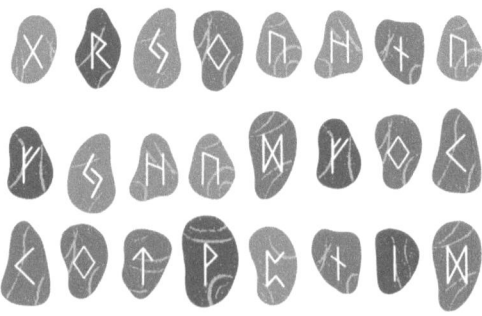

The 24-Rune Layout

Often done at the start of the year, the 24-rune layout contains exhaustive answers about, well, everything. This is done in a 3x8 grid.

The first row starting from the right to left shows:

- **First:** How you will achieve money and prosperity this year.
- **Second:** How you will achieve physical health this year.
- **Third:** How you will achieve defense or destruction this year.
- **Fourth:** How you will achieve wisdom and inspiration this year.
- **Fifth:** Which direction your life will take?
- **Sixth:** Any future wisdom that you'll learn.
- **Seventh:** The skills and gifts that you will be granted this year.

- **Eighth:** How you will achieve peace and happiness this year.

The second row from right to left shows:

- **First:** The future changes to your life.
- **Second:** The things that you need to achieve your goals.
- **Third:** The obstacles that are hindering you.
- **Fourth:** The successes and achievements that await you.
- **Fifth:** The challenges you will face and the choices you will have to make.
- **Sixth:** The inner skills that will manifest within you.
- **Seventh:** Your critical life situations this year.
- **Eighth:** Your guiding energy.

The third row from right to left shows:

- **First:** Your legal and business affairs.
- **Second:** How you will attain growth.
- **Third:** Friendships and relationships this year.
- **Fourth:** Your social status.
- **Fifth:** Your emotional status.
- **Sixth:** Sexual or romantic situations.
- **Seventh:** How you will attain balance.
- **Eighth:** Gain of assets this year.

Bind runes and How To Make Them

Bind Runes are two or more runes bound together to serve a magical purpose, such as making an amulet or to cast a spell. Combining different runes can invoke the gods for an outcome. Now, whether this outcome is good or bad depends on what runes you have used.

Bind runes bind spiritual energy into material objects for enhancement (such as a spell that can enhance someone's natural abilities) or enchantment (in the form of an amulet). Some common examples of bind runes include talismans that protect you from harm, enchanting items like weapons to become more powerful, and even empowering yourself to overcome challenges.

The two main types of bind runes are linear and radial.

Linear has two more sub-types, **stacked** (in which two runes share the same axis and are stacked upon each other) and the **same-stave** runes (in which runes are aligned along an axis). The linear ones can be used in spells to manifest a reality, while the same-stave ones can be used to attack a problem.

The **radial bind** runes contain a combination of runes that stem from a common center point. These are used as defense spells or amulets.

You are going to mix together runes, which can result in compounded effects, unknown effects, and even completely mystical effects that are so quintessential to the mysterious nature of the runes therefore before you can make bind runes, you must first understand the meaning of each individual rune as well as their positive and negative effects.

Do not be afraid. This is ancient wisdom that you are studying and using. Your mind and spirit will be elevated as a result of using this craft. So, rather than become paralyzed with fear at the prospect of wielding this magical power, be in awe and approach this discipline with reverence. You can use the Elder Futhark that we discussed in this chapter.

Step 1. Manifest what you want to achieve.

Think about the goal of your spell. What are you trying to achieve? Is it motivation? Are you looking for strength? Do you need clarity in your journey? Are you asking the gods for help? Are you lacking in strength? First, make it clear in your head what you want to achieve. It is only after you've manifested what you want to achieve that you can begin to select the runes that you need to use. Remember, without intent and visualization, it's going to be impossible to pick up the right runes. If you pick up the wrong runes, it can lead to unwanted consequences.

A spell should have a concise goal, its intent clear, and its meaning apparent.

Step 2. Select the runes.

After you've read about all the runes, their meanings, and their effects, select the ones that suit your purpose best. Do not overcomplicate things, especially if this is your first time working with bind runes. Just choose two or three runes. At the very most, pick up five.

This is the most important part of the process, as many runes have ambiguous meanings that can clash with the effect of other runes. You do not want to make the runes work against each other. You want to make them come together and work for you. So, be patient and take your time. Study more than one resource, cross-reference the meaning of the runes and their effects from different sources, and only after you're completely satisfied with their meaning and effect, move on to the next step.

Step 3. Create the design.

First, sketch the design on paper. Create many different combinations. Don't worry about right or wrong right now. Just work with your intuition and let your imagination fly. Draw to your heart's desire and draw whatever comes into your mind.

Give the drawings some time after you're finished. Go for a walk, read a book, watch a movie, or just disengage from the process of designing. After some time, the bind rune will come to you out of the blue. Then rush back to the paper and draw the design that came to you.

If that does not happen, then go back to your drawings and pick the one that vibes with you the most. Study that one and see if there are any reversed runes in there or if any hidden runes snuck into your drawing. These can alter the meaning of the spell. Re-draw the design without the unwanted runes and then finalize it.

· · ·

Step 4. Select the material.

If you want the bind runes to serve a long-term purpose, choose wood, stone, or metal. Ideally, something that can stand the test of time. If you just want to do something for the short-term, even cardboard can suffice.

If you want to create a pendant or amulet, choose comfortable jewelry you can wear for a long time without discomfort.

Step 5. Creating the bind runes.

It's time to give power to your bind runes. Before carving the bind runes, consecrate a space by lighting a candle and incense. Meditate in this place and clear your mind and align your intentions.

Then, carve the runes individually, thinking about how each rune's meaning and effect can help you, and then join these together in the final design.

Once you are done, meditate again and think about the intent of this bind rune, whether it's an amulet or a carving. In the end, thank the gods and goddesses you have invoked for their help. Leave an offering for them.

Step 6. Using the bind runes.

Use the bind runes carefully. If you have an altar at home, place the bind runes there and make sure they are nearby and at hand. Keep your bind rune close until you achieve the goal that you set out to attain. Once that has happened, you can get rid of the bind rune. If it's paper, burn it. If it's wood or stone, bury it or cast it into a lake. Just make sure you don't cause any pollution.

Thank the gods and goddesses once more after you've achieved your goal and leave another offering for them. How you can leave offerings for the gods and goddesses and how you can venerate them will be discussed in great detail in the upcoming chapter.

Storing the Runes

If you have runes in your possession, know that they must be treated with care and respect. If you do that, you'll find that the runes are very powerful allies. They have to be cleaned and empowered and stored properly.

It's critical to clean them, especially if they are new and have been touched by many hands before. They are considered a personal item. You need to keep them with you as much as possible so that they can tune into your personal energy, allowing them to give you more accurate readings.

When cleaning them, you should wait for a full moon night and then place them outside for the entire night. You can also leave them in the sun for twenty-four hours if you want. You may smudge them with wafting smoking herbs like sage and lavender and releasing their purifying properties to clean the runes. Lastly, you can clean them with natural water from a river, creek, stream, spring, or well. Never use tap water for that purpose.

After they're cleaned, you must empower them. Empowering can be done by laying out the runes in the midday Sun and then retrieving them at dusk. You can also place the runes on a piece of cloth and then sprinkle sea salt on them to empower them with the element of Earth. Then, run the runes through incense smoke while empowering them with Air. You should then pass them through a candle flame to empower them with Fire. Lastly, sprinkle rainwater or spring water on them to empower them with Water. Empowering has to be done regularly if you work with the runes frequently.

Store them in a bag made of natural fiber like cotton or silk. Use an exclusive bag for them, as the bag comes into contact with the runes and contains their pure energy. That bag is their home. You may use a piece of fabric for wrapping the runes and for laying down as the casting cloth.

This chapter was extremely thorough and quite lengthy, but given the subject matter, this was required. Now, you have a detailed insight into what the runes are, how they originated, what they mean, how to cast them, how to bind them, and how to store them.

Not only did we study each rune in detail, we learned about different casting methods. Your takeaway from this chapter should be to practice the casting and binding as much as possible while re-examining the meanings and effects of the runes. The more you are in tune with the runes, the better you'll be able to cast and the better you'll be able to bind them.

Treat this discipline with the reverence and respect it deserves, as runes are extremely powerful in terms of magic, spirituality, and mystical potency. This is just the beginning of our foray into the world of Norse Magic. In the next chapters, we will examine different rituals such as Seiðr, Spá, and Galdr. We'll discuss how we can incorporate Norse magic into our daily lives, how to build altars, and how to practice rituals like Blót and Sumbel.

CHAPTER 7
NORSE MAGIC

Unlike the profaned status that magic has been relegated to today because of Christianization and the dominance of Abrahamic faiths, wherein magic has been cursed as the art belonging to the devil and demons, in the Old Norse world, magic was revered as a part of nature, an elemental force that could help people see into the future, shift into other forms, and fathom the mysteries of the universe. It was as much a part of the Norse folks' life as hunting, raiding, and farming was. While there were practices within magic that were seen as off-limits (perceived to belong to the gods and goddesses and not to men and women), magic was at large a regular part of the community, with people inviting the practitioners into their homes or visiting them for all sorts of things, whether they were related to divining the future or asking the favor of the gods for better crops, or even victory over their enemies in the battlefield.

The Norse folk respected the practitioners of magical arts greatly, often coming to them for their services. Predominantly, magic was seen as a feminine craft, although men did partake in it as well. But in doing so, they recognized that they were adopting a feminine craft. For the men, adopting magic sometimes meant endangering their masculinity in the eyes of the community. There are exceptions to this rule, of course, even in mythology. Odin learned how to perform seiðr from Freya, who was the best in the business. But that had more to do with Odin's quest to become more knowledgeable than anyone else.

The reason why magic was seen as a woman's art in those days was that women were seen as holy vessels imbued with magical powers and possessing the capability of reaching out to the divine for prophetic purposes. This reverence for womenfolk endured in Scandinavia until Christianity arrived, which was and remains to this day, a thoroughly patriarchal religion.

Before Christianization, magic was considered a part of the everyday life of the Norse folk. It wasn't seen as blasphemous or unholy. Quite the opposite, actually. Those who were able to divine the future were thought to possess the ability to communicate with the gods and the Norns. The Norse practitioners of magic used their understanding of the world and their perception of the gods to decipher dormant truths laid out in the world and in the cosmos. For them, magic was a force like any other force, and it could be used to discern destiny, foresee the future, and shape someone's fate.

A völva or gyðja—a divine seeress—would carry out magical rites, rituals, blóts, and other ceremonies. The magicians were also known as seiðkonur or spákonu, which meant the ones who "speak" and "send." The men who delved into magic were known as goðar, galdramaðr, or seidhmadhr.

Seiðr

The translation of this Nordic word means to seethe or to send. Magical practices that were related to divination, astral projection (also known as soul travel), channeling the soul sheath, necromancy, and even cursing someone. There was a ceremonial and esoteric nature to seiðr, with much of it being somewhat similar to shamanic rituals.

A völva could perform more than just the art of divination. Besides seeing into the future, she could put curses, lift them, form protective boundaries that saved someone from physical and spiritual harm, and even manipulate destiny in some cases. The völva could cast benign spells as well, such as love spells, spells for prosperity, and charms that had to do with friendship and loyalty.

When seiðr was performed in a group setting, the rites were called utiseta (which involved sitting out) and the völva's song (in which vocals were utilized to raise collective energy). The spoken incantations were called galdr, which were used to reach altered states of consciousness. These states would also be ecstatic in nature and could be used to get in touch with the spirits of one's ancestors, as well as other spirits. In these altered states, the völva would ask questions while divining, and the spirits would help her perceive the answer.

One particularly powerful aspect of seiðr was to change fate, the principle being that if you could see the future, you could take steps to avoid that future from coming into being, therefore changing the course of destiny, and the second principle being that the use of magic changed the course of fate by making events happen that otherwise would not have happened, eventually changing fate.

The archaeologist Neil Prince provided a good summary of seiðr. He said that the seiðr rituals were concerned with clairvoyance and seeking out hidden truths within the mind and in physical locations. According to him, seiðr could be used to heal the sick, bring good luck, control the weather, for calling animals and fish for hunting, and divination. But these were benign uses of seiðr, as per his summary. He said that seiðr could be used with malevolent intent by cursing someone, blighting the land and making it barren, inducing illness, killing someone, telling false futures, injuring people, and invoking hate in someone's heart for another.

Mythologically, seiðr was seen as the domain of the Norns, who used magic of many kinds to tell the shape of the future of all living beings. But among the gods and goddesses, Freya and Odin were seen as the foremost authorities on seiðr.

Historically, the völva used to wander from town to town and farm to farm. There, they would come across people who'd commission them to perform acts of magic in exchange for room, money, board, animals, or anything else that the völva would ask for. The most popular story concerning a völva comes from the saga of Erik the Red.

In his saga, a völva was asked to come to a steading so that she could divine for the people when their famine would end. Upon her arrival, she was treated with much respect and given a meal comprising the hearts of animals that were difficult to hunt.

Then, she sat in a raised seat that had a cushion made from hen feathers. A woman sang a song to invoke the spirits who'd help the völva go into a trance. The völva prophesied when the famine would end and answered other questions for other members of the steading. She was adorned with a specially crafted costume and wielded a staff with a brass knob.

This tale shows us that the völva was set apart from the rest of society, both exalted and reviled at the same time. It also provides us with a basic framework for how seiðr works. A seeress sits on an elevated platform to perform her magic. Chants are sung to bring the seeress into a state of trance and the subsequent prophesizing.

When it comes to performing seiðr, there are three main steps to follow.

- The **first step** involves learning about the altered states and gradually going into them, i.e., going into trance. Sometimes, the act of going into a trance is also known as seething (which is one way this practice got its name) because, in this state, the person convulses a lot. In the first step, you have to learn how to block out the world around you and focus on just the ritual itself. Go inwards, meditate, and seek within yourself. This is not meant to be vague advice. This is exactly what you have to do. Following the fundamental principles of meditation, you must first empty your mind, regulate your breathing, and then let yourself be empty of all thoughts. In the old days, sometimes the völva would use herbs and drugs to get into a trance-like state. The mystical nature of the song sung to them by their assistant would also catalyze their going into a trance. The song served to open the doors to the otherworld and to let the seeress become more immersed in her meditation.

- The **second step** is concerned with soul-traveling. This is done after the trancelike state is attained. Most of the work the seeress performs is done in this state. This stage is also called faring forth, path walking, journeying, and sitting out, as in sitting outside of your body, walking the spiritual path, faring forth into the realm of wights, and journeying into the mystical dimension of souls. It is a complex but intuitive part of the process wherein you will have to direct yourself where you have to go. If you're going to answer questions about the future, you'll have to fixate on the person who is answering the questions. In case you're performing it for yourself, you'll have to direct your focus within yourself. In this stage, spirit guides and animal totems can come to your aid to assist you with your questioning. They're also called the fylgja, animal forms that accompany you throughout your life. With enough practice, a seeress or a shaman performing siedr can even shape-shift (first in an astral capacity, then later, potentially in physical form as well). You can even perform spirit possession in this state, where you can allow your body to be a vessel for the gods, goddesses, and spirits, who can then work through you.

- The **last step** is about rhythm. A rhythm throughout the ritual can help you maintain the trance as well as come out of it. The singer, often the assistant to the seeress, would sing rhythmically, first creating a rising tempo in her song and later subside it to reach a trough that would prompt the seeress to come out of her altered state. A drum would also be used, its initial striking forceful and fast, and its ebb slow and deliberate. The rhythm is used to further one's concentration when performing seiðr. It controls the ritual's pace and dictates when it starts and ends.

Spácraft

Yet another form of spiritually focused magical practice, spácraft, was considered more practical and much more readily accepted by the people. This form of magic was practiced by women who were deemed to have healing abilities and a psychic inclination.

Spácraft /Spá could determine orlog through intuition or meditation. The spá-kona were the practitioners of this magic form and could use it to foretell the future and one's fate by directly interacting with the strands of the wyrd.

Historical records, such as the one written by Tacitus, tell of a prophetess named Veleda, who prophesied the victory of the Vikings over the Romans. She said that there would be an uprising that would result in success for her tribe. In the end, what she had prophesied came to pass, thus granting credibility to this practice in a historical context.

Another example of spácraft was when Thorgeirr, the Lawspeaker, went under the cloak for two days and then gave a prophecy about Iceland's religious future in which he saw the Christianization rapidly spreading through the area. To preserve the religion, he suggested that the Norse lore be written down and preserved. Had it not been written down, much of what we know today would have been lost.

Practicing spácraft is relatively simpler than performing seiðr or galdr. It is even easier if one has a psychic inclination. Spácraft was seen as a matter of psychic sensing without the utilization of much skill or effort. If you want to practice it, start by paying attention to your sixth sense and to any feelings of foreboding that come your way. Say you get an intuitive thought about an event coming to pass. Write it down. A few days, weeks, or months later, if that event does come to pass, know that you have an innate ability for spácraft. Now, to become adept at it, there is more to it than paying attention to your personal emotions and observing outside omens. You need to be able to do it at will.

To perform spá at will, you have to tune in to your intuitive and psychic abilities and focus them on a particular question or problem. You may fixate your thoughts on the matter and gather all the emotions that you feel when you think about that particular event. If those emotions remain uniform for a while, note them down. Do this for several different questions, events, and forebodings. Notice how your accuracy goes up almost tangentially the more you practice spá. When you start practicing spá, begin with smaller events. The upcoming results of an exam, for instance. Start from the microscopic before you learn to foresee the macroscopic.

Because of its similarity to seiðr, spá, and seiðr had a lot of overlap in both a historical context and in the present context. The two schools of thought in this matter state that a) either spá is a specialized form of seiðr meant to be practiced by only those who have earned the title of völva or b) that spá is a more positive aspect of the same soul work of which seiðr is a darker aspect, that they're two sides of the same coin.

Given that spá was used to prophesize the results of battles, harvests, sailing, childbirth, trading, and foretelling an individual's fate, one can see how the two forms are similar.

Spá wasn't always all about intuition. Sometimes, trancework techniques were also performed, such as mound sitting (in which the practitioner sat upon a burial mound) to communicate with the dead.

Galdr

Galdr involved singing incantations. The songs sung during this practice were considered to be imbued with magical powers. Surprisingly, this bit of magic was not exclusive to the Norse people. Performing magic through singing—especially singing in varied notes —was common practice in Indians, Indigenous Americans, Arabs (particularly pre-Islamic Arabs), and in the Aztec civilization as well.

A common misconception regarding galdr is that they were used to vocalize the sounds and meanings of the runes. While that was one form of galdr, it was hardly all that galdr constituted. Those who performed galdr used more than just runes. Songs could be sung to venerate the deities, elements of nature, one's ancestors, and other spirits.

While men who practiced seiðr and spá were considered to be ergi (unmanly), they weren't considered so when they practiced galdr, as it was considered a craft fit for both genders. In some instances, it was considered to be a more masculine form of Norse magic, with men being preferred to perform it as opposed to women.

Most of the formal incantations were performed in the poetic meter of galdralag, the meter of spells. But there were also cases where impromptu and extemporaneous songs were sung to perform galdr. It was all about poetic composition and how one could creatively use words to wield the power of poetic language in the form of song.

In many cases, women sung to delivering mothers to ease their childbirth. In other cases, someone could be rendered mad by singing a particularly chaotic song to them. Gven the musical portfolio of some modern pop singers, it's understandable how someone could be driven mad by a mere song.

A master of galdr could, through their singing, make sharp swords blunt, make distant ships sink, raise storms, bring about drought, and even decide the victory or defeat of an army.

Many Eddas mention galdr by name. Odin is said to know 18 galdrar in Hávamál.

The principle of galdr extends beyond just singing or chanting. It is more than just stringing together notes and hoping for something to happen. There is pattern, rhythm, intent, and form. When these are combined for a single purpose, the song manifests a tangible magical change.

Domestic and Healing Magic

In Norse culture, spinning is connected to fate and magic. Even the web of fate is said to have comprised many threads woven together. Spinning had religious philosophy behind it. People believed that the goddesses of spinning inspected the distaffs and spindles of women of a household and judged her as either industrious or lazy, rewarding the former with good luck and punishing the latter with disaster. The skill of a spinning woman automatically dictated the luck of the family.

This belief extended very exhaustively toward the children. The people believed that the fate of a child could be made, changed, and even harmed through spinning. The Swedish women would draw blood from their fingers in the seventh month of their pregnancy. They would use a sewing needle and then use the blood to mark a strip of wood with protection spells and symbols. Then they would spin linen thread that was dyed red, black, and white. This strip was burned, and its ashes were mixed with beer or mead. A burning twig was taken from the fire and used to burn apart the linen threads. Later on, the three threads would be used for individual purposes. The white cord was used to tie off the umbilical cord of the baby. The red one was tied around the baby's wrist for protection. The black one was burned to ashes, and then the ashes were buried. The afterbirth was buried under the tree on which the linen threads were dried.

Spindle whorls were discovered by archaeologists that acted as prisms when spun in the sunlight.

Magic could be woven into clothes as well for protection.

Beyond household magic, pagan societies applied it in healing as well, for the treatment of physical and mental illnesses. This was done in the form of amulets and curing stones. Curing stones were used to ease childbirth and staunch bleeding, as well as granting wishes to the wearer and making them invisible.

A mother would lay her hands on her son before a battle and would divine where he'd get wounded in the battle. The son would then take extra caution to protect those particular body parts, thus saving himself from a terrible fate.

Although these were the main forms of magic used by the Norse people, this list is far from exhaustive. Sadly, many such magical traditions have been lost with time. Today, we have an inkling of an idea about the kind of magic that the Norse folk used, but we do not possess the full picture.

Luckily, modern revivals such as Ásatrú and Vanatru have not only revived the old practices of magic but also added their own flair to the practices to keep the tradition alive while also innovating just about enough to keep the practices compatible with the times.

It is my belief that all that is lost is not lost forever. The gods and goddesses once communicated with the people thousands of years ago and directed them in their lives, taught them magic, and provided them with sustenance. I believe that they still do it today if one's intent is pure and one's connection is sincere.

In the next chapter, I'll discuss how to venerate the gods to open a line of communication with them.

Who knows, maybe the once-lost rites and rituals will make it back to us by communicating with the gods directly.

CHAPTER 8
PRACTICING NORSE MAGIC

This chapter deals with practical magic, which includes a step-by-step guide to working with the gods, performing blót and Sumbel, and understanding how naming ceremonies and weddings were also rituals that were imbued with magic at their core.

Working with the gods

In the Hávamál, the 144th stanza summarizes the skills needed for runecraft while also laying down the groundwork for Norse religious practices.

> *Do you know how to carve, do you know how to interpret,*
>
> *Do you know how to stain, do you know how to test out,*
>
> *Do you know how to ask, do you know how to sacrifice,*
>
> *Do you know how to dispatch, do you know how to slaughter?*

The first two verses, as stated by the High One, indicate towards carving, interpreting, staining, and testing out the runes. The next two encapsulate the essence of Germanic religious practices.

Do you know how to ask? This refers to supplication. One can ask the gods for anything. A good harvest, healthy progeny, success in endeavors such as battles, and so forth.

Do you know how to sacrifice? The word in the original text is blóta, which refers to sacrifice. Back in the olden days, this referred to the sacrifice that had to do with bloodletting and dedicating meat to the gods and eating it.

Do you know how to dispatch? A more fitting word for the translation would be to send. As in, do you know how to send? This indicated to the sending of something to the gods. The next line clears it up as to what is being sent.

Slaughter. People slaughtered anything from animals to their foes in battle to send to the gods.

The two main elements that come into light from these verses are prayer and offerings.

Praying to the Gods

Prayer, according to the Old Norse religion, was the act of communicating with the gods rather than merely worshipping them. The words and acts involved in performing a prayer varied significantly.

One prominent example of a prayer was the greeting the Valkyrie Brunhild used for Sigurd.

Hail to thee Day, hail, ye Day's sons:

hail Night and daughter of Night,

with blithe eyes look on both of us,

and grant to those sitting here victory!

Hail Æsir, hail Asynjur!

Hail Earth that givest to all!

Goodly spells and speech bespeak we from you,

and healing hands in this life!

Here, the prayer includes requests and salutations. We can get a blueprint of what a prayer constitutes from this passage. It hails the powers that identify the god, attracts their attention by declaring their traits, and honors them through veneration. Brunhild requests skills in communication and in performing magic. She does this by calling upon the powers of nature and the gods and goddesses as a whole.

There's also a prayer to Thor preserved in Snorri Sturluson's work by skalds, who prayed to him by saying:

> You smashed the limbs of Leikn;
> you bashed ðrivaldi;
> you knocked down Starkadhr;
> you trod Gjalp dead under foot.

Historian John Lindow compared this prayer to other surviving prayers from Indo-European traditions, stating that such prayers included two components of praise to the god, followed by a request to that deity.

From this, we can construct a formula for prayer, which can be something like this:

> *Hail (to the god using their best-known name), (a descriptive epithet),*
>
> *Child of (their parent's name), lover of (their spouse's name)*
>
> *You who dwell in (the name of their hall),*
>
> *You who (summarize their deeds),*
>
> *With your (their weapon or tool)*
>
> *Come quickly to aid me,*
>
> *As I (state your problem)*

Invoking a god's help can be done through chanting their names, referencing their attributes and their monickers, and even stating out loud their endeavors from their mythologies.

Offering to the Gods

Praying to the gods was just one part of paganism. One of the oldest practices of their faith was to offer things by way of sacrificing to them. Besides blood sacrifice, food was offered to the gods as well as any offerings that the worshipper deemed suitable and fitting for the god. For example, grain, flowers, fruit, alcohol, and hair cut from the forelock were some of the primary offerings. You could even offer a verbal vow as an offering.

When animals were sacrificed, their heads, hearts, and hides were also hung as offerings while their blood was poured on the shrine and sprinkled on the people. The meat from those animals was consumed in a communal feast.

These sacrificial feasts were also part of the yearly traditions and festivals that marked the turning of a season, weddings, funerals of noblemen, or even to gain the favor of the gods in times of disaster.

When sacrificing animals, special care was taken to ensure that the animals were healthy and perfect in every way. The animal was washed and garlanded with aromatic herbs and flowers.

Today, heathens offer a diverse range of offerings as a sacrifice, which include:

- Nuts
- Fruits
- Meat
- Cheese
- Butter
- Mead
- Beer
- Spirits
- Animal Effigies
- Baked goods
- Grains

It's important to note which god and goddess prefers which gift.

When making an offering to Freya, effigies of animals like cats, boars, falcons, rabbits, and horses would do wonderfully. She'd also love naturally shed cat hair or claws. You can offer her mead, wine, and honey. Perfumes are another of her favorite offerings. A goddess of sensuality, she has a special corner in her heart for aphrodisiacs like chocolate and strawberries. She's also got quite the sweet tooth and loves apples and raspberries. Additionally, you can offer her silver, gold, copper, necklaces, and stones like emerald, jade, citrine, and amber. As I said earlier, you can also pledge a vow as an offering. When it comes to Freya, if you vow to care for cats or to devote time of your day to taking care of local flora, she'll be very pleased and inclined towards you.

The gods and goddesses have a certain affinity for discipline. Dedicating an altar space for them and placing altar offerings for them is yet another surefire way of getting them to notice you.

When you devote an altar to Odin, you'll be, in a sense, offering him a gateway to come to you. You can set up the altar by decorating it with the Hanged Man tarot card, the Othala rune, the Ansuz rune, raven feathers, effigies of wolves, horseshoes, mead bottles, and beer. The All-Father is also fond of red meat, tobacco, and spirits.

You must understand that modern Norse Paganism does not condone human sacrifice and acknowledges that those practices were inhuman practices that have no place in modern paganism today. People are not a resource to be given away.

. . .

Performing Blót

Considered the most sacred and most important ritual in Paganism, performing a blót requires some pre-planning and understanding of what it means. The literal translation for blót is sacrifice.

But why should we blót?

Offering something to the gods isn't necessarily a transactional dynamic. You can consider blót as a device to engage in the gifting cycle with the gods. And what is a gift? When you gift someone something, you do not expect something in return. There is no obligation there. Showing the gods that you acknowledge them, love them, and venerate them through gifting offerings to them is one of the primary reasons why we do blót.

It's not like the gods need our gifts or sacrifices. They have existed long before us, and they'll exist long after us. So it's not like they're dependent on our offerings. We give to the gods because they give to us. By offering things to them, we're reflecting their divinity to them, letting them know that we're also capable of generosity and goodness.

Even though there's no obligation, the gods have your back. They're good for it. They will come to your aid with their generosity and their benignity; of course, they will. They will give you something back tenfold or even a hundredfold. That's their nature. They like to reward those whom they deem good, honorable, and sincere. They like to gift back.

Sacred Space

Performing a blót requires access to a sacred space, and since most of us do not live in the vicinity of temples, you can designate a certain area as a sacred space by performing ritual purification. It is in this space that you and your fellow pagans can feel safe, guided, protected, and comfortable conducting the blót.

For this purpose, you can use a natural spot in the woods, a room in a community center, your backyard, or any space where you can connect with your fellow venerators and with the gods.

Performing the Blót

For the blót, we're going to need the following things:

- Mead as an offering (beer can work too)
- A drinking horn
- A bowl for collecting the libation
- Sprig of evergreen

The worshippers have to stand in a circle facing each other inwards.

Start by pouring the beverage into the horn and invoking the god/goddess that you wish to invoke. Raise the horn and say the toast to the deity. Then drink from the horn. Pass the horn around to everyone in the circle, and one by one, they have to raise and toast and drink.

After the horn has reached the first person, pour some of it as a libation in the bowl.

Now do another round of drinking, this time toasting the heroes of yore. Pour the remaining libation into the bowl.

Do a third round for boasts and toasts, then pour the remaining as a libation in the bowl.

Dip the sprig in the mead bowl and sprinkle the people with the mead, using the sprig as a blessing.

Lastly, pour the libation onto a sacred spot.

A Modern Variant

You can add a modern twist to the blót, such as the one Ásatrú members have been practicing since the 2000s.

In this variant, you need an offering (see the list mentioned earlier), a beverage that can be offered as a libation, a bowl to catch the libation, and a sprig of evergreen for aspersion.

You also need fire and water for blessing and for purifying the sacred space as well as the offering.

You can use candles or torches for the fire. Additionally, if the sacred space has room for it, a brazier or fire pit can be used for the sacrificial fire.

For the water, a single jug of clean water can be used so that everyone can wash their hands and face before touching the offerings.

You can stand around the sacrificial fire in a circle, or you can all stand on one side of the fire while the goði stands near the fire. Both formations are completely fine.

For the modern version of the blót, first, set up the sacrificial fire with some wood. You can use an accelerant for this purpose as well. Now pour some fresh water into a jug and also get a bowl for the water.

Whatever offerings you have planned to sacrifice, gather them together. Then, distribute torches or candles to the people gathered for the offering. Light these candles and walk over to where the sacrificial fire is going to be. You can now hand the torch to the goði so they may light the sacrificial fire.

Pour some water into the bowl and let the goði wash their hands and face. Dispose of that water.

Let the goði speak a prayer that may invoke the gods and goddesses. Following the prayer, the supplicants should pray, chant, sing, and dance as the goði sanctifies the offerings at the sacrificial fire.

Now, these offerings may either be placed at the fire, or they can be left out on an altar. If libation is involved, it should be poured out and caught in the bowl for the blessing.

It is at this time that the dancing should stop. Around this time, when the offering is being made, you should kneel or prostrate as you see fit. While the sacrifice is happening, the chants and the songs should continue until it is done.

The goði will leave the sacred space, bless the gathered people, and announce the beginning of the feast.

Sumbel

The Sumbel, also spelled as symbel and sumbl, is the practice of sitting together and drinking together. Participants pass the horn to each other as they make toasts and boasts and vow oaths. They also make speeches, give gifts, form alliances, make agreements, and hear each other's oaths.

The Sumbel was used to strengthen pre-existing bonds and form new ones within a holy setting. While a blót can be done alone, Sumbel is entirely communal.

The religious significance of this ritual was to boast your past deeds, your ancestor's past deeds, and the deeds of the great heroes so that those who have passed might live on through their memory. Oaths and promises made during the Sumbel took on a more sincere and strengthened form, allowing the individuals and the group to shape their wyrd. To ensure sincerity, Sumbel made sure that those who made false promises or words without worth were punished through a distorted shaping of their wyrds that would eventually bring them harm.

The intent behind the Sumbel is to celebrate the community, strengthen it by bringing it closer together, and venerate one's gods and ancestors by boasting about them. It is by venerating them in such a communal spirit that one's ancestors can take place within the Sumbel like visitors, and the gods can be harkened to witness this ritual.

Performing Sumbel

The ritual demands that you sit, unlike standing, which is done in blót. Sumbel also takes place indoors, unlike blots, which can be performed both indoors and outdoors. In the sagas, it was described that halls had rows of benches and high seats. The head of the hall sat at the high seat while others sat on the benches. Today, however, Sumbel is performed by sitting in a ring, rectangle, or any other shape wherein you can sit facing others while remaining close enough to them.

Since it's exclusively a drinking-related ritual, Sumbel was historically arranged after dinner. It usually begins by offering a basin of water and a towel to the gathered people so they may wash and dry their hands.

Whether it's ale, cider, beer, wine, or mead, the Sumbel begins with the filling of the drinking vessel with the preferred drink. Then the leader speaks a blessing or a prayer (in some cases, both) over the filled horn and then toasts. This toast is traditionally made to a god or goddess or a group of them, such as the Æsir and the Vanir. This toast can be something as simple as Hail Thor! Or it can be something as complex as a full-fledged poem written in skaldic meter. The leader then swallows the drink, in response to which the assembled people also say hail!

Then the horn is passed from one person to the other. If it's a larger gathering, the horn goes around the room via a horn-bearer who gives each person the horn, hears their toast, acknowledges it, and then takes the horn to the next person. In the end, the horn-bearer gives their toast.

After the first round, the drink leftover from the drinking vessel is poured into the blessing bowl to give the gods their due.

There can be three rounds of drinking, one for the gods and goddesses, the other for the heroes and ancestors, and the third for anything that the participants choose.

. . .

Naming Ceremony

A name is considered a gift that gives the newborn its status as a human being and a member of the family. Historically, the father took the child, sprinkled water on the child, and named them. This was called ausa vatni, which means sprinkling of water.

The materials required for a naming ceremony include a pitcher of water, a cloak for the parent to wrap the child, the naming gift, and a ceremonial bowl, preferably one that belongs to the family. For the procession, you'll need the godparents, the father's parents, the mother's parents, and the parents with their newborn child. In Asatru the goði, performs the salutations and invocations. After the salutations are said to the guests, invocations are made to Freya, the Alfar, and the Disir, and then the water is poured into a bowl by the officiants.

The godparents present the child with the name-fastening gift and place it next to the water bowl.

The grandmothers approach the baby and recite the blessings of the Disir:

> *Hail the dead.*
> *Hail the wives, mothers and sisters.*
> *Hail our ever-faithful friends!*
> *Look on us*
> *with kind eyes,*
> *That we may*
> *Bless a new life and name.*

The child is given a first and middle name.

The grandfathers then approach the baby and recite the blessing of the Alfar:

> *Hail the dead.*
> *Hail the husbands, fathers and sons.*
> *Hail our ever-faithful friends!*
> *Look on us*
> *with kind eyes,*
> *That we may*
> *Bless a new life and name.*

The child is then given a family name.

The priest comes forth holding the naming gift over the child, then recites the blessing Freya:

> *Hail, day!*
> *Hail, sons of day!*
> *Hail night and her daughter!*
> *Look on us*
> *with kind eyes,*
> *That we may*
> *Bless a new life and name.*
> *Hail Aesir,*
> *Hail Asynjor,*
> *Hail the holy giving Earth,*
> *Bless us with goodly speech and wisdom*
> *And healing hands in life.*
> *Hail Freya Vanadis.*
> *Hail Gracious Lady.*
> *Hail Queen of the Disir.*
> *Look on us*
> *with kind eyes,*

> *That we may*
> *Bless a new life and name.*
> *Hail the Joyful One.*
> *Hail Frith Weaver.*
> *Hail Luck Bearer.*
> *Bless us with goodly speech and wisdom*
> *And healing hands in life.*

The priest then gives the newborn to the father, who'll fold the child in his cloak. The mother is given the water bowl.

The parents then recite the blessing of the sprinkling of water. They name the child with the full name and sprinkle the newborn's head with water.

Wedding Ceremony

Let's break down the wedding ceremony into ten steps. Note that this is a modern paganistic reconstruction of the original Norse wedding rites.

- Receiving the guests
- The Hallowing of the Rite
- Attesting to the characters of the bride and groom
- Invocation of the gods
- Speaking the Oaths
- Giving Gifts
- The Blessing of Thor
- Announcing the Couple
- Commencing the Feast
- The Honeymoon

Receiving the guests

It begins by receiving the guests at the entrance of the venue and inviting them in. Following the guests, the couple comes in.

Back in the old days, the woman passed from her father's protection to her husband's. Today, you can see this reflected in the modern custom where the father walks the bride down the aisle and gives her away.

Hallowing a rite

The leader of the ceremony begins this ceremony by announcing the purpose of the ceremony.

Witnessing the characters

The family members of the couple are asked to speak about the man and woman's good qualities and their suitability for marriage to each other.

Invocation of the gods

Now, this is where the magic comes in. First, the leader invokes the gods and goddesses, and then the ancestors of the couples so that they may come and hear the oaths and bless the marriage.

Speaking the oaths

The woman brings a horn of drink to the man, who drinks it, then takes her hand and swears his oath. The woman can do this as well. The remaining drinks from the horns are then placed into a bowl as an offering to the gods.

Giving gifts

Both partners give each other gifts. Historically, weapons were exchanged, wedding bands given, and keys to the house given by the groom to the bride to signify that she now held dominion over the household. In modern times, you may choose suitable gifts of your choosing.

The blessing of Thor

Thor's hammer should be placed on the bride's lap to hallow the ceremony. The hammer is also a phallic symbol meant to signify fertility in the upcoming days. This invokes Thor, who turns his attention to the wedding and blesses it, being the patron god of the Midgardians.

Announcing the couple

The leader then pronounces the man and woman as married.

Commencing the feast

The men and the women from both sides of the family race to the feasting hall. Those who lose have to serve the drinks to the winners. Once at the feasting hall, mead is drunk, and food is eaten, while much talk is had and songs are sung.

Honeymoon!

The couple is then sent forth on their honeymoon, preferably with some honeyed mead so that they can drink, loosen up, and get in the marital mood, so to speak.

You might wonder why I included the naming ceremony and the wedding ceremony in a chapter related to magic rituals.

Well, what is magic, if not the utterance of special words, invoking the deities, and performing a ritual to bring about a certain manifestable change in the world? Is the naming of a child, not a change? When the destinies of two people intertwine to become one, isn't that a change brought about by invocation, supplication, and performing the necessary rites?

The Norse understood that magic was imbued in their everyday lives, from the most ordinary thing, such as tilling soil, to the most special rite, such as marriage.

In this chapter, we learned how to work with the gods through offerings and prayers. We discussed how to perform blót in detail and then did the same for Sumbel. Lastly, we looked at two major rites, the naming ceremony and the wedding ceremony, and understood them within the context of the rituals that they are in that they involve supplication, offerings, veneration, and praying.

You might be wondering where to go from here, given that there is such a rich reservoir of information that you can access and implement in your life, from divining runes to performing rites strengthened with magic.

On that note, intuition was considered a magical trait in Norse Mythology. It still is. Intuition is one form of wisdom, an innate wisdom that can serve to guide you when the paths are many and the directions are vague.

The hardest part is to begin. Once you do begin, let your intuition guide you. Use this book as a reference and find your way to the gods and goddesses. Divine the mysteries of the secret world all around you, the world where Jörmungandr still stirs around the world, where Sleipnir strides across the skies, and where Thor prompts lightning to fall by wielding his hammer.

That world is not lost. It's still there. Just as your ancestors are still there, living inside you. Just as the gods and goddesses are still there, watching over you. Just as you are here, uncovering this ancient truth, the greatest of truths—that the magic is real! It was always real all along.

THANK YOU

Thank you for letting me be your guide through the fascinating history and mythology of the Norse. Now, I'm sure you're wondering how you can help others experience the same joy and fulfillment that you have gained from reading this book.

Leaving a review can be a great way to help others learn about Norse Paganism. Your review can help people discover the book, and it provides an opportunity to share your own experience and what you've learned on your journey. All you need to do is >>Click here to leave a quick review

If you are reading this in hardback or paperback, type in this link on your device: http://amazon.com/review/create-review?&asin=B0BP1CVBQG

AFTERWORD

If you think that this is the end of our journey together, it is not. We may yet meet again, whether as fellow travelers on this great road that we call life or as readers and writer again in a different narrative.

When I set out to write this book, I had one goal in mind. I wanted to make sure that you, the reader, would discover as much as you could about the wonderful world of Norse Mythology, understand the pantheon of the Norse gods and goddesses, and learn how to harness your knowledge of mythology and paganism in its many forms and utilize it in your daily life.

I would be all too glad to learn from your feedback if I have managed to achieve my goal.

Let us review what we have learned so far in this book.

- We began with an introduction to Norse Magic, wherein we discussed, among many things, Odin and his tale of sacrifice, what magic is, what power

language possesses, and how mystery and history are intertwined when it comes to Norse Paganism. I briefly shared some details about me as well as discussed why you should read this book.
- Then we went back to the beginning of it all, to the beginning of Norse cosmology. We understood the distinction between folklore, myths, and legends. Then we dived into the history of the world, from the Ginnungagap to the creation of the Nine Realms.
- No mention of Norse Paganism, Magic, and Mythology would be complete without shedding light on the Nine Realms and the World Tree. In the second chapter, we looked at each realm in detail.
- In the third chapter, we looked at the gods who helped shape these worlds and then resided in them. From the Æsir, such as Odin and Frigg, to the Vanir, such as Nerthus and Kvasir, we took a look at the major gods of the Norse pantheon before taking a deep dive into the A-listers of Norse Mythology.
- In the fourth chapter, we studied Odin, Frigg, Thor, Baldur, Vidar, Tyr, Bragi, Idun, Loki, Heimdall, Njord, Freya, Freyr, and Mimir. This encompassed their histories, their traits, and their powers.
- We got to the meat of the book in chapters five and six. The fifth chapter was all about Norse Paganism and what it entailed. We discussed its characteristics, the beliefs that it espoused, and the rituals that were performed by the pagans.

- In the sixth chapter, we dwelled upon runes, first going through their history, then looking at each and every symbol, meaning, and usage. We learned how to cast runes, bind runes, and store them.
- In chapter seven, I introduced you to various elements of Norse Magic, such as seiðr, spá, and galdr, while shedding light on domestic and healing magic.
- In the final chapter, we discussed how some rites were practiced back in the day and how we can practice them today. These included working with the gods through prayer and offerings, blót, Sumbel, the naming ceremony, and the wedding ceremony.

I will admit that a book of this length cannot be exhaustive when it comes to teaching magic, helping you divine the runes, while also teaching you everything about Norse Mythology and Paganism. But I have tried, and in my humble attempt, I have sought to give you a framework that you can use to adapt more magical practices in your daily life, perfect the ones that you've already learned about through practice, and understand the principle and the reasoning behind the many rites and rituals of Norse Paganism.

The accounts told within these pages are not just stories. They are legends and myths from an era that has long since passed but whose ethics, values, and beliefs still live on in the hearts and practices of thousands of modern-day pagans. With the information provided in this book, you too can become a practicing Norse pagan and strengthen your connection with the Norse gods and goddesses. They are seeking you just as you are seeking them.

The purpose of providing such extensive historical accounts and facts was to prepare you for the future. Now that you know about the history of runes, their symbology, and their meaning, you can use them for runework, such as divination and binding magic.

With the historical context of seiðr, blót, Sumbel, spá, and galdr clear to you, you are more than capable in my eyes of carrying out those rites and rituals to transcend and communicate with the gods.

If you'd like other readers and kindred spirits such as yourself to find this book better, please do consider leaving a helpful review. This review will also help me and will allow me to write further books exploring Norse mythology, paganism, rituals, and rites in more detail.

Thank you for embarking on this journey with me. And remember, this is not goodbye. We may yet meet again.

But until then, farväl!

FREE GIFT!!
FREE BEGINNERS KIT

Just starting out on your Journey learning about the magic of Norse Paganism?

Click here https://norsepaganwisdom.info/optin-page2bxjr47c or use the QR code below to get all the resources you need at your fingertips!

What it includes:

- A copy of the Elder & Younger Eddas
- The Die Germania by Cornelius Tacitus
- The Hávamál
- The Heimskringla
- The Codex Regius

RESOURCES

THE NORDIC BIG BANG

- Where do myths, legends and folktales come from? (2019, March 15). Retrieved March 13, 2023, from https://www.torch.ox.ac.uk/article/where-do-myths-legends-and-folktales-come-from
- How did our legends really begin? (2014, July 29). Retrieved March 13, 2023, from https://www.independent.co.uk/arts-entertainment/books/features/how-did-our-legends-really-begin-9634148.html
- How the great myths and legends were created. (n.d.). Retrieved March 13, 2023, from https://writersstore.com/blogs/news/how-the-great-myths-and-legends-were-created
- Mark, J. (2023, March 13). Mythology. Retrieved March 13, 2023, from https://www.worldhistory.org/mythology/
- Myths and legends of the world. (2023, March 13). Retrieved March 13, 2023, from https://www.encyclopedia.com/humanities/news-wires-white-papers-and-books/norse-mythology
- Groeneveld, E. (2023, March 10). Norse mythology. Retrieved March 13, 2023, from https://www.worldhistory.org/Norse_Mythology/
- Norman. (2018, June 30). The origins of the Norse mythology. Retrieved March 13, 2023, from https://thenorsegods.com/the-origins-of-the-norse-mythology/

- Skjalden. (2022, July 18). Creation of the world in Norse mythology. Retrieved March 13, 2023, from https://skjalden.com/creation-of-the-world-in-norse-mythology/
- The history of the Nordic region. (n.d.). Retrieved March 13, 2023, from https://www.norden.org/en/information/history-nordic-region
- The creation of the cosmos. (2018, July 24). Retrieved March 13, 2023, from https://norse-mythology.org/tales/norse-creation-myth/

THE NINE REALMS

- Mark, J. (2023, March 10). Nine realms of norse cosmology. Retrieved March 13, 2023, from https://www.worldhistory.org/article/1305/nine-realms-of-norse-cosmology/
- Milligan, M. (2021, August 26). Yggdrasil and the 9 norse worlds. Retrieved March 13, 2023, from https://www.heritagedaily.com/2018/08/yggdrasil-and-the-9-norse-worlds/121244
- Ásgard and the nine worlds of Norse mythology. (n.d.). Retrieved March 13, 2023, from https://www.history.co.uk/articles/asgard-and-the-nine-worlds-of-norse-mythology
- Muspelheim. (n.d.). Retrieved March 13, 2023, from https://www.britannica.com/topic/Muspelheim
- Niflheim. (n.d.). Retrieved March 13, 2023, from https://www.britannica.com/topic/Niflheim
- Midgard. (2018, June 30). Retrieved March 13, 2023, from https://norse-mythology.org/cosmology/the-nine-worlds/midgard/
- Vanaheim. (2017, July 09). Retrieved March 13, 2023, from https://norse-mythology.org/cosmology/the-nine-worlds/vanaheim/

- Jötunnheim. (n.d.). Retrieved March 13, 2023, from https://kids.britannica.com/students/article/Jötunnheim/311926
- Svartalfheim. (n.d.). Retrieved March 13, 2023, from https://godofwar.fandom.com/wiki/Svartalfheim
- Hel (the Underworld). (2017, July 09). Retrieved March 13, 2023, from https://norse-mythology.org/cosmology/the-nine-worlds/helheim/
- Alfheim. (2017, July 09). Retrieved March 13, 2023, from https://norse-mythology.org/cosmology/the-nine-worlds/alfheim/

Chapter 3 —The Pantheon of Norse Mythology

- HistoryExtra. (2022, August 30). A brief history of the Vikings. Retrieved March 13, 2023, from https://www.historyextra.com/period/viking/vikings-history-facts/
- Delgado, D. (2020, May 29). Legendary characters from Norse mythology. Retrieved March 13, 2023, from https://www.megainteresting.com/history/gallery/legendary-characters-from-norse-mythology-741590756208/1
- Vanir. (n.d.). Retrieved March 13, 2023, from https://www.newworldencyclopedia.org/entry/vanir
- Aesir. (n.d.). Retrieved March 13, 2023, from https://www.newworldencyclopedia.org/entry/aesir
- The aesir-vanir war. (2018, July 04). Retrieved March 13, 2023, from https://norse-mythology.org/tales/the-aesir-vanir-war/
- Owen.pham. (2022, July 01). The difference between the Aesir and Vanir. Retrieved March 13, 2023, from https://www.wondriumdaily.com/the-difference-between-the-aesir-and-vanir/

THE A-LIST GODS OF NORSE MYTHOLOGY

- Smith, M. (2022, February 22). 15 Norse mythology gods and goddesses list - with names & info. Retrieved March 13, 2023, from https://education.onehowto.com/article/norse-mythology-gods-and-goddesses-list-13342.html
- A guide to norse gods and goddesses. (1970, October 29). Retrieved March 13, 2023, from https://www.centreofexcellence.com/norse-gods-goddesses
- Seven of the most important gods and goddesses in Norse mythology. (n.d.). Retrieved March 13, 2023, from https://www.history.co.uk/articles/seven-of-the-most-important-gods-and-goddesses-in-norse-mythology
- The norse gods. (n.d.). Retrieved March 13, 2023, from https://thenorsegods.com/
- Gods and creatures. (2018, July 14). Retrieved March 13, 2023, from https://norse-mythology.org/gods-and-creatures/
- The aesir gods and goddesses. (2018, September 04). Retrieved March 13, 2023, from https://norse-mythology.org/gods-and-creatures/the-aesir-gods-and-goddesses/
- The vanir gods and goddesses. (2018, September 04). Retrieved March 13, 2023, from http://norse-mythology.org/gods-and-creatures/the-vanir-gods-and-goddesses/

NORSE PAGANISM

- Routes North. (2022, June 20). Norse paganism: What is it, and what do its followers believe? Retrieved March 13, 2023, from https://www.routesnorth.com/language-and-culture/norse-paganism/
- The Old Nordic Religion Today. (n.d.). Retrieved March 13, 2023, from https://en.natmus.dk/historical-knowledge/

- denmark/prehistoric-period-until-1050-ad/the-viking-age/ religion-magic-death-and-rituals/the-old-nordic-religion-today/
- Nomads, T. (2023, January 05). Norse paganism for beginners: Quick introduction + resources. Retrieved March 13, 2023, from https://www.timenomads.com/norse-paganism-for-beginners/
- Pagan religious practices of the Viking Age. (n.d.). Retrieved March 13, 2023, from https://www.hurstwic.org/history/articles/mythology/religion/text/practices.htm
- Staff, Sigurþórsdóttir, S., Gunnarsson, O., & Helgason, M. (n.d.). 11 things to know about the present day practice of ásatrú, the ancient religion of the Vikings. Retrieved March 13, 2023, from https://icelandmag.is/article/11-things-know-about-present-day-practice-Ásatrú-ancient-religion-vikings
- Mythology. (n.d.). Retrieved March 13, 2023, from https://www.cliffsnotes.com/literature/m/mythology/summary-and-analysis-norse-mythology/the-norse-gods-8212-odin-thor-balder-frey-freya-and-loki
- Lafayllve, P. (2022, August 31). Modern Norse pagan practices for beginners. Retrieved March 13, 2023, from https://www.spiritualityhealth.com/norse-paganism-for-beginners
- Nikel, D., Warren, R., Evelake, Paula, Heimdallr, Raven, . . . Brown, D. (2020, December 03). Viking religion: From the Norse gods to Christianity. Retrieved March 13, 2023, from https://www.lifeinnorway.net/viking-religion/?__cf_chl_rt_tk=Ns7il0FW1D9MkUis2eT7mt2WF55N.Cq1iX_nROH3eR8-1678716442-0-gaNycGzNCtA

THE RUNES

- Rune guide - an introduction to using the runes. (n.d.). Retrieved March 13, 2023, from https://www.holisticshop.co.uk/articles/guide-runes
- Groeneveld, E. (2023, March 10). Runes. Retrieved March 13, 2023, from https://www.worldhistory.org/runes/
- Shelley, A. (2023, March 01). Futhark runes: Symbols, meanings and how to use them. Retrieved March 13, 2023, from https://andreashelley.com/blog/futhark-runes-symbols-and-meanings/
- Talisa + Sam | Two Wander. (2022, September 27). Rune meanings and how to use rune stones for divination. Retrieved March 13, 2023, from https://www.twowander.com/blog/rune-meanings-how-to-use-runestones-for-divination
- Wigington, P. (2020, January 31). What is rune casting? origins and techniques. Retrieved March 13, 2023, from https://www.learnreligions.com/rune-casting-4783609
- Nomads, T. (2023, January 29). Rune magic 101: What are and how to make bind runes. Retrieved March 13, 2023, from https://www.timenomads.com/rune-magic-101-what-are-and-how-to-make-norse-bind-runes/

NORSE MAGIC

- Women and magic in the sagas: Seiðr and spá. (n.d.). Retrieved March 13, 2023, from http://www.vikinganswerlady.com/seidhr.shtml
- Owen.pham. (2022, September 03). Magic in old norse: Seith, curses, and blessings. Retrieved March 13, 2023, from https://www.wondriumdaily.com/magic-in-old-norse-seith-curses-and-blessings/

- Manea, I. (2023, March 11). Viking witches and Norse Magic. Retrieved March 13, 2023, from https://www.worldhistory.org/video/2735/viking-witches-and-norse-magic/
- HistoryExtra. (2023, February 01). Gods, myths and rituals: What we know about viking religious beliefs. Retrieved March 13, 2023, from https://www.historyextra.com/period/viking/viking-religion-gods-myths-rituals-ship-burial-sacrifice-odin-thor-loki/
- Seidr. (2018, July 04). Retrieved March 13, 2023, from https://norse-mythology.org/concepts/seidr/
- Garis, M. (2021, March 15). How to make a home altar that honors your personal power. Retrieved March 13, 2023, from https://www.wellandgood.com/how-to-make-altar-home-design/
- Basics of Sumbel. (n.d.). Retrieved March 13, 2023, from http://www.thewhitegoddess.co.uk/articles/general_pagan/basics_of_sumbel.asp

PRACTICING NORSE MAGIC

- Worshipping the gods. (2012, April 09). Retrieved March 13, 2023, from https://hrafnar.org/articles/dpaxson/norse/worship/
- Blot: Heathen rituals. (n.d.). Retrieved March 13, 2023, from https://thetroth.org/resources/rituals/blot-Ásatrú-rituals.html
- Symbel: Heathen rituals. (n.d.). Retrieved March 13, 2023, from https://thetroth.org/index.php/resources/rituals/symbel
- Naming ceremony: Ausa Vatni. (n.d.). Retrieved March 13, 2023, from https://thetroth.org/resources/rituals/naming-ceremony

- Ásatrú wedding ceremony. (n.d.). Retrieved March 13, 2023, from https://thetroth.org/index.php/resources/rituals/Ásatrú-wedding-ceremony

EMMA KARLSSON

GUIDE TO
NORSE PAGANISM

A COMPREHENSIVE GUIDE EXPLORING NORSE PAGAN
HISTORY & CULTURE, VIKINGS, MYTHS AND LEGENDS OF
THE NORSE GODS & GODDESSES, CREATION OF THE
UNIVERSE, RUNES, RITUALS, SYMBOLS, AND DIVINATION.

FREE GIFT JUST FOR YOU!!!
2023 NORSE GOD & GODDESSES CALENDAR

Norse God & Goddesses Calendar

Use this link https://norsepaganwisdom.info/squeeze-page1679502439646 to get it delivered straight to your email!

OR scan the QR code below:

INTRODUCTION

A white-bearded figure walks through a green field against a splendid backdrop of snow-covered mountains. Donning a weathered robe and a long, pointed hat and wielding an adorned cane that, upon closer look, reveals a concealed spear, this mystical figure wanders with poise, and as he walks, you see that two wolves match his gait at his heels. Above him, two ravens fly close by, cawing, crooning, keeping a weather eye on the horizon.

Above him, the sky broods with storm clouds and the deep roar of thunder. Below him, the seas send tide after tide to clash against the jagged rocks on the Scandinavian cliffside.

You do not take long to realize that you are in a state of trance. This is a vision. You see the wanderer from far across the fjord as he traverses across the countryside.

It is only when he turns in your direction, and his piercing blue eye gazes into your soul do you realize something.

It is no coincidence that you are here.

The roots of the Yggdrasil run deep, binding the world together and beckoning seekers from far and wide. I will say it again. It is no coincidence that you are here. If it is dissent from modern organized religion that has turned your heart away from the fulfillment that faith can offer, you are in the right place. If you seek deific mysteries passed through the ages, mysteries that speak of godly figures that once walked this realm, mysteries that painted this common world of ours into a place of wonder and fantasy, you are in the right place.

If you seek to break free of the tethers that have confined your belief to monotony, if you yearn to unleash the acolyte within, you are in the right place. Here we ditch conforming norms and wear the pagan garb, divining deeper meaning in runes and fostering harmony with arcane lore that will help you reveal the truth about yourself.

Before we delve into the intricacies of this beautiful creed, I want to welcome all, wherever it is that you may have come from, whatever your background is.

It may be that:

Modern Renditions in Pop-Culture Piqued Your Interest

You have seen the resurgence of Nordic lore in recent pop culture, from *Marvel's* adaptation of *Thor* to *Assassin's Creed's* portrayal of Vikings. If you are more of a bookworm like me, you might have come across modern interpretations of the Nordic pantheon of deities in works of literature such as *American Gods* by the venerable Neil Gaiman. That same author who gave us the beloved world of Sandman also wrote a concise history of Norse gods in his book, *Norse Mythology*, faithfully retelling ancient tales to a new audience. History Channel's critically acclaimed TV show *Vikings* conjures a sense of grandeur as it tells the tale of Ragnar Lothbrok. Young adult authors like Rick Riordan are infusing their works with Norse mythology. Video games franchises such as *God of War* have made use of Norse mythology's rich culture and have placed their game setting within locations such as Midgard. Many notable works of fiction, such as *Lord of The Rings,* have taken a huge amount of inspiration from Norse mythology.

Present-Day Religions Have Failed To Inspire You

You have explored modern interpretations of Abrahamic religions such as Christianity, Judaism, and Islam and have felt disconcerted by their organized and restrictive nature. This disconcertment has led you to explore other creeds and faiths wherein you feel more in tune with the world around you, are more of an active participant in religious activities, and feel accomplished after having performed your rites. The sense of freedom that Norse paganism offers will come as a welcome change of pace, reorienting your entire worldview.

You Seek A Deeper, More Meaningful Existence

The primal nature of Norse mythology speaks to you. Many of us feel tied into the cyclical nature of our daily lives, unable to escape from the dystopic web that late-stage capitalism, organized religion devoid of spirituality, and the debilitating blandness of our routines have woven around us. I'm talking about a life that's impeded by subpar, processed food that doesn't nurture, an unending barrage of entertainment thrown in our faces in the form of infinitely scrollable social media feeds, binge-able episodes of seasons after seasons of media meant to sedate us, and a listless existence centered around keeping oneself trapped in a loop of earning and spending money. In the face of all this, the old Norse religion comes bearing liberty, letting you harness your primal self and allowing you to unlock your spiritual, physical, material, and emotional potential.

Your Quest for Knowledge Has Left You With Many Questions

As with any topic that possesses a substantial history, ties to a certain region, and a culture that dates back thousands of years, Norse Paganism, encompassing all its beliefs and practices, is a deep subject that requires an equally deep understanding of the nuances of its beliefs, evolution, and history.

- You might be wondering what Norse Paganism is, who its followers were, and how is it different from other religions.
- Have you wondered how many gods there are in the Norse pantheon? What their powers are, what traits do they carry, and what elements do they have control over?
- Is there a form of worship that allows you to harness the spirituality associated with those gods?
- How do I become a Norse Pagan?
- What do Norse Pagans believe in?
- What are the different types of religious practices I can follow as a Pagan?

- What benefit—spiritual or material—do I stand to gain from following this religion?

If these are some of the questions that you have pondered over, I have glad tidings for you. First off, you are a kindred spirit, and I welcome you in this quest to uncover ancient truths and wisdom. Secondly, you are in the right place. Throughout this book, I will help answer all the questions that you might have, provide you with a direction, and instill awe for the wonders that Norse Paganism has to offer.

What Exactly Is Norse Paganism?

Norse Paganism encompassed the beliefs, customs, practices, and world views that the Northern European civilizations followed before Christianity pervaded throughout the region.

Modern-day Norse Paganism is an adaptation of the spiritual beliefs and practices of the Norse folk. The Norse were a diverse group of people in terms of their crafts, occupations, lifestyle choices, and values. For example, the term Vikings, although used synonymously with Norse people, was just one of the many roles that the Norse people had adapted. Despite their different roles, the Norse folk shared a common belief system which gave rise to their religious practices.

Norse Paganism differs from other religions because it is:

- Polytheistic
- Orthopraxical
- Pluralist

- Decentralized
- Animistic
- Immanent

Now, what does that mean?

Polytheistic

While Abrahamic religions such as Christianity and Islam believe in one god, Norse Paganism is polytheistic. It believes in multiple gods. The most prominent deities in the Norse pantheon include Odin, Thor, Loki, Balder, Frigg, Heimdall, and Tyr. Each god bore specific characteristics associated with the domain they held power over. Thor, for example, was the god of thunder and therefore harnessed the powers of thunder using his weapon, Mjölnir.

Since the religion was decentralized, different gods had different levels of devotion in different places at different times. A fishing hamlet by the sea might have venerated Njord, the god of the wind and the sea and all the riches it contained, while at the same time, a mountain village might have worshipped Ullr and Skaði, the deities associated with winter.

Its polytheistic nature allowed quite a bit of liberty in terms of choosing which deity to venerate.

Orthopraxical

When it comes to religious thought, there exist two main schools—orthodoxy and orthopraxy. Orthodoxy means "the right belief," whereas Orthopraxy means "the right practice." While some religions take a polarized approach to these schools of thought, employing one instead of the other, some religions utilize both aspects. However, Norse Paganism believes in orthopraxy.

Orthopraxical religions prioritize and incentivize experience, the integrity of one's practice, the creation and continuation of one's lineage, and one's legacy. In sheer contrast, orthodox religions prioritize adherence to dogmas, doctrines, creeds, and faith above action.

Orthopraxy also means what's the right action for a certain individual rather than what's been deemed right for them according to some religious authority.

Pluralist

All religions have philosophies rooted in them, which serve as the building blocks of the faith and its practices. The philosophy behind doing virtuous acts is that one will be granted rewards in the afterlife. Such philosophy can also serve as the foundation of religious morality. This philosophy can also be used as a device to spiritually relate one thing to another.

Norse Paganism follows a pluralistic philosophy. Pluralism, in contrast to the dualist and monist philosophies, believes that everything contains profound multitudes, that even the most ordinary of things have different principles, and that the truth behind things is not absolute. Rather, it takes multiple forms and is even bound to shift.

The plurality of Norse Paganism creates a nuanced worldview where things, entities, people, and forces are viewed as more than just good or evil. Pluralists believe that everything is multifaceted, possessing both a light side and a darker side, and it is within the balance of both sides that one can look at a picture clearly and decipher its meaning.

Unlike Norse Paganism, Christianity, Judaism, and Islam have a dualist philosophy, where the categorization of good and evil is used to describe things. Sin and virtue, heaven and hell, and angels and demons are just some dualist aspects of these religions.

Some branches of Sufism and Pantheism can be considered monist beliefs, where everything is just an expression of the Universe or its Creator. Monists believe in the Source and believe that all things come from a place of singular origin.

Decentralized

Christianity's centralized source of instruction comes from the Bible. With Judaism, it's the Torah. In Islam, Muslims adhere to the guidelines as noted in the Quran and Hadith. This makes these religions centralized, with a singular source serving as the foundation of ideologies, laws, and practices.

Norse Paganism is a decentralized religion with no singular authority or ideology behind the religion. There aren't any central holy books, religious figures, scriptures, doctrines, or dogmas that a Norse Pagan has to adhere to.

Given that most religions have a demanding nature wherein they require a commitment of time and resources, selecting authorities, delegating orthodox beliefs, and behavioral codes that include rules of dress, diet, and sexual practices, it might come as a shock to people that Paganism, unlike its counterparts, does not carry such a rigorous eligibility criterion, thanks to its decentralized nature.

An argument can be made for the authenticity of Norse Paganism because of its decentralized nature. Since there's not one singular source but many, many of those sources corroborate each other, validating each other's beliefs, thus bringing credibility to the religion's beliefs because its multiple sources substantiate the same thing.

The decentralized nature of Norse mythos and Paganism meant that it grew organically throughout a community via local customs and oral narration of traditions.

The Prose and Poetic Edda, while considered exhaustive texts with much lore and mythology, are not deemed religious scriptures.

Animistic

Animism is a belief that recognizes that all objects, creatures, and places possess a spiritual essence. From rocks to rivers, plants to planets, everything—even words—is considered animated or alive. When you view things from an animistic perspective, you understand that everything, from the minutest of objects to the largest of beings, plays an integral role in the ecosystem that it exists in.

The existence of animism in Norse Paganism eliminates the distinction between holy and unholy, sacred and cursed. There's no concept of sinning in Norse Paganism. Your actions in the world are attributed to your existence rather than serve as a metric for some reward.

By assigning a spirit to every object and creature, animism opens the doors to near-infinite reserves of spirituality, giving birth to special rituals that can let you communicate with the spirits of the departed or form a bond with a deity by venerating them directly.

Immanent

Faith can be considered transcendent or immanent. Most faiths fall in either of these categories, although sometimes, some can have elements from both.

Transcendent faiths focus on *transcending* to a reality beyond our current one. The purpose of these faiths is to align your actions with a given set of instructions to fulfill the criteria to attain a desirable afterlife. In Christianity, your life choices will serve to bring you closer to God or drive you away from Him, determining whether you'll go to heaven or hell.

Immanent faiths, instead, focus on the actualization and fulfillment of your present life and the relationship that you have with the people and the world around you. Immanent faiths seek to improve the quality of your immediate reality.

Norse Paganism prides itself in being a religion that improves upon your current life by equipping you with skills, beliefs, principles, and practices that will improve your relationship with those around you, both people and nature, and let you experience living in a more primal manner. Many Pagans believe that we will be rejoined with our ancestors after we die unless we choose something else, such as a warrior's death which will result in us attaining an afterlife in Valhalla. But there is no pressure to live your life in a certain way to attain a desirable afterlife, unlike in Judeo-Christian religions, where heaven has to be earned.

What Will This Book Entail?

When I set out to write this book, I wanted to create something that would initiate a newcomer to Norse Paganism with the prerequisite knowledge that will help establish a clear understanding of Norse Mythology and Paganism in their mind and provide them with tangible and followable guidelines on how to align themselves with the teachings and principles of Norse Paganism.

To that effect, we are going to study the following topics:

1. How you can become a Norse Pagan
2. The rich history and culture of the Nordic people
3. The creation of the world according to Norse mythology, what the nine realms are, and what the world tree, Yggdrasil, is
4. The Norse calendar, holidays, festivals, and celebrations
5. The Gods and Goddesses of the Norse Pantheon
6. The Many Magical Creatures that populate the Norse mythos
7. The afterlife according to Norse mythology. Here we shall explore topics such as Valhalla and Ragnarök.
8. Discovering the magic and mysticism of runes
9. The rites of passage and rituals associated with the natural cycle of birth, growth, and death.
10. What it means to be a Norse Pagan in the modern world.

After going through the contents of this book, you will have a blueprint that will allow you to practice Paganism on your own or with a community of like-minded souls. The purpose of this book is more than just to inform. I want to instill the same awe of Norse mythology and paganism in you that runs in my veins. I want to open your eyes to the wonders of this ancient world and show you that magic still exists. I want to empower you to such a point that you can harness that magic yourself.

A Little About Me

I'm Emma Karlsson. Ever since I could remember, the stories of the old gods and goddesses have been there by my side. Growing up in Kungsträdgården, Sweden, I was surrounded by Scandinavian heritage. For me, the tales of Loki were more than just stories told to me at bedtime; for me, they were accounts of what had happened long ago, in a land where frost giants dwelled and warred with the armies of Odin.

I used to dress up as Freya and would ride a makeshift chariot that I made by tying my cats to a cart. I'd spend days upon days dreaming about the gods and goddesses who inhabited a wondrous, enchanted world, perfusing it with their magic.

It was my love of Norse mythology and culture that helped me develop a robust working knowledge of my religion and its roots. Although I was raised Christian, I always felt disconnected from Christianity. This wasn't the religion of my ancestors. Why was I following it?

In an attempt to connect with my ancestors and form a mutually respectful and loving bond with nature, I became a follower of Ásatrú, one of the modern interpretations of Paganism. I have devoted much of my learning to reading runes and understanding what it means to be a follower of the Old Norse Paganism belief systems. I continue to develop my knowledge base to share with my readers around the world. I believe that the magic of the world around us is precious and plentiful enough for all of us to experience. I want to bring that magic to you and share my love and passion for Norse Paganism and culture with kindred spirits such as yourself.

So let us venture forth and immerse ourselves in a world of wonders. Welcome to the realm of Norse Mythology.

CHAPTER 1
THE FRAMEWORK FOR BEING A NORSE PAGAN

The world as we know it has been rendered monotonously uniform as a result of aggressive corporatization, capitalism, and cultural wars that span centuries and continents.

Whether you're standing at the center of Times Square on New Year's Eve or backpacking through India after college, there's always a McDonald's nearby. Grocery stores all over the world contain the same Coke, the same Froot Loops, and the same Axe Body Spray. This rapid homogenization has taken the magic out of life.

Multimedia companies have ensured that we're all watching the same TV shows and movies, regardless of our location. Streaming platforms have morphed what was otherwise an enjoyable activity reserved for the weekend or date nights into a FOMO machine where if you haven't watched episode number x of show number y, you're going to miss out on all the great conversations surrounding that show on social media, almost forcing you to watch it just so you don't feel left out.

We have deviated from our traditions. Where are the old ways that our ancestors once used to live and thrive by? Is there no place for spirituality in the 21st century? Why has this rat-race-natured modern living robbed us of the mystical fulfillment that comes with following a creed?

Surely, you must have also thought along those lines at some point in your life. Perhaps that served as a crossroads, leading you here, imploring you to seek deeper meaning in life, uncovering the ancient ways, the old religions that our ancestors used to follow.

If so, congratulations. You are a seeker. And it would please you to know that you are sought just as much as you seek. The old gods still live among us today, keeping an eye on those who possess the prerequisite spark that can be ignited into a fire of passion, devotion, and otherworldly satisfaction. It may very well be that your intrigue has fascinated the gods, and they have—through the means they possess—paved the way for you to uncover the truth.

It is your intrigue and fascination that have brought you this far. Going further, you are going to have to do some research into what Norse mythology entails and what constitutes some of the practices of Norse Paganism. This homework is necessary, as it's going to set you apart from someone just curious about what it means to be a Norse Pagan and will start you on a journey to becoming one.

The framework for becoming a Norse Pagan includes the following steps:

Learning the fundamentals. This includes acquainting yourself with the history of Norse Paganism as well as the general mythology that encircles Norse beliefs. Once you learn what's out there, you will form an opinion about it. As it's a whole new dimension of belief, one that you aren't used to, it's going to take some time to wrap your head around more complex topics, such as the cyclical nature of time in Norse mythology. Here, you will learn that the gods and goddesses are not perfect beings without any flaws such as the Abrahamic god. The gods of the Norse pantheon are complex beings with anthropomorphic characteristics, flaws, strengths, emotions, and fully-developed personalities.

Understanding the Deeds. Paganism includes several practices such as Blót, Veneration, Rune Divination, Sumbel, and Norse Magic. Norse Magic includes practices such as Spadom, Galdrastafir, and Seiðr. Seiðr, for example, is associated with prophecy and manifestation. In modern-day, Seiðr is associated with spiritual work such as inducing trances, seeing visions, and astral projection. To become a Norse Pagan is to first understand the meaning of different practices and deeds and then integrate them into your daily life to attain your goals, whatever they may be—spiritual elevation, the manifestation of desires, emotional contentment, and so on.

Doing one's homework. First, we have to understand that Norse mythology and, subsequently Norse Paganism are very decentralized entities. Unlike modern religions that come from a singular source, you have to read from different sources and form a coherent narrative for yourself that allows you to make sense of Norse mythology and its practices. Norse Pagans rely on sources such as the Prose Edda and the Poetic Edda, which are collections of Nordic stories and poems. As you expand your knowledge base, you will come across books such as Íslendingabók and Landnámabók that provide further detail about Norse myth and the accounts of the settling of Norse Vikings in places such as Iceland in the 9th and 10th centuries.

Taking part in celebrations, rites of passage, offerings, and rune magic. Once you have learned the fundamentals, understood the meaning behind the deeds, and done your homework, you are ready to take part in the Norse celebrations that the Pagans celebrate throughout their calendar year. Yule, Ostara, and Midsummer are some of the celebrations that the Norse used to celebrate at different points in the calendar period. You might want to learn about the rites of passage associated with Norse mythology and implement them in your life. At this stage, you are ready to include offerings and rune magic into your daily life as well, allowing you to truly become a Norse Pagan.

Learn the Norse Pantheon. A good starting point for your research would be finding out about the gods and goddesses of Norse mythology. Norse Paganism is a polytheistic religion populated with many gods and goddesses with their own set of abilities, strengths, domains, and characteristics.

As Norse mythology was largely passed down orally for centuries, the exact number of gods is hard to ascertain. Snorri Sturluson, an Icelandic figure most well-noted for his poetry and contribution to Norse history, did write down the mythologies in the form of the Eddas and the Heimskringla, which gives us a basic understanding of the gods, among other things.

In Norse mythology, the gods governed as mentors, guides, allies, protectors, and beings worthy of worship. According to Norse lore, the gods, being polytheistic, are not all-powerful or limitless. Each of them has a certain domain that they have mastery over. Understanding which god rules over which domain will give you a better understanding of what their true forms are like.

Perhaps one of the redeeming features of the Norse gods is their imperfection. While in conventional religions, the image of a monotheistic god is associated with perfection and flawlessness, the Norse gods have a much more relatable and approachable nature *because* they are imperfect. It's not just within the physical traits that they are imperfect—such as missing body parts or bearing battle scars—but it's also within their actions that they are flawed.

Where modern religions associate holiness with infallibility, Norse mythology presents its gods as fallible beings capable of error. Rather than paint the gods in a negative light, their imperfections cast light on the aspects that they are the gods of. For example, Loki, the god of mischief, is by his nature a god who relishes in deception and cunning, providing insight into the workings of what mischief is and what its limits can be. Similarly, Thor, known for his temper and his brute strength, resonates with the powers and traits of thunder.

The Norse gods were split into two categories:

- The Æsir

- The Vanir

. . .

The Æsir

These are the gods associated with humanity in a societal context such as through law, war, conflict, and labor. Odin, Thor, and Loki are some very famous Æsir gods. Other Æsir gods include Baldr, Foresti, Ullr, Bragi, and Iðunn.

Take Odin, for example. He is probably one of the most complex gods in Norse mythology. He is known as the Many-Named God because of his attributes, titles, and honors. He was seen as a god of war and death, but he was so much more than that. He is synonymous with the quest for knowledge, taking extreme measures to attain his goal whether it's losing an eye or hanging upside down from the World Tree.

The Vanir

The Vanir are gods associated with humanity's connection to nature, such as in magic and fertility. Some famous Vanir include Frey, Freya, and Njord. The Vanir are inherently different from the Æsir as they offer an understanding of how man is connected to the world around him. The Vanir have a mystical element that implores a learner to seek a deeper understanding of his relationship with the biosphere he lives in.

Freya, one of the Vanir, is considered the goddess of femininity, passion, and wisdom. Freya is also adept in the art of seiðr, a magic that she even taught to Odin. Besides being wise, strong, and beautiful, Freya was also able to shapeshift into a hawk and a falcon using her feathered cloak. Her very image evokes respect for nature.

The Jötnar

The Jötnar are considered gods by some practitioners. They are the gods of the wilderness, associated with raw forces of nature such as those that exist in the depths of oceans or wildfires. The Jötnar are associated with the elemental forces of nature including nature (earth) itself. You may consider them gods of deeper wisdom. Ymir, Surtr, Jord, Aegir, and Ran are some of the Jötnar.

These three clans have had a very complicated history with each other, sometimes warring with each other and sometimes seen establishing friendly relationships with each other, even marrying from each other's clans. When it comes to these gods, things aren't exactly split into clear black and white—there's no distinct divide between what constitutes good and evil. Ask yourself this: Can thunder be evil? Does fertility possess the capacity to be a dark force? Can the sea be a malevolent entity?

Of course, there are some gods and creatures who exist beyond any category: Hel, Níðhöggr, Fenrir, and Jörmungandr are all magnificent beings who embody primordial forces that are much more powerful and vast than any of the other gods from the previously mentioned categories. Hel, for example, is the guardian of the dead, connected to the spirits of those who have passed. Jörmungandr is a giant serpent who circles all of Midgard, representing the limits of all that is known.

. . .

What Is the Norse World?

All the gods and goddesses that I mentioned thrive in the Norse world, a realm that contains multitudes in terms of mysticism, lore, and locations. The Norse Pagan world contains four main realities:

1. The World Tree Yggdrasil
2. The cyclical nature of the universe, starting from its birth and ending in Ragnarök
3. The spirits that thrive all around us in the world
4. The web of fate that encompasses everything

These realities—or *truths*—shape the perception of the Norse world.

Yggdrasil and the Nine Realms

The world tree is the spiritual backbone of the Norse world. This great ash tree has roots that spread in every direction, extending into the nine realms and digging deep into the world to take its water from three wells, the Urdarbrunner (the Well of Fate), the Hvergelmir (the Roaring Kettle), and the Mimisbrunnr (Mimir's Well). Each of these wells has a rich history of its own.

Mimir's Well, for example, is the source of wisdom and contains waters for which Odin sacrificed his eye.

Upon the Yggdrasil, rest the nine realms. You may consider these parallel dimensions ruled by their own laws and governments. There's a hierarchy to these realms based on their respective position on the Yggdrasil.

The top two realms of Asgard and Vanaheim are at the top of the Yggdrasil and are home to the Æsir and Vanir gods. The gods of these realms use the Bifrost to travel from their realms to other realms. The Bifrost is a rainbow bridge guarded by Heimdall, one of the gods.

Near to these two realms lies the realm Alfheim, home of the powerful spirits known as the Alfar.

Then, halfway down, is Midgard. Midgard is basically our land. The Middle Realm. It's the realm containing the earth. The great beast Jörmungandr encircles Midgard's outer limits. This serpent holds its tail in its mouth.

Near Midgard is the land of the Jötnar, Jötunheimr. On the other side of Jötunheimr is Nidavellir, the home of the dwarves.

At the base of the Yggdrasil, there are two realms opposite each other. These are the realms of fire and ice, Muspelheim and Niflheim, respectively.

The final realm on Yggdrasil's base is Helheim, the land where the dead reside. It is here that the souls of the departed rest eternally.

At the root of the Yggdrasil, there's a dragon named Níðhöggr, who keeps gnawing away at the roots of the tree. His hunger will never be sated.

Yggdrasil's iconic position as the nurturer and nourisher of all the worlds makes it one of the most important fixtures of Norse Mythology.

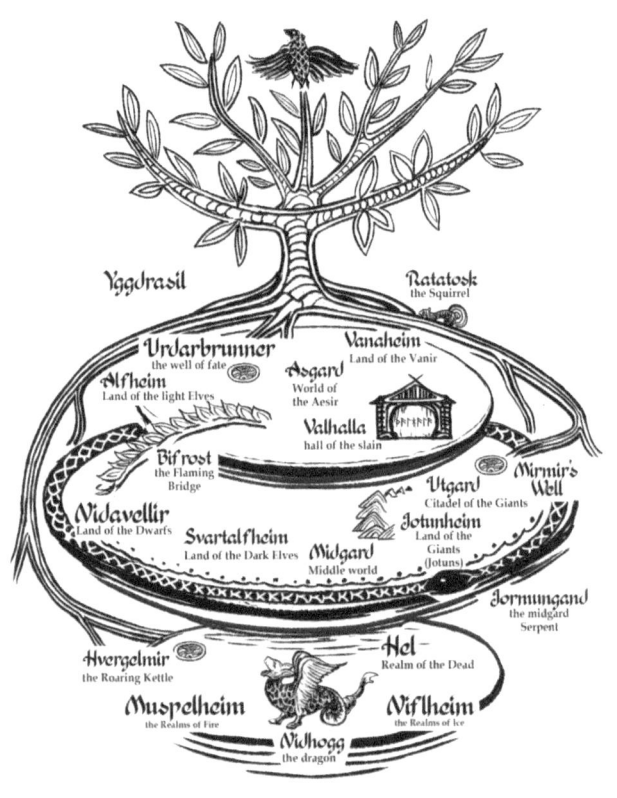

The Cyclical Nature of Reality

The story of creation, as told in the Eddas, bears remarkable similarity to how the creation of the universe is detailed in modern science in the form of the Big Bang. In Norse mythology, there was nothing in the beginning except for a humongous void known as the Ginnungagap. This gap was surrounded by the fire of Muspelheim and the ice of Niflheim. And then, no one knows how long ago, a cosmic clash took place as both ice and flame met with vigor, causing an explosion the likes of which was never seen before.

This caused the great cow known as Auðumbla and the ferocious giant Ymir to come forth from the steam issuing from the explosion. While Ymir gave birth to the giants, the first of the Jötnar, from his body, the cow Auðumbla unearthed the first of the Æsir by licking away mist off the rocks. The first of the Æsir was Búri. Búri had children with a giant, including a son named Bor.

Bor then had three sons with a frost giant: Odin, Vili, and Ve.

Together, these brothers ended the age of the Great Giants and ushered in a new era.

Odin and his siblings slew Ymir after they couldn't take any more of their poverty, given that Ymir was hoarding Auðumbla's boons for himself. Ymir's body was used to craft existence as we know it.

Midgard was created after the gods decided upon the details through consulting with each other. The first humans began inhabiting Midgard.

And just as this creation took place, so too will cyclical destruction take place, known as Ragnarök. Foretold by the Nameless Seeress, Ragnarök is the end of the world in the aftermath of a great battle.

Heimdall shall sound his horn for the first and final time, summoning the gods and their kin to battle. A time of bitter cold known as Fimbulwinter will bring forth frost the likes of which has not been seen before. The great wolf

Fenrir shall break free and wreak havoc. Jörmungandr will rise from the sea and cause the land to be flooded. Surtr shall gather an army of fire giants in Muspelheim.

The armies shall battle with each other. Surtr will fight Frey. Thor shall wrestle Jörmungandr and perish. Odin shall be devoured by Fenrir. A big hound called Garm shall come out and slay Tyr, the god of war and justice. Loki will arrive with his forces and cause further cacophony on the battlefield.

Surtr shall set everything alight by striking the base of the Yggdrasil. Odin's son Vidar will seek revenge for his father's death by tearing Fenrir into two pieces. Thor's children shall salvage their father's hammer.

Two humans, Lif and Lifrasir, will wait out the end of the world and will bring forth new humanity into the world. The slain god Baldr will rise to join the new gods in a new world created from the ashes of the previous one.

And so, like Ymir's downfall gave birth to our current reality, Ragnarök will give rise to a new reality, and the cyclical nature of reality shall continue.

We shall discuss creation and Ragnarök in detail in respective chapters. Here, the purpose of summarizing these two events was to shed light on the cyclical nature of the world in Norse mythology.

Spirits Thriving All Around Us

Animism, as we discussed earlier, is the belief that all things are essentially living things containing a spirit. Norse Paganism takes this belief and applies it to the entire world. Animism demands that everything be treated with a certain amount of respect, as everything has a role to play in the grand design.

The spirits of natural places were known as Vættir.

Norse Paganism treated everything as if it was alive, and the purpose of its rituals was to foster a harmonious relationship with these things. Yes, the gods were important as well, but so were everyday things like trees, rivers, meadows, and clouds.

The Web Of Fate

Finally, the last truth central to Norse mythology is fate. In Norse mythology, fate is more than just an unchangeable destiny that will come regardless of what we do or act; in Norse mythology, fate is akin to an alive being. It is active and changing, depending on the actions that you take in the immediate present. The two main forces that shape fate are known as Orlog and Hamingja.

Orlog is the base of fate. You can consider it those things that have already been determined by previous actions that are beyond your control, such as the time of your birth, the place where you live, and how your life is affected by the consequences of other people's actions.

Hamingja, also known as luck, is comprised of your conditions, your skills, your resilience, and anything else in your life that you are capable of changing through positive or negative action.

Norse Paganism is about accepting the fact that you can change your fate rather than sit idly and wait for fate to change you. Given paganism's immanent nature, it is recommended that you take positive action using your faculties to achieve the reality that you desire and in doing so, change your fate for the better.

What Kinds Of Paganism Are Being Practiced Today?

Given Norse Paganism's decentralized nature, it should come as no shock that in different regions, different types of Paganism are being followed. Some of the prominent ones include:

- Ásatrú
- Vanatru
- Rökkatru
- Shamanism
- Theodism
- Thursatru
- Odinism
- Lokeans
- Tribal Heathenry

Even though we're going to discuss these in great detail in a later chapter, I saw it fit to give you a basic overview of the prominent types of beliefs that are being followed today, so that you have an idea of what to expect in terms of paganism beliefs and practices.

Ásatrú

Ásatrú revives the ancient practices and beliefs of the old Norse faith. The word Ásatrú means Æsir faith, referring to the Æsir gods. The clergy in this religion are known as goðar. This religion was revitalized by Sveinbjörn Beinteinsson in 1972, to bring back the worship of the Norse deities.

Ásatrú's modern beliefs are along the vein of humanism and even reconstructionism, where the deities are reimagined as metaphorical rather than actual beings. However, this reconstructionist belief varies from follower to follower, as some followers still believe in the deities being actual entities. Deities venerated in Ásatrú include Thor, Odin, Freya, and several of the Æsir.

Ásatrú's beliefs emphasize one's positive actions in this world rather than transcendental actions meant to attain an afterlife. The practitioners believe in the creed "you are your deeds."

The central ritual in Ásatrú is known as Blót; wherein sacrifice is made to the gods and goddesses in a commemorative, communal setting through the use of alcohol. Several texts are followed by the followers of Ásatrú, including the words of Snorri Sturluson. Other texts that Ásatrúans follow include collections of runes, Eddas, books, sagas, and poems such as the Hávamál.

Those who congregate as part of Ásatrú are known as Kindreds. The priest of a Kindred is known as a Gothar. The congregants are known as Folk. The ceremonies performed are called Blóts, and the altars upon which the Blót is performed are known as the Stalli.

Vanatru

As Ásatrú is "true to the Æsir", Vanatru is "true to the Vanir." Vanatru takes spiritual practices inspired by the Vanir. Vanatru focuses on the Vanir-centric aspects of heathenry, including divination, being attuned to nature, folk magic, and witchcraft. Gods and goddesses venerated in Vanatru include Njord, Freya, Frey, Nerthus, Ullr, Frodi, and so forth. Since the Æsir are considered gods of order, war, civilization, and justice, and the Vanir are considered the gods of nature, those who are drawn to Vanatru tend to be more earth-centric. This is the key difference between the two practices.

In Vanatru, importance is given to the individualistic nature of worship, where each god and goddess is worshipped or venerated in a way that's unique to them.

Rökkatru

Those who focus on the third pantheon of the gods, such as Hel, Loki, Surtr, and Jörmungandr took upon the name Rökkatru. This religion originated in New Zealand. The word Rökkatru means "worthy of the gods" or "true to the gods."

It should be noted that venerating the Rökkr gods does not mean condoning evil. The correlation of darkness with evil is a very Christian concept. When we talk about darkness in the context of Rökkatru, we are talking about necessary forces that ensure that the world is balanced. Death is not perceived as evil. Without death, there would be no cycle of life. Similarly, mischief is yet another aspect of life without which there would be no order or honor. When Surtr sets forth the gears of Ragnarök, he is not being an evil entity. He's performing his role as delegated. Without

Hel to preside over her realm, there would be no one left to oversee the portion of the dead that she receives.

Other practices such as Odinism, Shamanism, Thursatru, and Theodism all fall under the umbrella of paganism, with their specific practices, beliefs, and rituals. Whatever their differences may be, the foundation remains the same: venerating the Norse gods, understanding the old creed, and becoming a better person through the religious practices that allow you to focus on the here and now.

What Literature Can I Peruse?

Even though Norse mythology and paganism draw from a preliterate society where books were not seen as the primary source of conveying information, today, thanks to the works of devotees, we have several foundational texts available that you can peruse to give yourself a better understanding of Norse mythology and paganism.

The Eddas and the Sagas

Around 1200 AD, an unnamed editor compiled traditional Norse mythical poems and named his compilation The Poetic Edda. In the Poetic Edda, the poems about the gods and goddesses of old are preserved. The Poetic Edda is considered to be a very raw and unabridged compilation of Norse poetry.

However, despite their anonymous nature, the poems are arranged coherently, starting from the creation of the world. This poem is known as Voluspa.

Then, there's a poem known as the Hávamál where Odin talks to the reader directly, offering his wisdom and insights. Similarly, there are poems about the gods Frey and Thor as well.

In 1222, Snorri Sturluson took some of the stories in the Poetic Edda as well as some folklore that wasn't written in the Poetic Edda and compiled a book called Edda. Modern scholars differentiate between the two works by calling one the Poetic Edda and Snorri's work the Prose Edda.

The Prose Edda is one of the most approachable written works for someone interested in getting into Norse mythology, as they detail everything chronologically.

Similarly, the Icelandic Sagas, written in the 13th and 14 centuries, detail the stories between the settlement of Iceland until the 11th century, describing the events that took place among the Celtic and Nordic inhabitants of Iceland. These sagas offer great insight into the pre-Christian religion followed in the region as well as the culture that dominated that geographical region. These sagas provide us with accurate historical accounts of medieval Scandinavian societies and kingdoms, allowing us to make sense of what transpired historically.

Íslendingabók

This text contains the history of Iceland and some of the earliest recorded Norse mythology about the battle of the gods. Within this book, the creation of Midgard is also detailed. This narrative text also tells us of the advancement of Christianity in Iceland during the 13th century. A database by the same name is created by a biotech company called deCODE genetics, attempting to record the genealogy of Icelandic people.

Landnámabók

Also known as the Book of Settlements, this medieval Icelandic text describes how the Norse people settled in Iceland in the 9th and 10th centuries. Divided into five parts and told over a hundred chapters, this book contains information on important events, family histories, and settlements. It also provides genealogical accounts of the settlements and their settlers. There are stories told in the book as well which gives it a narrative structure. This book is also one of the primary sources of heathenism and the pagan religion, followed by the Norse folk.

The Germania of Tacitus

Written in the 1st century, this is the most complete account of the religion and society of the Germanic tribes who settled in Germania. Tacitus's work provides not just the historical account of the Germanic tribes but also includes symbolism and allusive storytelling that grants us a deeper understanding of the ancient Germanic worldview. Tacitus's work is still being interpreted and reinterpreted to this day.

Runes

These ancient alphabets that originated in Germanic and Scandinavian countries are used by many Pagans in their divination and magic rituals. According to Norse lore, Odin was directly responsible for the runes becoming available to us, as he discovered these runes as part of his trial wherein he hung from the Yggdrasil for nine days.

Understanding the history of these runes, their modern usage, and their historical context, as well as their application in divination and magical rituals, will pave the way for you to get a deeper understanding of how such symbolism relates to Norse mythology.

Modern Research in Archaeology, History, Linguistics, and Anthropology

Lastly, stay in touch with modern discoveries of science, archaeology, history, anthropology, and linguistics as work is currently being done in the present to gain a nuanced understanding of the historical significance of Norse mythology and Norse Paganism. Every day, more discoveries pave the way for a clearer understanding of the rich history that the Norse folk have left behind.

One such way of going about it is creating a Google alert for Norse mythology news so that you can get alerted about any new developments that might take place. Another excellent method is to join a community of kindred spirits who can keep you in the loop and boost your enthusiasm in the meantime.

The more research you conduct, the more intuitively Norse Paganism will come to you. You might even feel the draw of certain gods and goddesses, allowing you the opportunity to explore your spirituality further. In doing your homework, you will uncover many mysteries that will make you question what you know about this world and completely recontextualize life as you know it.

CHAPTER 2
THE ORIGIN AND HISTORY OF NORSE PAGANISM

You are the living link to history. Stored deep within your soul, within the DNA that you are made of, and within your mind, there are memories of your ancestors. It might sound like I'm taking a leaf out of the *Assassin's Creed* games, but the fact remains that all of us contain a stamp, a signature, of our ancestors dating back to the first humans.

If we seek to live a more meaningful life and experience a deeper connection to our reality, it is in our interest that we learn about where we came from and who our ancestors were. To that end, we should also put on our Indiana Jones hats and go on a little archaeological expedition to unearth the origins of the old Norse way.

It is only when we learn about the origins of Norse Paganism will we realize that the chronological chain of events attests to the authenticity of the religion. We will understand that these are not just stories. Everything within these pages is not a work of fiction. The Vikings were real people. The Norse folk followed Paganism devotedly, spending their entire lives venerating the gods and goddesses they believed in. Through our understanding of their history, we will borrow some of their belief and lend credence to everything that we will learn along the way.

What Do We Know Of Norse Paganism?

Norse Paganism as we know it today rose from the beliefs and practices of the Old Norse Pagans before Christianity pervaded Northern Europe. The acts, beliefs, and practices of the heathens of pre-Christian Scandinavia, especially during the age of the Vikings, are collectively referred to as the Norse religion. Other terms used to describe the old religion include Germanic paganism, Norse mythos, and Germanic religion.

Around the 7th century, Anglo-Saxon England was converted from Norse paganism to Christianity. Similarly, Scandinavia was converted three centuries later. After that, the Norse religion seemed to fade away in history, but despite efforts to completely wash it away, many traditions of paganism survived in Christian practices.

Most of what we know today was transcribed long after Christianity had spread through the area, which, unfortunately, means that there's no way to gauge how much Christianity influenced those transcriptions. However, there's still some pure knowledge preserved in the form of archeological records, temples of old, and burial mounds. One can also ascertain the real version of the religion and lore by cross-referencing different texts (the sagas and the Eddas) to create a coherent narrative that is relatively unsullied by the Christian influence.

The very least that we can ascertain from the reference material that we do have is an understanding of the community that thrived long ago, how it lived, how it worshiped different deities, and how their religion inculcated teachings and rites throughout their lifestyles.

Those who followed Paganism believed it to be an advocative religion of the land. The Norse people who followed it believed that their religion was supposed to evoke a kinship between them and everything around them.

The people focused on Nordic and Germanic deities, rituals, and folklore. Their animistic beliefs lend credence to the ideology that everything occupied a soul and that certain rituals would allow them to connect with that soul. As a result, they had rites, both complex and simple, that included everything from chanting to divining runes. Sometimes, the followers would sing songs up until the point that they'd reach a spiritual reverie where they would be possessed by the old gods.

Those who followed this religion were known as the Norsemen. Collectively, the Norsemen were a cluster of different groups spread throughout that geographic region. They rose to prominence during what we call the Viking Age. Several marked differences made the Norse people stand apart from the other civilizations of their time. The women, for one, were treated as equal in status. They could fight in battle, divorce their spouses, vote, and even acquire property.

There came a time when the Norse people were converted to Christianity during the Middle Ages. Before that happened, they used to ascribe to their native religion, the centerpiece of which was Norse mythology. These stories and their faith in them gave the Vikings' life a purpose and provided them with the foundation to shape their religious practices.

The creed that the Vikings followed rigorously reflected their relationship with the world. Rather than view the world as something to gain mastery over or think of it as an antagonist to their lives, they marveled at the world as it was, cherishing nature and acknowledging that earthly life was filled with struggle and hardships. Their faith celebrated it when the Norse people rose to the occasion, braved the hardships of the world, and accomplished great deeds for their and their people's benefit. If Vikings were being true to themselves and performing these great deeds, then they were upholding their creed.

When you read the word "Viking," it might conjure up an image of a bloodthirsty, barbaric warrior tearing through civilization wearing horned helmets, flailing axes, drinking mead, and destroying everything in his path. That image is nothing but Christian propaganda, meant to dismiss the rich lives of the Norse people by painting them as brutes.

In reality, the Vikings were so much more than that. They were brave warriors, seafaring raiders, conquerors, explorers, settlers, and traders originating from what is modern-day Norway, Sweden, Denmark, and Iceland. The Vikings quested through much of the world during the Viking Age (A.D. 793-1066). They explored North America five hundred years before Christopher Columbus did. They traveled as far as Baghdad in the East.

They conversed in the Norse language, wrote in runes, and practiced their ancestral faith.

The Vikings had a very nuanced social structure in which the hierarchy was divided between the Jarls at the top, the common folk in the middle, and the slaves at the bottom.

Those who ruled over the common folk were chieftains who had cultivated power and strength through military expertise. These chieftains commanded raiding warriors who traversed across Europe, ushering in a golden era in the Viking Age. This was before Scandinavia was a unified land. Back then, chieftains and Jarls, both small and large, ruled over certain areas. They were always competing with each other for power.

Unlike the barbarians that they're depicted as, the Vikings were a very nuanced people, strictly following a complex law.

It is because of the Old Norse poems, treatises, and sagas, available to us in written form, that were transcribed after the Viking Age that we have an idea of the faith and practices that they followed. These records grant us the understanding that the Old Norse religious beliefs, rather than being uniform throughout the region, were varied based on time and space. These varied beliefs and practices were based on social conventions and differences in environment (people who lived near the sea would have different practices compared to those who lived by the mountains). There were variations based on the profession of the people as well. Warriors, farmers, and hunters would adhere to beliefs specific to them rather than follow a general practice. Their religion was also influenced by the Viking's social contact with people who lived outside of the Nordic areas.

. . .

The Timeline of Norse History

Let us take a brief look at the timeline of Norse history, which shall serve as the backbone of a detailed look into what the Viking Age was, and how the Norse folk thrived, spread throughout the region, and eventually disbanded because of Christianization.

8000 — 4000 B.C.

Before this time, glaciers used to cover the region, making it impossible for people to come to Scandinavia. However, during this era, the glaciers started to retreat, allowing people to come to Scandinavia and settle down.

4000 B.C.

Often, people traverse large distances for the sake of sustenance. Similarly, in this era, the hunting tribes pursued reindeer in Scandinavia, particularly in the southern region. These people are the ancestors of the Sami people. There are rock drawings discovered that date back to 4000 B.C.

1550 B.C.

Tribes begin to form and settle between what is modern-day Sweden and Norway. At this time, amber was considered a commodity in those areas. A trade route known as the Amber Route formed from the Baltic Sea down to the Mediterranean. This route was named so because of the availability of amber along that route.

1000 B.C.

Indo-European tribes come and settle down in Scandinavia. Around this time, the language that was spoken in that area, Proto-German, began forming its characteristics.

500 B.C.

The Scandinavian Iron Age begins after contact with the Celtic civilization.

450—50 B.C.

Scandinavians and Celts begin trading with each other. At this time, the Celts occupied most of the European continent, competing with both Greeks and Romans for land.

200 B.C.

The Scandinavian tribes also start their inquests, moving into Germany and Eastern Europe. By doing so, they displace the Celts in the region. The Celts, as a result, move into the British Isles and Ireland. It is here that we see the formation of Old Norse through the evolution of the north branch of the Proto-Germanic language.

150 B.C.

As language evolved, so did inscriptions. Around this time, the first runes start to appear. What they were used for and what significance they had remains a mystery to this day. We know this much about those runes: they evolved from the Old Italic alphabets.

120 B.C.

Many movements take place during this time: the Romans settle in Europe, and the Scandinavians, by then known as Goths, moved from Sweden into central Europe.

A.D. 150

The evolution of boats becomes prominent. By A.D. 150, the boats began to look like how Viking boats are depicted in modern media, with masts, sails, and end-posts made of oak, planks, and ribs. They even had long oars that were looped to rowlocks. These boats evolved into fast and agile vessels, allowing swift movement on the seas.

A.D. 325—500

Christianity starts to show up in central Europe thanks to the Romans. Germanic and Roman people engage in tribal skirmishes. Pirates start plundering and looting on the seas. The Huns weaken the Roman empire and subsequently make it fall in A.D. 476.

A.D. 450—650

West Germanic tribes invade the British Isles and settle there.

A.D. 550—790

The upper eastern part of Sweden known as Uppsala becomes an economic force to be reckoned with, exporting many things like iron, fur, horses, and slaves.

A.D. 500—1160

The Frankish tribes from the south are impeded by the Danes, who built walls to keep them out.

A.D. 772—785

The ruler of the Frankish Kingdom begins his campaign to exterminate pagans, including the Norse.

A.D. 790—1066

This is known as the Viking Age. The Vikings raid Scotland, Ireland, England, Spain, Wales, Germany, and France. The Norwegians wage battle against the Danes to gain control of Ireland. The Norse also discover Iceland in A.D. 860, then settle there. When Alfred the great forces Christianity on the Danes, the Danes and Norwegian people flee to Iceland.

By 912, Vikings take over the Northern Frankish lands. In 947, Norway starts adopting Christianity. Denmark follows Norway's lead. The Vikings settle in Greenland after Erik the Red discovers it.

In A.D. 1000, Iceland also converts to Christianity. Around that same time, Leif Eriksson discovers North America but is fended off by the natives.

Soon after, the Norse descended Normans invade Italy and Sicily and later on take over England. But after this point, the Viking invasions and inquest die down, and slowly, the belief in the old gods also dies down, bringing an end to the age of the Vikings.

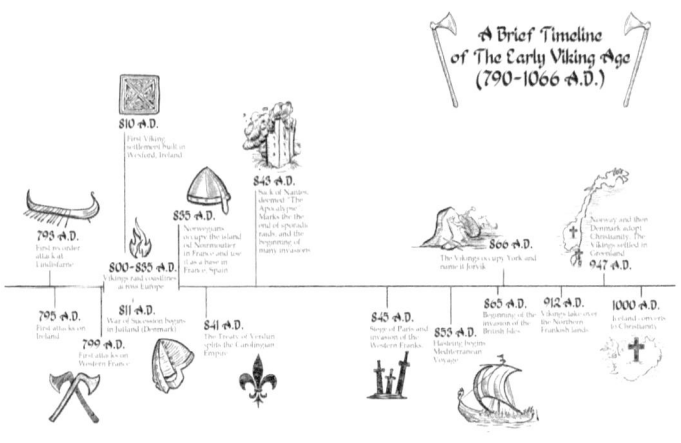

What was the Viking Age?

The Viking Age, starting from A.D. 790 and ending only with the Christianization of Scandinavia, saw the rise of Norse or Viking culture. The Norse people had an agrarian economy, relying upon farming as a source of sustenance and trade. This also made it convenient to delegate roles to different types of people. Farming was one of the primary purposes of the Norse people during the Viking age. They would farm crops like rye, oats, barley, and wheat. Their homes would be on farmsteads, enabling ease of access to their farmlands.

The work would be divided between men and women. While the men did tackle the majority of farming, the women were in charge of work inside the house. Women were charged with producing clothes and preparing food.

They would cook and bake and produce things such as cheese, milk, mead, and beer. The women would milk the animals as well. As fresh food was not always readily available, women were also charged with preserving food by salting and pickling it.

Meanwhile, the more physically demanding activities were tasked to the men. Agricultural roles such as those of fertilizing, plowing, sowing, and harvesting would fall in the domain of men.

Besides farming and agriculture, the Vikings would travel and conquer. The grandiose desire to seek fame and fortune was embedded in their nature, ushering them to travel to the far expanses of the globe to fulfill their purpose. This allowed them to discover places such as North America and Greenland.

Their style of warfare and raiding made them feared throughout the land, providing them with a competitive edge against their foes. It was this style of combat that ushered in the Viking age.

When the Vikings attacked the Lindisfarne monastery in England, which is the first recorded Viking raid, that's when the Viking Age officially began. This happened in 793. It ended in 1066 when the last Viking King known as King Harald Hardrada was defeated in the Battle of Stamford.

In the Viking age, the Vikings discovered many different people, locations, and riches as their raids, looting, colonization, and trading brought them face-to-face with their rivals in the land. But this was not all that they did. The Vikings were also founders of cities and colonies. Dublin and Normandy are two popular locations that the Vikings founded. The Vikings also colonized Iceland, which made it possible for them to colonize Greenland as well.

This might beckon you to think how such a populace of scattered tribes so few in numbers was able to conquer so much area. Well, the Vikings were characteristically brave, fierce, and courageous. They reveled in the face of danger, often taking risks that lesser warriors would not even think of. The reason they were able to conquer so much land in such a short amount of time was their ability to brave their way through any loss they suffered. Their opponents used to think that the Vikings did not fear death.

But the Viking ideology expands beyond just pilfering and pillaging; they were also peaceful traders and, as we mentioned, farmers. Sometimes, their expeditions avoided bloodshed entirely, focusing instead on bartering with the people they came across.

As glorious and fantastic as their reign was, it eventually came to an end just as all the ages preceding them did. Just as the Stone Age was consumed by the Bronze Age and the Bronze Age was overshadowed by the Iron Age, the Viking Age as well came to an end due to the shift in religion.

By the time the 11th century came around, Christianity was taking hold of most of the world, not just Scandinavia. Perhaps one of the reasons the Viking Age came to an end was that during the Viking Age, there was not a single unified ruler of the lands. Warlords and chieftains occupied specific portions of land.

The Christianization of Scandinavia didn't happen at once. It took more than a century's worth of missionary work and conquests for the Christianization to fully take effect.

But despite the efforts of the Christians to propagate their religion and eliminate Norse Paganism, it survived and is still alive today.

Why Did the Viking Age End?

There are several factors besides just Christianization that caused the Viking Age to end. The Vikings did not exactly go extinct or die out or disappear from history. They assimilated into other cultures, became residents of other countries, and assimilated into other civilizations.

Most Vikings Didn't Leave the Nordic Lands

The Viking Age caught traction after the fall of the Western Roman Empire, granting Vikings the opportunity to take advantage of mostly unconquered, lawless land. However, by the 11th century, Europe was coming into its own. William the Conqueror was making the English kingdom a stronghold while the Frankish Kingdoms were morphing into the Holy Roman Empire, propagating their version of order across the lands. Back in Scandinavia, the Viking kingdoms were evolving as well, taking the shape of the medieval monarchies of Norway, Sweden, and Denmark. The rulers of these kingdoms did not see it fit to send off their warriors overseas, finally putting an end to the Viking raids in the face of the political certainty that had taken hold of Europe.

The Vikings Assimilated into Other Societies

The Vikings began to assimilate into the countries where they had settled. For example, in Normandy, the Frankish rules were so vexed by the constant pillage and plunder of the Vikings that King Charles of France offered them a small area of land in the early 10th century to permanently occupy. The Viking Jarl Rollo invited more of his people from Scandinavia, and here, the Norsemen assimilated with the local inhabitants.

They Were Offered Luxury and Riches

Christianization was not only gradual, but it also came with political advantage, material riches, influence, and diplomatic ties. Getting marked with the Christian cross allowed the converts to receive rewards and also enabled them to continue trading in Christian establishments, towns, and cities. The trade routes were controlled by Christian believers, who demanded that to continue trading, the Vikings had to give proof that they believed in Christ.

The Christian missionaries also coaxed the Vikings by saying that the Vikings had a polytheistic faith, so why not accept one more deity (the Abrahamic God and his son, Jesus Christ) when they were already worshipping multiple gods?

This gradual and constant coaxing with riches and ease eventually led to the Christianization of Scandinavia, seemingly wiping away the Norse Pagan religion.

However, as I mentioned at the start of this book, old roots run deep. It took its time, but eventually, Norse Paganism made a resurgence in the modern era, and today, thousands of followers can be found not just in Scandinavia but all over the world.

Today, in both America and Western Europe, Paganism is one of the fastest-growing religions. According to population data, Ásatrú is one of the fastest-growing religions in Iceland now.

Moving forward, we will take a closer and much more detailed look at the story of creation, the nine realms, and Yggdrasil. Once we understand the historical context of the events of creation and the significance that the nine realms and the World Tree hold in Norse Paganism, we will delve into the Norse calendar and study their holidays and traditions.

CHAPTER 3
THE CREATION OF THE COSMOS

Almost every ancient religion that has survived the ages and is still being practiced contains its unique lore that deals with questions larger than life such as "Where did we come from?" or "How did the world come to be?" or "Where will we go after we die?" Such questions are natural, and in some religions, such as Judaism, asking such questions is encouraged so that the followers can gain a closer understanding of their god, their self, and their role in the universe.

Each religion gives the story of creation a lot of significance, and it is sometimes competitively contested as to which particular creation lore aligns most with the modern scientific understanding of this universe's creation.

In Hinduism, the universe is said to have been created by the god Brahma, who fashioned everything out of himself. The stories in the Hindu Vedas tell of a lotus flower growing from Vishnu's navel with Brahma sitting atop it. Brahma then cleaves the flower into the heavens, the world, and the sky.

Greek mythology tells us another tale entirely, stating that in the beginning, there was only a singular primordial condition known as Chaos, out of which arose Earth (Gaia), the Underworld (Tartarus), Desire (Eros), Darkness (Erebus), and Night (Nyx). Together, they created the rest of the primordial creatures, such as day, the sea, and the heavens.

In Christianity, it states that in the beginning, there was nothing, and then God said, "Let there be light." And then it took him six days to create the heavens, the earth, hell, and everything else in the universe.

In Islam, similar to Christianity, Allah commanded with a singular word "Be!" all the matter that was compacted together blew apart, spreading the universe in every direction.

But what does Norse mythology tell us about the creation of the cosmos? Is there a grand fable befitting the magnificence of Norse mythology and paganism that provides a thorough explanation of the story of creation?

The answer is yes. And for all of us who ascribe to the beliefs of Norse Paganism, the good thing is that the story of creation's spiritual and metaphorical elements serves perfectly to satiate the grandest questions of all: Who are we, where do we come from, and what's our role in this universe?

An Unparalleled Story of the Birth of The Universe

In the beginning, there was just the great empty gap known as Ginnungagap. One can describe Ginnungagap as an endless abyss that existed before the creation of the nine worlds. Norse mythology has a poetic ideology that tends to demarcate the universe into a cyclical order of creation and destruction. So, as Ginnungagap existed once before the creation of anything, so too shall it exist upon the destruction of everything.

In the poem *Völuspá*, often cited as one of the most prominent poems in the Poetic Edda, the seeress describes the state of un-creation as:

> "That was the age when nothing was;
> There was no sand, nor sea, nor cool waves,
> No earth nor sky nor grass there,
> Only Ginnungagap."

The word itself is a concatenation of two words, *ginnung* and *gap*. The word ginnung abstractly means something that is charged with magic or a primordial force. The word gap pretty much means the same as it does in English. So, the barebones definition of Ginnungagap that we can form is that of a magically charged gap. Other sources translate the name to "yawning gap" or "chaotic chasm."

To the north of this great gap was the Hvergelmir that gave water to Yggdrasil, the World Tree. Not all water went to Yggdrasil. The leftover water started freezing, as the Ginnungagap was a polarized region, with its north being extremely cold and its south being hot.

As the water started freezing, the ice world of Niflheim came into existence.

And as the south of the Ginnungagap began growing hotter—one can assume, to keep up with the cooling of the north region to conserve the polarity of the gap—this heat gave birth to the land of fire, Muspelheim.

Some of the heat that emitted from Muspelheim slowly began traveling the gap, and by the time it reached Niflheim, it was nothing more than mild warmth. However, this mild warmth was enough to melt some of the ice, causing droplets of water to drip downwards into Muspelheim.

From this seemingly aberrant chaos, order began forming. As the water reached Muspelheim, sparks started emitting, causing the fire and heat to mix in the Ginnungagap. And it is here that the first sentient creations come into existence. When the iciness of Niflheim met the blazes of Muspelheim, it gave rise to Ymir. Ymir was the first of the jötunn. Ymir is also known by another name, Aurgelmir.

These mists and rime also gave birth to Auðumbla, the primeval cow. Her name means "hornless cow rich in milk" or "abundance of humming," depending upon different sources. She nourished Ymir with her milk. As for herself, she survived by licking the salt gathered on the ice of Niflheim.

Together, Ymir and Auðumbla created life in the Ginnungagap.

Two things happen in quick succession to one another.

Firstly, Ymir started sweating because of the heat coming from Muspelheim. He began sweating and as the sweat flowed under his arms, two giants—a male and a female—were born. Furthermore, Ymir, possessing the capability to produce offspring on his own asexually, joined his legs together and created a third son named Thrudgelmir. This bizarrely formed group of giants was now the first family of frost giants in the universe, also known as the jötnar. They all nourished themselves from the cow's milk.

Now, as this was happening, of course, Auðumbla, was also sustaining herself by licking off the salt from the ice. As she kept licking, some hair emerged from the melting ice. This hair was soon followed by an entire head. On the third day of her constantly licking the ice, an entire body came out.

Here was born Búri, the first of the gods. She fed Búri the same way she had fed the giants. As he had been born a fully-formed being, much like Ymir and Auðumbla, Búri did not have to go through the process of growth from childhood to adulthood. However, the cow's milk gave him quite a lot of strength.

As to how Búri managed to bear a child, it is unknown. The existence of the mother is not confirmed in the mythical texts. It could be that he created his son Borr by mating with one of the giants or from another god freed from the ice, or asexually from his own body.

Búri also had a daughter named Bestla. Her mother, most probably, was a giantess. Now, Borr married his sister, and together, they had three sons.

Here, Odin, Vili, and Vé enter the story of creation.

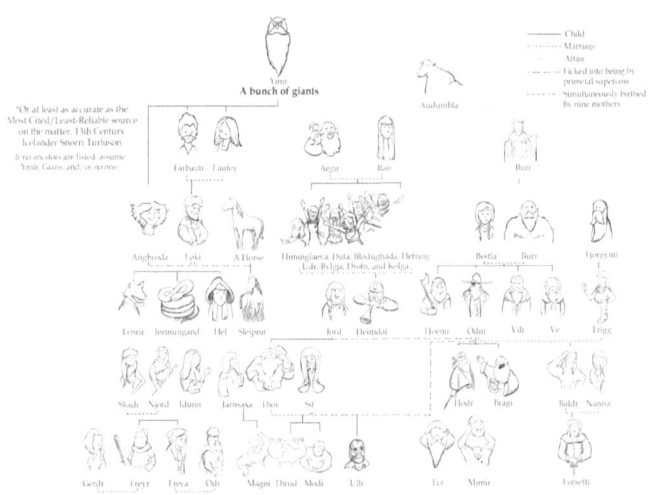

I n the Eddas, it is mentioned that Ymir was very vicious, bordering on cruelty. His behavior was depicted as that of a cruel entity. His children, in turn, were also cruel like their father. This evil behavior manifested itself when the giant and his children started oppressing the other creation, particularly the first gods. In the Gylfaginning, it is stated that when the sons of Borr finally revolted against Ymir, they slew him with such ferocity that the blood from his wounds drowned out the entire race of the frost giants except for a single giant who saved himself with his household. This giant was Bergelmir, who escaped with his wife. All the other frost giants descended from him.

This deluge of blood was not the end of Ymir. Now that the primordial giant was dead, the god-brothers decided to carry on the process of creation using Ymir's body. Such immense was his body that it required to be moved to make place for other realms in the Ginnungagap. Rather than completely shift it elsewhere, they decided to fashion a world out of it.

Ymir's flesh turned into land. His bones and teeth turned into mountains, fjords, and cliffs.

All of his blood was collected to create the water of the oceans, rivers, and lakes. His skull was used to create the dome of the sky.

They took his brain and threw it into the sky to create clouds. In some instances, it is said that both his eyes were plucked out. One became the sun, while the other turned into the moon.

All of his hair and beard were morphed into the grass and trees that covered the earth.

And yet, despite this process of intricate creation, the sky still felt barren. So, the three brothers took some sparks that were emitting from Muspelheim and trapped them in the earth's dome to appear as stars.

Knowing very well that Ymir's descendants would come for some form of revenge, the gods took the eyelashes of the giant and made a palisade around the land.

It is also mentioned that the gods sent Night and Day into the sky in horse-drawn chariots to create a full day. Night rode on a horse named Hrimfaxe. Every night he bedewed the earth. Day rode upon Skinfaxe and lit up the sky and the earth using his mane.

Some accounts stated that the Sun and the Moon were gendered and conscious beings, set along paths in the sky, forever to run fast so that they may keep outrunning the wolves who pursued them.

While Odin and his siblings were creating this new world from Ymir's corpse, worms kept coming out of the rotting body of the giant. These worms then evolved into the first dwarves. Odin, Vili, and Ve, concerned about the sky's integrity, worrying that it might fall if not held properly, told four of the dwarves to go and hold the sky up, sending them into the four major directions.

The dwarves are known as Nordi, Vestri, Sundri, and Austri, i.e., North, West, South, and East. The rest of the dwarves made their home in the land known as Svartalfheim. In time, the dwarves became experts in crafting tools. Some of the most powerful weapons in Norse mythology, such as Thor's hammer, Mjölnir, come from the dwarves.

Thus was born Midgard, also known as Middle Earth or the Middle Enclosure. Named for being placed along the middle of Yggdrasil's length, this land was to serve as a home for a new race entirely. The gods decided that they would not live here.

So they plucked some twigs from the World Tree and carved them into humanoid shapes. One was named Ask, and the other was dubbed Embla, the first man and woman.

It is fascinating to note that when the gods went about creating Midgard, they wasted no part of Ymir's corpse.

Around this time, new worlds also formed. Odin and his brothers built Asgard on the plains of Idavoll, a fabled location where the gods would meet. In yet another part, the escaped offspring of Ymir started dwelling in Jötunheimr.

Let us now take a look at the nine realms upon the World Tree, Yggdrasil, and understand the significance of each of these realms. By now, we've seen how the humans came to inhabit Midgard, how the dwarves sought refuge in Svartalfheim, how the gods went to Asgard, and how the frost giants went to Jötunnheim.

Yggdrasil — The World Tree at the Center Of All Life

Norse Mythology considers the World Tree extremely sacred, considering it to be at the center of all creation. The origins of this tree are shrouded in mystery. The Poetic and Prose Edda mentions this tree, but there are few fables or poems that describe the creation of this tree itself. What text exists are open to different interpretations that have resulted in several different explanations.

Some claim that the Nine Realms lay along the trunk of the tree. Others deciphered that it meant that the worlds were nestled in the tree's branches. Norse artwork is very vague in terms of its representation of the worlds within the context of the World Tree, not exactly showing where the worlds existed on the tree. In general, though, all depictions, whether literary or artistic, depict it supporting the nine worlds, which is an integral belief in Norse mythology.

And where exactly did the tree itself come from? How long did it exist before the creation of the realms? Was it there in the Ginnungagap? Alas, this too is shrouded in mystery with only speculations about its origins.

The most coherent speculation that we have is that Yggdrasil was there long before any of the nine realms, any other forms of life, and even the Ginnungagap itself. All that came later. It is described, though, that the gap itself was as long as the length of the tree.

An alternate source claims that the Yggdrasil grew from a seedling and that there was a far more ancient world that existed before it.

The reason we have such obscurity about Yggdrasil is that the Norse authors considered this tree a well-known and well-understood archetype. As in its existence was broadly perceived and considered for granted or quintessential.

Yggdrasil's Ecosystem

Besides being the cradle of the Nine Realms, Yggdrasil had a complex and diverse ecosystem, supporting different manners of fantastical life.

A humongous eagle perches atop the topmost branches of the tree. On that eagle's head, between its eyes, there was a smaller hawk. The hawk's name was Vedrfolnir. It flew between worlds to gather news and bring back vital information. Some people believe that the giant eagle was Odin himself, who possessed the ability to shift his form.

Below, in Niflheim, the world of ice, there was a dragon or serpent-like creature known as Níðhöggr who thrived on one of the roots of the Yggdrasil, gnawing at it. The implication here was that the creature was trapped by the roots. It would eventually free itself and escape at Ragnarök.

The giant eagle and the dragon bore enmity towards each other. While Níðhöggr was unable to attack the eagle, the eagle was also unable to leave its perch because of Níðhöggr's presence below.

This did not mean that the two did not communicate. There was a squirrel named Ratatosk, whom they both used to exchange slurs and insults with each other. The squirrel ran up and down the tree, passing down hate-filled messages between the eagle and Níðhöggr.

And then there were the four stags and harts who dwelled within the tree's branches. These four were known as Dainn, Dvalinn, Duneyrr, and Duraþror. They reached up to the branches and fed on their leaves. Some scholars connote their existence to that of the four seasons, the major elements, or the directional winds.

Lastly, upon the destruction of the world as a result of Ragnarök, two humans named Lif and Lifþrasir will seek refuge in the tree, surviving the destructive events of the end of the realms. There they shall survive on the tree's leaves. Then they will emerge, much like Ask and Embla once did, and continue the cycle of creating new humans in a post-Ragnarök new world.

The Sacredness of Yggdrasil

Ancient Germanic religions such as Norse Paganism held sacred trees in the highest regard. Trees had symbolic, spiritual, and metaphorical strength in these old European religions.

Yggdrasil was considered the ultimate sacred tree, the embodiment of the highest order of holiness. This was its primary function. The support it provided the nine realms was a result of its holiness.

Sacred trees such as Yggdrasil were believed to connect the realms of mortal men with those of the gods and the realm of the dead. People prayed at designated sacred trees to ask favors from higher powers and to remember those who had passed.

Sacred trees were believed to be sites where sacrifices to the gods were conducted. Even Odin, the All-Father, sacrificed himself by hanging from Yggdrasil in his search for wisdom. The ultimate sacrifice by the ultimate god to the ultimate symbol of sacredness. In his words, according to the poem Hávamál:

> "I know that I hung on a windy tree
> Nine long nights,
> Wounded with a spear, dedicated to Odin,
> Myself to myself,
> On that tree of which no man knows
> From where its roots run."

The Root Wells of Yggdrasil

Yggdrasil required a source of water to feed itself. The three main sources of water that Yggdrasil drew from were known as the well of Mimir, Hvergelmir, and the well of Urd.

Mimir's well has a fascinating backstory behind it. Mimir's head sits next to the well. The well itself is infused with Mimir's powers. Anyone who drinks from the well will get Mimir's powers and would be able to decipher ancient knowledge.

Mimir's backstory goes back to creation itself. Considered to be the wisest of gods, Mimir's knowledge expands to limits far beyond even Odin himself, who is a powerhouse of knowledge as well. He is the son of a giant named Bölþorn. His sister, Bestla, married Borr.

When war broke out between the Æsir and the Vanir, Mimir was beheaded by the Vanir and his body was left to decay. His head was sent to Odin, presumably as a message. Odin, knowing very well the station Mimir held in the realm of knowledge, tried to preserve the head and even went as far as to succeed, bringing Mimir's head back to life.

After being rescued, Mimir was given charge of a well that came to be known as Mimir's well or Mimisbrunnr.

Odin tried to reason with Mimir's head, begging him for wisdom. The two had mutual respect and held each other in high regard. One could even venture to say that they were friends. They held long talks with each other, pondering over the wisdom of the universe.

Odin pleaded with Mimir to allow him to drink from the well, but Mimir demanded that there should be a sacrifice to gain the privilege of drinking from the well. And so it was that Odin sacrificed his eye and threw it into the bottom of the well to attain wisdom.

The very same well that nourishes one of the roots of Yggdrasil.

The second well, bubbling in Niflheim, was Hvergelmir. This well was considered to be the source of major rivers. It is within this well that Níðhöggr the dragon dwelled, constantly gnawing away at the root of the tree to free himself. His venom started seeping into the root of the world tree gradually.

The third well, the well of fate, was a place where the Norns met. These were the goddesses put in charge of tending to the tree. They could also tell the future and manipulate a person's fate. It is said that the Norns deciphered the fate of all beings and would etch it on Yggdrasil itself.

Yggdrasil underwent decay as time went on, what with the dragon chewing its roots and seeping its venom into the tree, the squirrel Ratatosk also using its rodent teeth to weaken the tree, and the four stags constantly eating away the leaves.

The Norns in the well of Urd tended to the tree and made sure to restore it by pouring water over its rotting wood. But try as they might, eventually, the tree will succumb to decay, catalyzing Ragnarök itself. Of course, after that battle, it will flourish and return to its previous healthy status.

The Nine Realms

The colossal World Tree nestles the Nine Worlds, home to different beings and species, such as the gods, the elves, and the dwarves. These realms include:

- Midgard, where humans dwell in their civilization.
- Asgard, home of the Æsir gods.
- Vanaheim, the realm where the Vanir gods lived.
- Jötunheimr, a world filled with frost giants.
- Niflheim, the primeval world of ice.
- Muspelheim, the primordial world of fire.
- Alfheim, the realm of the elves.
- Nidavellir/Svartalfheim, the sanctuary realm of the dwarves.

- Helheim, the world of the goddess Hel, where the dead dwell.

Midgard

Once it was populated by Ask and Embla, the newly formed Midgard soon became home to the rest of the humans who descended from Ask and Embla. The Bifrost connects Midgard to Asgard, allowing the gods to access this realm.

There is much symbolism at play here. Midgard does not only represent Earth but the middle ground between order and chaos. Within Midgard, it is peaceful, hospitable, safe, and inhabitable, allowing humans to thrive in order. Outside the palisade built from Ymir's eyebrows, there is chaos in the form of dangerous creatures, giants, and a harsh climate.

There is yet another layer to this metaphor of order and chaos. Two figures from Norse mythology play an important role in Midgard's fate. One is the god of thunder, Thor, seen as the protector of Midgard and a champion of its people. The other is Jörmungandr, the world serpent coiled around Midgard. Thor represents order, whereas the serpent represents chaos.

While Thor was seen as a favorable figure to Midgard, often traveling there with many companions and protecting this realm from dangers, Jörmungandr was the danger itself, prophesied to destroy Midgard during Ragnarök. Jörmungandr was born to Loki and the giant Angrboða. He had a brother Fenrir and a sister Hel, both of them immensely powerful beings. These three siblings would inevitably bring the destruction of the world. In an attempt to delay Ragnarök, Odin separated these three beings. He threw Jörmungandr into the seas of Midgard.

Instead of perishing, the serpent grew in size and became so huge that he encircled the world completely, creating a circumference around it and then biting upon his tail. Upon Ragnarök, Thor, representing order, would face Jörmungandr representing chaos, and together they'd fight to the death. Thor would crush the serpent's skull and kill it but also die due to the serpent's venom.

Asgard

This spectacular home to the Æsir gods was one of the most written-about worlds in the Eddas. This is where Odin dwelled with the rest of his kin. Those who died honorable deaths also came to this land to dine in Valhalla.

Asgard was majestic. It had beautiful halls, serene fields of green, and lustrous forests. It was protected with fortifications. Everything about it spoke of grandeur. Its halls had hundreds of rooms. Its lunches were lavish. The essence of magic was imbued in this world, shaping it into a sort of utopia.

As far as its creation is concerned, the historical accounts give a lot of detail about how Midgard was formed, but there's not a lot of information given about the rest of the realms.

The god Heimdall watched over from the Bifrost to ensure that no one would assault Asgard. However, this was not the only form of protection Asgard had. Back when the Æsir and the Vanir fought each other, Asgard's walls were destroyed.

So, the gods hired someone to build the walls better than they were. This mason arrived with a single horse and claimed that he could build the wall within a year. He stated that as a reward for his timely job, he would marry Freya. If he lost, he said, he would do the entire work for free.

Freya did not want to marry this strange mason. Loki took the matter into his hands to reassure Freya. He said that it would be impossible to build a wall in a year without anyone's help.

But the strange thing was, this man and his horse worked very fast, and they were well on their way to finishing before the deadline. This put Loki in a tight spot, as he had been the one to prompt the gods into accepting the bet.

Now, on the last day, when merely a couple of slabs were left to be placed, Loki shifted into a mare and seduced the man's horse. It was because of his horse that the man was able to work so quickly and drag the massive slabs so efficiently. It isn't explicitly mentioned what Loki did with the seduced horse. At least, not so much in words. It does say in Gylfaginning that the horses ran together for the rest of the night until dawn, but here's the kicker. Loki disappeared after that.

But now that this stranger's plan had been thwarted and he was unable to finish the wall, he revealed his true identity as that of a giant named Gangleri. He had disguised himself as a mason to trick the gods into marrying him to Freya.

The gods killed him. The wall had been built, and Freya was safe.

As for Loki, well, he reappeared after many months with an eight-legged foal. Its name was Sleipnir. Loki gifted this horse to Odin.

There are several realms within Asgard itself. Some of them include:

- Valhalla, the hall with more than five hundred rooms where the Einherjar, the brave warriors who died in battle, came to dine with Odin after their death. This hall was a place of endless merriment and drinking and feasting and fighting.
- Hlidskjalf, which was a throne in Odin's palace from where he could look into all the realms.
- Bilskirnir, the grandest hall in all of Asgard, where Thor lived, celebrated, and feasted.
- Thrúdheim, the place within Asgard where Thor ruled.
- Fólkvangr, a field belonging to Freya where she welcomed those who died in battle. According to lore, Freya gets to pick the brave warriors who died in battle first. Half of them went to Fólkvangr while the other half went to Valhalla.
- Breidablik, where Baldur lived. It was a bright place where evil could not exist.
- Himinbjorg, a place on the border of Asgard near the Bifrost where Heimdall lived.

Unlike Greek mythology, where the gods had to share a single mountain, Asgard was huge and had realms within itself where each god could thrive and rule.

Vanaheim

This realm is home to the Vanir gods. The Vanir are a race of gods as old as the Æsir. They are the masters of fertility, wisdom, magic, and sorcery. They are also known to be tellers of the future. Vanaheim, unlike the other realms, is shrouded in mystery. No one exactly knows what it looks like or where in the hierarchy of the realms it is placed.

One of the prominent events in the history of the Vanir is the war they had with the Æsir gods. The Vanir destroyed the fortifications of Asgard and breached into the land. One of the reasons this war erupted was because both races of gods had opposing views on rules and societal structure. The Æsir believed that the world should follow strictly the rules laid down by the lawmakers, while the Vanir believed that the world should have a much more laidback attitude.

An example of this is the marriage between siblings. Æsir gods completely prohibited this whereas the Vanir commonly married among siblings. Njord, a Vanir god, was married to his sister. Together they were parents to Frey and Freya, who also married each other.

Upon the end of the war, Njord, Frey, and Freya were sent to Asgard as a token of peace. The marriage between Frey and Freya was annulled, and they were married to other gods. Hoenir and Mimir were sent to the Vanir by the Æsir.

Jötunheimr

Home to the giants, this realm comprises wilderness, dense forests, rocky plains, and snowy regions. The giants survive on a diet of fish that they get from the outer shores of the ocean. Jötunheimr is depicted as a barren place where fertile land is nonexistent.

Some of the most prominent characters of Norse mythology come from this land. Loki is one of the Jötunn.

As far as the land itself is concerned, it is a place where chaos rules. The place is home to deception. Nothing is as it seems there. Normal laws of the universe do not apply in Jötunheimr. Realities and dreams tend to intermix there, leaving a visitor perplexed.

Niflheim

This dark, cold region in all the realms is one of the two primeval worlds that existed before creation. Here, the bubbling spring Hvergelmir served as a river, providing water to the root of Yggdrasil. This land is inhabited by ice giants. It is said that most cold rivers that flow in the world come from Niflheim.

Muspelheim

This land of fire is one of the primeval worlds that caused the creation of the universe. This fiery place, burning with lava, flames, sparks, and spread with ash, is where the fire demons, fire giants, and the giant Surtr lived.

Surtr bore enmity to the Æsir. Upon Ragnarök's arrival, he will ride out with his sword and attack Asgard, turning it into a hellscape. His destruction will be the final flourish to the chaos and desolation that Ragnarök will cause.

Alfheim

Cradled right next to Asgard, this realm is home to the most beautiful creatures in Norse mythology, the light elves. Frey rules over the light elves, who in turn serve as the guardian angels of common folk. You may even consider them minor gods in the sense that they have control over magic and fertility. They can use this prowess to help human beings. Like the muses in Greek mythology, the elves of Alfheim can help poets and writers with inspiration. They also have a keen understanding of music and can assist musicians in coming up with symphonies, melodies, and songs.

Given the bright nature of the elves and their role as assisters, some scholars have concluded that the light elves are the Norse equivalent of angels.

Nidavellir

The realm of the dwarves is cavernous, filled with mines, forges, and resources that the dwarves can use for their crafting. The dwarves have historically provided many of the strongest weapons and artifacts that the gods have used. Odin's magic ring and his Gungnir spear came from the dwarves as well as Thor's hammer, Frey's ship, and the enchanted chain that bound Fenrir, the wolf.

Helheim

Ruled over by Hel, the goddess of the realm of death, and daughter of Loki, this land is cold, dark, depressing, desolate, misty, and downright unpleasant. There is no escaping from this realm as the impassable river Gjoll hinders any who try to break free. Once someone enters Helheim, they cannot leave, not even if they are gods. Odin couldn't save his son Balder from Helheim.

Those who die of disease or old age and those whose deaths were not as a result of battle go to Helheim. Garm, a humongous beast, and Modgud, a female guardian, guard the entrance to this realm. At the edge of this world sits the giant Hræsvelgr, making the wind blow in his eagle form.

At the end of the world, Hel will sail to Asgard alongside Loki in a ship made from the fingernails and toenails of the dead. Her realm and the residents of her realm will play a significant role in Ragnarök.

We have discussed at length the creation of the cosmos, the details about the nine realms, and the mysticism of Yggdrasil. Moving forward, we are going to understand the Norse gods and the Norse calendar and holidays, allowing ourselves to immerse further in the rich lore of Norse mythology. It is only through understanding the lore and its implications that we can integrate Norse Paganism into our lives.

CHAPTER 4
THE NORSE CALENDAR AND PAGAN HOLIDAYS

Cast your mind back to the old Norse days with me and imagine a world where science and technology have not made any of the modern strides yet. There are no tall buildings, no such concept as electricity, and when night falls, it is not bright neon lamps or arc-sodium lights that illuminate the villages but the clear night sky with its myriad stars and the luminescence of the moon.

To anyone who lived during that time, the world was filled with mysticism, with faith being the propelling force behind most beliefs instead of factual scientific data. Magic was seen as a likelier explanation of the wonders of the cosmos as observed from the standpoint of an observer looking up into the sky.

It is a feeling that we cannot perceive, knowing what we know. To someone living in the Norse era, the sun set in the west and rose in the east. To them, this was certain. Irrefutable. Of course, the sun came up from behind the mountains, and of course, it dipped into the sea. They did not know the orbiting nature of the earth around the sun.

Their worldview was that of unbridled fantasy and belief in forces and beings far more powerful than themselves. A purer, stronger belief that left no place for doubt, allowing the average folk to delve freely into the depths of their religious beliefs.

As time went on and as the theories and knowledge of the European world pervaded, these beliefs gradually dwindled, aligning with the modern worldview that we know today, a world where astronomy is a science and explains the details of how constellations are formed, what planets are, and why forces like gravity exist.

But let's go back to that old age, where common folk believed in uncommon things—there was still a semblance of order to their actions. They followed a calendar devised from the phases of the moon, dividing the year into twelve months of thirty days, and in leap years, there were four extra days every fourth summer called the Sumarauki. They adhered to solstices and equinoxes as most civilizations did at that time.

The Norse people lived so far up north that they noticed the solstices and equinoxes far more clearly, as these astronomical events are much more visible in the northern regions of the earth. This allowed them to predict the arrival of different seasons, which were critical for their farming and agriculture. Another stark difference between them and us is that they only had two seasons: summer and winter.

. . .

The Lunar Calendar

Norse folk made sense of the passage of time through their lunar calendar, wherein they counted each month from new moon to new moon or full moon to full moon. Even though the moon had a very critical role in their understanding of time, the sun played a more important role. To understand why this was so, you must know that Scandinavia is and was a very cold and dark place. The sun was heralded as a bringer of light and warmth, allowing the people to grow their crops.

Dividing the year into summer and winter, the Norse people had designated moon cycles as the following months:

Skammdegi — the Winter Months

- **Gormánuður** — known as slaughter month, lasting from mid-October to mid-November. In the olden days, slaughtering an animal was a complex task as there was no way to refrigerate its meat. You had to either cook the entire animal or risk spoiling it. But when the weather was cool, the meat was able to stay fresher for a longer time. The winter months were times when it was very hard to feed farm animals, given that they were utilizing valuable crops. So, to deal with this, the farmers slaughtered most animals other than their breeding stock. The cold of October and November allowed them to preserve this meat for longer. It is in this month that a feast called Winter

blót is held to honor Frey to thank him for the harvest.
- **Ýlir** — lasting from mid-November to mid-December, the Yule month, is connected to Odin. Yule comes from one of Odin's names, Jolnir, which originates from the word Jol. During this time, Odin traveled a lot around Midgard, visiting the locals. Kids filled their socks with hay to feed Sleipnir, Odin's horse, so that Odin would give them a gift. This month also has significance in terms of fertility and cultivation of the earth.
- **Mörsugur** — literally known as "fat-sucker month," was between mid-December to mid-January. In the harsh winter months, the Norse folk had to survive the months by consuming animal fat. This was a time when nothing grew on the land in terms of crops. Besides animal fat, people consumed bone marrow as well. Winter solstice was held this month.
- **Þorri** — from mid-January to mid-February, the frozen snow month was observed, its name coming from Thor. During this month, the feast known as Þorrablót was held. The night before this month begins, the women walk outside their homes and welcome the month inside as a guest. Some speculate that Þorri was a winter spirit or an entity. This month was also observed as a month for men, and men could choose a day within this month to be celebrated. At this time of the year, people used to eat some hardy food such as sheep heads, rotten sharks, testicles of rams, and jelly made from meat. Liquor was also consumed heavily in this cold month.

- **Góa** — between mid-February and mid-March, this month was celebrated. This month was observed as women's month. It was the penultimate month of winter.
- **Einmánuður** — from mid-March to mid-April, the lone month was observed. It was referred to as the single month or the lone month because it was the final month before summer arrived. This month was dedicated to young boys.

Náttleysi — the Summer Months

- **Harpa** — starting from mid-April and ending in mid-May, this was considered the first month of the Norse calendar year. This month was dedicated to girls, as Harpa is a girl's name. As for which deity this month was named after, it is unclear as there are no records of a goddess existing under that name. The summer blót was held in this month, serving as a feast in veneration of Odin to ensure that victory comes to warriors and all the travelers reach their destinations safely.
- **Skerpla** — from mid-May to mid-June, this month, named after a forgotten goddess, was the second month of summer and considered a time of new life.
- **Sólmánuður** — the third summer month from mid-June to mid-July was when summer solstice was held. This was the brightest time of the year in Scandinavia, with some days even lasting for twenty-four hours. That's why this month got the name "the sun month."

- **Heyannir** — the fourth summer month from mid-July to mid-August was a time for haymaking. This was when the people dried and harvested the hay. In some parts of Scandinavia, this month was known as worm's month or snake's month. One can assume this was so because these creatures infested the harvested hay.
- **Tvímánuður** — from mid-August to mid-September, the Tvímánuður, meaning two months arrived, heralding sunny times, fall foliage, and a cold snap in the air. People harvested grains during this month. This was the final month of summer.
- **Haustmánuður** — from mid-September to mid-October, people observed the month of Haustmánuður, which was treated more as an autumn month and a preparatory month for winter. People believed that summer was behind and that now it was time to harvest and brace for the upcoming winter months.

All the months of the Norse calendar began with the same day of the week. This calendar gave the Norse folk a timeline to observe Norse holidays and celebrations.

The Norse Holidays

Festivals and holidays are plentiful in the Norse calendar. The Icelandic people loved to celebrate. Their primal lifestyle came with its fair share of difficulties, both in battle and in times of peace, but whenever they overcame their adversities, they made sure to mark that occasion with a well-deserved celebration.

- **Þorrablot** — This mid-winter celebration, also known as husband's day, was a time when people honored the fathers and husbands. Held in honor of the winter spirit Þorri and the god Thor, this festive celebration included locals coming together to sing, dance, and eat specific delicacies that they washed down with strong alcohol. Locals used to eat Þorrablot particular foods such as rotten shark meat, boiled sheep's head, picked ram's testicles, wind-dried white fish, and dung-smoked lamb. Then they drank a potent drink known as Black Death. After dinner, the folks sang together heartily, played games with each other, and partied until the morning.
- **Góublót** — This holiday took place on the first day of Góa in honor of all women, especially mothers and wives. This celebration also served to mark the coming end of winter.
- **Sigrblót** — Taking place on the first day of Harpa, this holiday was to mark the victory of light over dark. In other words, the victory of summer over winter. During this holiday, people made offerings to Freya.
- **Mid-summer**— The celebration of the light, warmth, and one's connection to the earth, was a festival for the summer solstice. People joyously venerated fertility, magic, and light during this celebration. The nature of the celebrations included feasting, dancing, and building a bonfire.

- **Alfarblót—** This holiday marked the first day of winter. There were certain reasons for this much more sober celebration. The people had done their last harvest of the year and so were thanking Freya for bestowing fertility upon the land. It was a much more toned-down celebration, mostly held inside the privacy of people's homes. Rather than the men, the women of the house led the celebrations.
- **Yule** — The Norse folk celebrated the midwinter solstice by drinking, feasting, and sacrificing to the gods for twelve consecutive days. This holiday was in celebration of Odin, believing that he would ride across the night and visit them in their homes.
- **Dísablót** — This holiday honored female deities including the goddesses, the ancestors, the Valkyries, and the prominent figures of Norse mythology. As to when this was celebrated, it's a bit unclear. Some sources stated that it was celebrated at the start of the winter while other sources claimed that it was celebrated at the end. And then some say that it was celebrated on both.

Heathen Holidays

Building upon the existing lore of the festivals, the calendar, and the significance of certain days, a Heathen calendar was created by Steven McAllen in the late twentieth century. However, this calendar took inspiration from the Wiccan wheel of the year and then assigned Nordic names to celebrations that had already existed within Northern Europe.

It is considered by some to be a more contemporary alternative option for celebrating holidays. Some contemporary heathenry borrows from both Wicca and paganism and has evolved into an amalgamation of different religions. This particular calendar designates the following days for the following celebrations:

- **Disting/ Dísablót** — On the 2nd of February, the Dísablót celebrations marked new beginnings and preparing the crops for planting.
- **Ostara** — On the 21st of March, Ostara was celebrated to mark the rejuvenation of the land and to celebrate fertility.
- **May Eve** — On the 30th of April, May Eve was celebrated, associated with Frey and Freya, to celebrate fertility and the arrival of spring.
- **Midsummer** — on the 21st of June, Midsummer was celebrated by burning corn dollies, playing music, and dancing around bonfires to mark the summer solstice.
- **Frey Feast** — On the 1st of August, people thanked Frey for the yearly harvest and baked a loaf of bread as an offering to Frey.
- **Fall Feast** — On the 23rd of September, upon the Autumn equinox, the coming of Fall as well as the second harvest of the season, was celebrated. This celebration marked a time for gathering food for the upcoming winter months.
- **Winter's Nights** — On the 31st of October, this celebration took place to mark the end of the

harvest season and to herald the time for hunting animals. This celebration venerated Hel, the goddess, as this was considered a time when the veil between the world of the living and the world of the dead thinned down.
- **Yule** — Celebrated between the 20th of December and the 1st of January, Yule marked the beginning and end of all things. This was considered the time when the gods were closest to Midgard and when the dead returned to the earth to feast with their living family members. It was a time when magic was thought to course freely through the earth.

The Days of the Week

The fascinating story of the Norse calendar doesn't just end here. Did you know that the days of the weeks were named after the Norse gods?

- **Monday** was known as Mandag, named after the god Mani. Mani's parents named him after the moon, which made him suffer a terrible fate in turn. He had to drag the moon across the sky with his chariot for his entire life.
- **Tuesday** was known as Tirsday, a day devoted to Odin's son, Tyr, whom many knew as a god of war and a god of the sword. The Norse folk, especially the Vikings, held the belief that the best day to start a war was Tyr's day.
- **Wednesday** was named after Odin himself. It was called Onsdag. To commemorate this day, it is

recommended to indulge oneself in the pursuit of knowledge, as Odin did. Odin's old name was Woden, which is where the name Wednesday comes from.
- **Thursday** was Torsdag, known as Thor's day. Hammer in hand, riding his chariot, emitting the roar of thunder, Thor was a symbol of divinity, power, strength, and bravery. It was believed that Thursday was the best day to do magic, as magic was fortified on this day.
- **Friday** or Fredag was dedicated to Frigg and Freya, the beautiful goddesses of love, fertility, and innate connection with one's inner self.
- **Saturday**, although gets its name from Saturn, was known as Lordag or Laugardagen, a day devoted to washing one's clothes. The Norse folk were very careful about their clothes, ensuring that they were clean.
- **Sunday,** aka Sondag, was named after Sol, the sun goddess. The gods did not like the pride with which Sol had been named after the sun, so they punished her for eternity by making her pull the sun in her chariot.

Although these customs, celebrations, festivals, and the old calendar diminished in use just as the Norse folk, many elements of them are still retained within our Gregorian calendar. We still use the same name for days, for instance. The Nordic celebrations affected many of the Christian holidays. Yule, for instance, heavily influenced Christmas. Originally, December wasn't even considered a time when Jesus was born. But to proliferate the teachings of the church, Christian missionaries tried to infuse Christian teachings with pagan beliefs to make them more palatable for those considering converting to Christianity.

Regardless, the revival of Norse Paganism in recent years has seen to it that these old rituals, customs, celebrations, festivals, and holidays are also revived and observed. Devotees and adherents to Paganism-centric beliefs, such as Ásatrú, follow the holidays and celebrations as described in the Norse calendar.

With the calendar and its celebrations clear to us, we will now move on to take a detailed look at the gods and goddesses of the Norse pantheon, understand their lineage, powers, and symbols associated with them, and how we can venerate them. Everything that we have learned so far brings us closer to a concise and thorough understanding of Norse mythology, the beliefs of paganism, the ideologies promulgated by this belief system in modern Paganism, and how all of these can be integrated into your life.

Learning about the gods will bring us one step closer to becoming better Pagans. Knowing particularly which god or goddess possesses what traits and abilities will allow us specificity in terms of whom to venerate and how to venerate them to ask for their help.

CHAPTER 5
THE NORSE PANTHEON OF GODS AND GODDESSES

I f there is one thing that can be said with certainty about the Norse gods, it is that they were magnificent in their splendor. And it was not just a predetermined grandeur such as the one we see in Greek mythology, where luxury was almost considered a requirement for the gods and goddesses of the Greek pantheon. Rather, the Norse gods and goddesses were rugged in their powers, more primal, and more connected to the realms they oversaw and the roles they were delegated. The physical characteristics of the gods were earned through toil and extraneous effort rather than just handed to them at godhood.

Odin, for instance, had to lose an eye to transcend his reserves of knowledge. When he hung from Yggdrasil, a spear was pierced through his side, scarring him. His visage and appearance were that of an aged man, giving his wisdom an extrinsic manifestation.

Thor, similarly, had an immense muscular and broad build courtesy of his adventures, his role as the god of thunder, and his reputation as a fierce warrior.

Goddesses such as Hel and Frey evoked respective emotions in the hearts of their believers. Hel drew fear because of her appearance, whereas Frey, one of the most beautiful goddesses, made onlookers' jaws drop in sheer awe.

They were fully-realized, deep personalities with redeeming traits, profound powers, and even some flaws such as becoming too prideful, resorting to wrath, or being conniving. But these flaws did not take away from their magnificence. Rather, they accentuated it by showing us that the gods, in whose image we were made, were also capable of folly at times, making us appreciate them more, resonate with them, and revere them for their fortitude, wit, wisdom, strength, and beauty.

The two primary factions of gods are the Æsir and Vanir. Historical sources such as the Eddas have paid more heed to the Æsir. What we know of the Vanir is all mentioned in sources within the context of the Æsir gods.

The Æsir and the Vanir were rivaling parties, which even led to a war between them, a war that ended with both sides exchanging "hostages" as a token of peace.

Both factions live in their respective realms. The Æsir have made their home in Asgard, while the Vanir live in Vanaheim.

Odin is the strongest and the most revered of the Norse gods. Ruler of the Æsir, he is married to Frigg, the queen of Asgard.

Every god, whether they were a Vanir or an Æsir, had unique characteristics that made them stand out from the rest. Loki was a mischief-monger, forever bent on creating trouble in the most creative of ways. Thor, who thought more with brawn than brain, was quick to anger. Freya, aware of her unmatched beauty, was always looking for new jewelry.

You might be wondering how the gods in the Norse pantheon could be as strong as they were and how they were immortal. The goddess of spring and rejuvenation, Iðunn, provided the gods with apples that ensured their long life.

Unlike the gods of other religions, the Norse gods did not cut themselves off from the rest of the world, forever residing in their heaven like home. Instead, they routinely made trips to other realms, interfering in affairs with the humans, and also interacting with other races such as the elves, dwarves, and giants.

As you'll know more about the gods, you are bound to pick a favorite, whether consciously or subconsciously. Let that happen. Let the magic take you.

Without further ado, let's talk of the gods.

Baldur — The God of Light

Said to be the most beloved of all gods, goddesses, and humans, Baldur represented light. And not just represented; because of his beauty, his grace, and his cheerful nature, he actually emanated light. It was said that such was his beauty that even the prettiest of flowers bowed as he walked past them. In Norse mythology, he was perceived as the epitome of perfection, not only in appearance but also in his benign wisdom.

He was very meek and mild, always speaking in a calm and tender voice. Where he lived was a place known as

Breidablik, the cleanest and brightest place in Asgard. His hall was considered the most resplendent in all of the realms.

His powers included the gift of wisdom and deep knowledge. He had precognition and could also make prophecies. His bright nature and his wisdom made him the arbiter of conflicts among men and gods.

It is no surprise that Baldur gets wisdom and knowledge, and light as part of his traits. He was, after all, the son of Odin and Frigg. Baldur had a loving wife named Nanna, and they had a child named Foresti, who was the god of peace and justice.

But that is where the cheery disposition of his story ends.

Once, Baldur's dreams began turning to nightmares showing his death. When he went to his mother, one of the wisest gods in the realm, and confided in her about this strange occurrence, Frigg became extremely worried about her son. A mother's love is a powerful force. Perhaps there is no force more powerful than it. Such was her adoration for her son that Frigg, to ensure Baldur's safety, went one by one to every single thing in the universe, taking an oath from them promising that they would not harm Baldur.

And all things agreed to this polite request put forth by Frigg.

Now, Baldur was invincible. His invincibility became a source of fun to the rest of the gods. So confident were they that nothing would harm him they would throw weapons at him and fling random things at him just to watch them bounce off him, leaving him completely unscathed.

For a little while, Baldur himself was content with this drastic measure, no longer concerned about dying as he had seen in his dreams.

But Loki, the trickster god, decided that this was the right time to create chaos through his mischief. Innocently he approached Frigg, asking her if she had indeed made everything take an oath in the universe or not. He feigned concern to appeal to her better nature and to come off as harmless. When her guard was down, she casually mentioned that the only thing she didn't take an oath from was the harmless and tiny mistletoe. She said that she considered it far too harmless to even take an oath from it. How could mistletoe harm Baldur?

But this sliver of information was almost too much for Loki, who fashioned a lethal spear out of mistletoe. He went to the blind god Hodr, who was also Baldur's brother, coaxing him into joining the let's-throw-things-at-Baldur-because-he-won't-be-hurt party. He gave Hodr the spear and sent him forth and watched with twisted glee as Hodr flung the spear.

Instead of bouncing off of Baldur, the spear pierced him and killed him on the spot.

All of Asgard fell in silent shock. The gods were torn with agony, having lost their favorite god. But they did not want to simply give up. After all, Baldur might be dead, but he was in Hel, the realm of the dead. Surely, he could be brought back from there through divine intervention.

Odin's son Hermod, Baldur's brother, decides to make the perilous trip down to Hel to appeal to Hel, the goddess of the realm of death, to return Baldur. He made the trip on

Odin's horse Sleipnir and rode down Yggdrasil till he reached the dark world of Hel.

Here he found his brother, miserable, stolen of his light, grim, pale, weakened, sitting in the seat of honor next to Hel's throne. Hermod, being a diplomatic being, asked Hel if she could release Baldur. Hel, of course, denied this at first, but after much persuasion on Hermod's behalf, she finally agreed on one twisted condition: Every living being in the universe would have to mourn and weep for Baldur to prove that he was as universally beloved as the gods claimed. Only then would she free him.

So Hermod went from Hel with a huge task on his shoulders, asking every being in the universe to weep and mourn for Baldur. But the whole world did indeed mourn him truly, and upon his asking, everything in the world did mourn for Baldur except one. When Hermod went to the goddess Þökk, she refused to weep for Baldur. It's believed that Þökk was Loki in disguise. And so it was that with Loki/ Þökk's refusal to weep that Baldur was forever doomed to remain in Hel's dark realm.

It's kind of ironic that the god of light would have to perish in the realm of darkness. It is also sickeningly depressing that the most beloved and friendliest of all gods would have to die in front of his family.

The gods decided to give Baldur a befitting funeral. They placed his body on the mightiest ship in Asgard and set it out to the sea. The ship was set ablaze as it went out into the sea.

Grief-stricken, Baldur's wife, Nanna, threw herself into the burning ship, not wanting to live a life without her husband. She hoped as she burned that she would be resurrected with Baldur after the events of Ragnarök. The gods assembled at the funeral threw all of Baldur's things in the fire, even his horse. As the ship burned and was carried off by the sea, the earth shook.

But do not despair too much about the death of the god of light. It is prophesied that he will return from Hel after Ragnarok and will be taking his place as the ruler of the new world alongside his blind brother Hodr.

This is not where the story ends, however. There is still the matter of Loki, who orchestrated Baldur's death. During a heated argument with the gods in the Aegir's halls, Loki confessed to being responsible for Baldur's death, which enraged the gods to such an extent that they chained Loki to massive rocks and placed a dangerous snake over his face. The venom dripped from the snake's fangs atop Loki, causing him unbearable pain. It is said in lore that Loki's punishment would last until Ragnarök.

You might be wondering how you can pray to the god of light. While it is true that he's still in Hel, his new position there represents a poetic role: He is the light that can be found even in the darkest of places. If you call on him, he can give you peace and solace in times of strife. In times of darkness, he can cast light your way.

While you can verbally venerate him by way of prayer at an altar or by reciting verses of poetry venerating him, you can also give an offering to Baldur by being kind to someone in need, by helping someone who is stuck in the darkness. And once you have done that, you can light a candle in the dark and then recite his name to invoke his aid. He will see that you have been carrying on his legacy, and he will answer with his help.

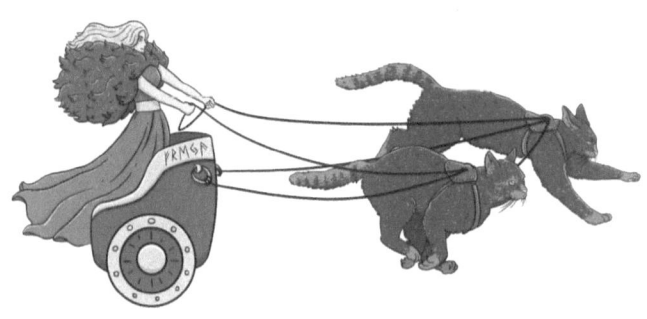

Freya — The Goddess of Fertility and Love

The goddess of fertility and love is more than just that. She is associated with magic, lust, sex, beauty, war, death, and gold. Her name, Freya, also pronounced as Freya, means "lady."

Although she is a Vanir goddess, she lives in Asgard with her husband, Odr. She has been made an honorary Æsir, called Asyunjur. After the Æsir and Vanir war, she was sent alongside her brother Frey and her father, Njord.

Freya's children, Hnoss and Gersemi, are known for their beauty. In the Prose Edda, there's a darker element to

Freya's tale as she constantly mourns her husband's disappearance. As to where he's gone, she does not know, but she goes out to find him while crying. Her tears fall into the sea and turn into amber.

She holds a monumental role in Norse mythology, given that it was she who taught the Æsir gods, including Odin, the magical known as seiðr. She was seen as a Völva in Norse mythology. A Völva is a seeress and sorceress who went from town to town, and in exchange for food and shelter, she would grant magic to those who helped her. It was because of her prowess in magic that she and her father were appointed as the high priests of sacrificial offerings.

When a warrior dies, it's not Odin who gets the first pick of whom to invite into the afterlife but Freya, who chooses half of the warriors for herself to stay with her in Fólkvangr while Odin gets the other half in Valhalla.

Her Völva persona was also granted credibility because of her love for travel. Her chariot that she used to travel on was one of a kind, being driven by two dark cats. She also had a cloak made from falcon feathers that allowed her to fly invisibly through the skies. Sometimes, she would loan the cloak to other gods and goddesses who needed to fly somewhere in a rush. The same cloak was borrowed by Loki to travel to the realm of the giants to rescue the goddess Iðunn. She also traveled using a boar named Hildsvini, whom Loki claimed was actually her human lover in disguise so that she could ride him in public. Many tales tell of Loki's spite towards Freya, one of them being his slanderous claim that she was bedding every single one of the gods and elves present in the halls during

Aegir's feast. Her father came to her side and said that Loki was utterly perverted for slandering her like that.

Her beauty was so famous among all the creatures in the realm that once a giant disguised himself and came to work as a mason, with his barter being Freya's hand in marriage if he were to build the wall within a year.

But then there are also stories of her promiscuousness present in the old fables, such as when she came upon a beautiful necklace being created by the dwarves, she asked to buy it, but when the dwarves said that the payment would not be in gold or precious stones but by sleeping with each of the dwarves, Freya agreed, sleeping with all four of them in exchange for the necklace.

She's been known to be a wild and free spirit, often reveling in parties and enjoying the pleasures of the flesh. That's how she is associated with fertility, not through agriculture but through her passion for lovemaking and conceiving children.

Praying to her and offering her sacrifices should be done with the utmost sincerity, as Freya cares about honesty, truth, and kindness. As she is the goddess of sexuality, you can make offerings such as honey, chocolate, bread, fresh fruits, and even poetry to her. Her role is not confined to being that of a fertility goddess. Freya has mastery of warcraft and can be considered a warrior goddess. You can offer feathers and bones as offerings, as this is symbolic of warcraft. Other offerings that you can place in honor of her include amber, amber incense, lavender, sunflowers, daisies, and ladybugs. When making offerings, leave them on a dedicated altar built just for Freya. On this altar, you can leave a picture of

Freya or an artistic depiction of her. Freya loved flowers, so add some flowers to the altar as well. If you want to delve further into her worship, consider learning the Futhark runes, as she was the master of these runes. They would even allow you to communicate directly with her. If you are inclined towards magic, you should learn and practice seiðr.

Frey — The Splendid God of Fertility

Son of Njord and brother of Freya, Frey's name stands for "lord." Associated with things that bring fertility, such as sunshine, rain, harvest, and material prosperity, Frey lives in the land of the light elves, Alfheim, which he received as a present.

Frey had a ship that he was famous for. It was a ship so big it could fit all the gods inside it, yet, when it was folded, it became so tiny that it could fit inside a purse.

Once, Frey snuck upon Odin's throne and looked at the nine realms. And as he was musing and looking, he saw a woman that was so beautiful that he became immensely captivated by her. Her name was Gerd, the daughter of the giants Gymir and Aurboda. Frey was so occupied with her thoughts that he stopped eating and drinking altogether to the point of sickness.

This made his father, Njord, very worried. When he inquired through his servant Skirnir as to what was wrong with Frey, Frey responded that he was in love with Gerd. To help his condition, Skirnir went to Jötunheimr to try to bring Gerd to Asgard.

But Gerd was not seduced by the promise of immortality or jewels. A vexed Skrinir started to threaten her with curses and said he would use the secret knowledge of runes to make her life perilous. This scared her enough to come to Asgard and marry Frey. But she had a condition. She wanted to wait for nine days before coming to Asgard, primarily to torture the lovelorn Frey psychologically.

Here's a particularly strange part of this tale. Skirnir, when he went to the land of the giants, took Frey's magical sword with him to protect himself. Skirnir took this sword as the price for bringing Gerd. According to legend, this sword was capable of fighting on its own. And it was because he lost his sword that he would perish during Ragnarök.

But his perishing would be just as legendary as his life. He would face Surtr, the fire giant, and kill him in battle. But this battle would weigh heavy on him and take his life as well.

When making an offering to Frey, remember that he is the god of fertility both in terms of sexuality and in terms of farming. So, offer him things like grains, nuts, legumes, seeds, apples, baked bread, and if you're feeling particular, you can even offer him pork, as pigs are a form of livestock. In addition, you can offer him things that are phallic in nature, as he's the sexual god of fertility. Traditionally, people used to leave the last sheaf of wheat standing in their crops as an offering to Frey. His Nordic nature allows you to sacrifice alcoholic drinks like dark beers and apple cider to him as well. Ideal times to thank Frey and offer him sacrifices is when you get a lot of abundance and fertility in your life. Think along the lines of financial gain, becoming a parent to a healthy child, or finding love in your life. That's when you should thank Frey by way of making offerings.

Heimdall — Protector of Asgard

With teeth fashioned out of gold, a tall physique, and beauty that rivals that of Frey and Baldur, Heimdall is the guardian god, protecting Asgard by guarding the Bifrost, the only way into the realm.

His birth must have been a strange occurrence as he had nine mothers. How he was born of nine mothers is a whimsical mystery unto itself.

He shone brightly and was considered the whitest of the gods. His unparalleled abilities made him the perfect choice to stand guard at the Bifrost. For instance, he slept less than a bird. He could see for thousands of miles in every direction, even in pure darkness. Such strong was his sight that he could observe blades of grass growing. He could also hear exceptionally well. It was said that he could hear the sound of wool growing on the back of a sheep.

He lived in a place called the Himinbjörg. When he was free from his duties, he liked to ride around on his horse named Gulltop. This horse was made entirely of gold, ergo the name "Gold top."

When he stood guard at the Bifrost, he had his sword, the Hǫfuð, to protect himself and to fight off any unwelcome people. For the direst of circumstances, when he needed to call upon the gods for help, he had a horn named Gjallarhorn. The gods would hear this horn upon the brink of Ragnarök, knowing that the end is near.

Like many other deities, Heimdall was Odin's son.

Heimdall had a fondness for human beings. For that very reason, he can be honored, venerated, worshipped, and offered sacrifices with relative simplicity. You can call on him with the purest of sincerity, and he will answer. To understand why you should bestow offerings unto him, it's important to know that he holds sway over several domains such as wisdom, purpose, focus, perception, commitment, protection, a familial bond, safety, communication, love, and devotion to one's duty.

Remember this when making an offering: He is sharp of sight and sees all that transpires, so approach him with honesty. Mead is an excellent offering to him. Coffee is as well. You should reflect upon Heimdall's purpose while meditating to understand his role and what he did, and how you can become a better person by being more watchful and careful in your life.

His is the domain of vigilance, so if you need more vigilance in your life, making a humble offering will do that for you. Pork, lamb, and mutton are excellent choices for offerings. In addition, anything caffeinated when offered will draw his favor to you. You can also guide others, help someone in need, and mentor someone who needs mentoring to honor Heimdall.

Frigg — The Goddess of Marriage, Motherhood, and Fertility

Queen of the Æsir, wife of the All-father Odin, and mother to Baldur and Hodr, Frigg was one of the most powerful goddesses in the Norse pantheon. She knew seiðr magic which she could use to alter the tapestry of fate. Frigg represented family, devotion, love, patience, motherhood, and nurturing. We have already seen one of her displays of maternal love when she tried to undo Baldur's fate by pleading to all the beings in the universe not to harm her son.

In terms of symbology, she is represented by the sky, the moon, mistletoe, silver, and the spinning wheel and its spindle.

Her role as Odin's wife was a very influential position. She could make her husband do things that she wanted, and he, loving her devotedly, always complied. A few times, he was even tricked into making a decision, but he never resented her for it.

Frigg was not only the mother to her two sons but also the stepmother to Thor, Heimdall, Tyr, Bragi, Vidar, Vali, and Hermod.

She played things close to the chest. Despite possessing the gift of prophecy, she never revealed what she knew.

She was the only other being in Asgard permitted to sit on Odin's throne to look at the nine realms. Her abode was Fensalir, a hall surrounded by wet marshes.

Her maidens always surrounded her. One of them, Fulla, was very close to her to the point that Frigg shared her deepest secrets. Gná was yet another maiden who tended to all of Frigg's needs and was her loyal messenger. When Frigg had to intervene or protect someone or something, she would send her maiden Hlín to do this vital task.

Frigg was a force of goodness, always looking out for others and caring for the smallest of things.

The All-mother should be given offerings that suit her stature. She stands for motherhood, familial strength, and homeliness. When venerating her, you should consider the things she is associated with. In terms of food, you can offer her something that contains cardamom. She will also appreciate savory meals like stews, porridge, and roasts. In terms of drinks, think along the lines of white wine, plum wine, sake, and even milk. If you clean your house while meditating about Frigg, her bounties will fall upon you. Since her home is in the marshes, things such as feathers from marsh birds and pictures of the marshes are also excellent offerings.

Hel — The Goddess of The Underworld

When a person dies from old age and illness or is considered too much of a coward or a dishonorable person unfit for the afterlife realms of Odin or Freya, they go to Helheim. And it is here Hel ruled. Daughter of Loki and a giantess named Angrboða, Hel's family extends to Fenrir, the wolf, and Jörmungandr, the world serpent.

Make no mistake, Hel is quite like the realm she rules over. She is ruthless, powerful, harsh, cruel, threatening, and filled with malignant malice. Norse mythology saw her as being very indifferent being completely unconcerned with the matters of living beings and the dead.

Her name does not imply any relation to the Christian concept of hell. Hel meant hidden, a word that also referred to those who had passed away, considering that they were hidden from the world of the living by way of being buried or cremated or that their souls were invisible to the living.

Descriptions of her were scarce in old texts, but the surviving texts described her as humanoid, half white and half blue.

Her trickery, which she notably got from her father, allowed her to hold Baldur in Helheim even though the gods wanted him back. It was said that she was thrown into Helheim by Odin who wanted to prevent the coming of Ragnarök for as long as possible. Once she was banished to this realm, she decided to crown herself queen and rule over this cold, dark, and desolate place.

Rather than fight her dark persona, she ultimately gave into it to the point where everything in her hall bore the name of some misfortune. Her dining table was known as hunger, and her knives were known as starvation. Her bed was called the sick bed, and the curtains in her room were named misfortune.

When dealing with the passing of a loved one, or when trying to overcome an existential crisis, especially within the context of death, you can turn to Hel and make an offering to her, venerating her for her role as the queen of the dead. If you're struggling with dark thoughts, depression, and mental anguish, you can also make an offering to her. Why? Imagine the mental fortitude and courage she must possess to thrive in a land as desolate and cold and devoid of light as Hel. She must possess a strong resolve, which in turn, she can grant you if you venerate her.

If you intend to propitiate Hel, attend funerals, visit the dead in graveyards, work on your mental health, offer help to those suffering from mental illnesses, or volunteer at a cemetery or a hospice program. You can also volunteer for roadkill cleanup and say a prayer for the spirit of the dead animals.

If you want a more traditional sort of veneration, then you can create an altar that contains animal fur, animal bones, skulls, horns, skeletons, black mirrors, black candles, wormwood, black roses, and grave rubbings. In terms of drinks, resonate with Hel by making a cup of black tea or black coffee. Apples can serve as an offering, too, as Hel has an apple orchard that she's quite fond of.

But most importantly, live your life to the fullest. It sounds like simple advice, but the truth is Hel appreciates those who don't live a half-dead, half-alive life. If you devote yourself to living fully, you will be ready for it when your time comes to die.

Loki — The Trickster

Before Tom Hiddleston donned his green robes for Marvel's Thor and Neil Gaiman portrayed him as Low Key Lyesmith in American Gods, Loki was not seen as a charming or swoon-worthy god, but rather a cunning god of mischief and trickery. The Poetic Edda dubbed him "the contriver of fraud."

He was the son of Farbauti and Laufey. While Laufey was an Æsir goddess, Farbauti was a jötunn. He was associated with the Æsir from his mother's side. And that's why he took the surname of Laufeyson when residing in Asgard.

You must not think him entirely evil. Mischief and trickery are different from evil. Sometimes, Loki used his trickery to help the Æsir gods, such as when he seduced a horse to hinder the efforts of a giant who wanted to make the walls of Asgard within a year to win Freya's hand. But his trickery was ambiguous, as he also used his cunning to send Baldur to Hel.

He was a chaotic character. That much can be said for certain. Once, when he was about to get killed by the giant Thiazi, Loki bartered his life by bringing him the goddess of immortality, Iðunn. And now that he had handed over Iðunn to Thiazi, the gods threatened him with death unless he brought her back. It was originally his mistake that Iðunn was captured by Thiazi. But he set matters straight when he went back to save her by shifting into a falcon and carrying Iðunn back to Asgard in his talons. Thiazi pursued Loki but was killed off by the gods when they burned him to death.

Rather than end here, the matter devolved into further chaos when Skaði, Thiazi's daughter, came for restitution, asking for revenge for her father's death. She demanded that the gods make her laugh, a feat that only Loki succeeded in doing by tying his testicles with a rope to a goat's beard. When the goat tugged, Loki writhed in pain.

This spectacle was so absurd and hilarious that Skaði began laughing.

After the horrendous events resulting in the death of Baldur, the gods tied Loki to chains in Muspelheim. They placed a venomous serpent over his head, forever to remain there until Ragnarök.

Upon Ragnarök, Loki will break free and fight alongside the giants against the gods in the last great battle.

Loki will take on Heimdall, and the two shall fight each other until their death.

One can argue that it was Loki's chaotic effect throughout Norse mythology that will eventually cause Ragnarök. His three children, Jörmungandr, Hel, and Fenrir, whom he had with the jötunn Angrboða, became elemental forces capable of wreaking unimaginable amounts of havoc. Odin took drastic measures and threw Hel into Helheim, cast Jörmungandr in Midgard's sea, and restrained Fenrir within Asgard—all in an attempt to put off Ragnarök as long as he could. Odin knew the prophecies and knew that these three characters would cause Ragnarök. And in the end, he was right, Loki, Jörmungandr, Hel, Fenrir, and Surtr will serve as the antagonistic forces causing Ragnarök.

But here is the paradox that will leave you undecided about Loki, despite his chaos, despite his plotting the murder of Baldur, despite his imprisonment: Odin referred to Loki as his brother, calling him the blood of his own blood. Thor often chose Loki as a traveling companion. Many gods and goddesses took his counsel, paying heed to his twisted wisdom. He was a force to be reckoned with.

He had a high standard for entertainment. His mischief was often to serve as his own amusement. And mischief was not his only domain. He knew different kinds of magic and was exceptionally skilled in shapeshifting. He had mastered the art of shifting into any living creature he wanted.

You can offer him meats, curries, and spicy foods at an altar. Additionally, foods that contain tons of sugar, such as cupcakes, brownies, candies, and chocolates, are bound to attract his attention. Loki drank alongside Odin. Whenever Odin drank, so did Loki. So, offering him strong alcohol, coffee, drinks with full-fat content, and anything delectable.

If you want to venerate him through your actions, then think about creating mischief. Don't do anything too drastic that will get you in trouble with the police or anything. Think stand-up comedy at the local Laugh Factory or practical jokes on your friends. Loki also has a whimsical side that appreciates novelty toys and puzzles, so that might be a great offering if you want to appeal to his fun side.

Njord — God of the Wind and the Seas

Njord, the Vanir god of the seas, ships, fishing, hunting, and the wind, was also associated with wealth, peace, prosperity, and fertility. After the Æsir and Vanir war, he came to live in Asgard with his two children, Frey and Freya. He made Nóatún his dwelling beside the sea, as this was a calm and quiet place where he could look at the sea, listen to its waves, and enjoy the salty wind coming from the windows of his home.

The surviving stories about Njord tell a sad tale of an unhappy marriage with Skaði. After the killing of Thiazi,

Skaði came seeking revenge but decided to reconcile in exchange for a few favors, one of whom was the gods making her laugh. The other was a far more serious proposition. She wanted to be married to a husband of her choosing. The giant was asked to choose her husband by looking at their feet, as their bodies were hidden behind a veil. Thinking that she had chosen Baldur, she mistakenly selected Njord.

The two were married, but this life was not a happy life for either of them. They started fighting right after marriage about where they would live. Skaði wanted to live in the high mountainous lands of her father's homeland, while Njord wanted to live alongside the sea. They came to a compromise, deciding to live for some days in Thrymheimr and some days by the sea. But despite this compromise, they complained to each other about each other's choice of dwelling.

They grew apart eventually, Skaði returning to the mountains and Njord returning to the seaside. Njord then had children with his sister, a common thing for the Vanir gods.

At the end of Ragnarök, Njord will survive and return to the Vanir.

Despite his troublesome life, Njord was a very generous god. In terms of offerings, when you offer him food, make sure it's seafood, as he loves things such as clam chowders, herring, rye crackers, and fried fish. Any food made in the shape of seashells will do just as fine as well. You can also offer him strong liquor, dark beer, vodka, and gin. Material offerings include seashells, spices, and things that can be used as currency, such as gold, beads, and stones.

He also has a fondness for tobacco, fishing gear, boats, and anchors. A miniature ship—such as a ship in a bottle—would be a thoughtful offering.

Odin — The All-Father, Ruler of The Gods

So much can be said about the most powerful god in Norse mythology. Words fall short of his magnificence. His wisdom is unmatched. His powers extend into the disciplines of wisdom, royalty, death, healing, poetry, the runes, magic, creation, diplomacy, and shape-shifting. Considered the leader of souls, both mortal and immortal, Odin truly personifies the monumentalism that befits Norse mythology.

You can trace his lineage back to creation itself. The grandson of the first Æsir, Búri, Odin was the son of Borr and the half-giant Bestla. He had two brothers, Vili and Ve. Together, these brothers created the world. Odin was married to Frigg, with whom he had Baldur and Hodr. Odin often visited Jötunheimr and was swept away by the beauty of the women living there. With them, he had sons, including Thor and Vali.

He was able to morph into the shape of any human or animal whenever he wanted. He would wander about wearing different guises, such as the guise of an old, cane-bearing, bearded man, listening to the matters of the world.

When he spoke, it was with such a soft and gentle voice that all who heard him believed that he was always telling the truth. It just was that he always spoke in rhyme and riddles. But his words possessed deep magic. With a single utterance of a brief word, he could make fire erupt from nothingness. With a gentle assurance, he could calm down the sea. His ability to speak entirely in poetry came from drinking the mead of poetry, which he stole from the giants. At certain times, he granted the gods favor by allowing them to drink from this mead.

An interesting fact here is that the drink's name is Óðrœrir, which means "the stirrer of Óðr." Óðr refers to ecstasy or inspiration. This is also the origin of Odin's name.

He was not a complacent god, although that was not his first nature. But whenever he did take part in a battle, he wounded his enemies to the point of blindness, deafness, or leaving them horrorstruck upon witnessing Odin's war visage. Furthermore, Odin had the power to infuse his men with powers to make them strong as bears and berserk with bloodlust. In his hands, ordinary items such as sticks or twigs turned into dangerous weapons.

Some of his powers came with grave weight. He could see the future and past of all beings. This meant that he knew of Ragnarök and knew there was nothing he could do to prevent its arrival. Yet still, he took some measures to ensure that it would be delayed.

One of his powers was the ability to travel to far-off lands and the ability to travel through other people's memories.

As he was the most powerful of gods, his thought was his will, and his will was absolute. He could kill someone or inflict them with a fatal illness just by thinking of it. The strongest of the Norse folk, the Vikings, offered him sacrifices to earn his favor in battle. People also made human sacrifices to him, especially by slaying their enemies in war. Sometimes, the sacrifice would involve spearing someone or tying them to a noose or even both at the same time. In combat, Odin's believers used to fling their spears while crying, "Odin owns ye all!"

Odin was also noted to have the power to communicate with the dead. He was even able to raise them from the dead.

Courtesy of Loki, Odin had the eight-legged horse Sleipnir as his steed. This magical horse was not only capable of crossing long distances in record time but it was fascinating in its appearance, beautiful to all who laid eyes upon it. It could travel in the air just as well as on land. Loki gifting Odin Sleipnir could be seen as a symbol of the bond that existed between these two gods.

Two ravens named Huginn (Thought) and Muninn (Memory) were a spiritual extension of Odin. He would send them out into the world to bring him news from all the realms. They would come to him in the evening and whisper what they saw and heard. When idle, these ravens sat beside Odin on his throne.

Odin also had two wolves named Geri (the hungry one) and Freki (the greedy one) as his loyal pets. These wolves would walk with him when he walked in the avenues of Asgard. Odin didn't need food to survive, so whenever food was placed in front of him on the table, he gave it to his wolves. He preferred drinking wine, anyways.

Among his most renowned weapons was the spear Gungnir, made from Yggdrasil itself. Odin carved runes onto his spear, imbuing it with magic, making it always hit its mark and kill his opponents.

He wore a ring known as Draupnir, out of which new rings dripped out every eighth or ninth day. This ring was given to him by the dwarves Brokkr and Eitri.

One of his most notable feats is the sacrifice of his eye as payment for drinking from Mimir's well. Odin became the wisest of all gods after drinking from the well, gaining all of Mimir's wisdom.

His quest for wisdom and knowledge did not stop there. He wanted to understand runes and learn their secrets. This could only be done through the ultimate sacrifice. So he pierced himself with his spear and hung himself from

Yggdrasil for nine days and nights. When he eventually fell from Yggdrasil, the meaning of the runes was revealed to him.

When you consider making sacrifices or offerings to Odin, remember that he's the god of sacrifices, whether it was losing his eye or hanging from the world tree. Self-sacrifice was sort of his thing. With that in mind, when you decide to offer something to the god of all gods, make sure it's something that you hold in high regard, something that's dear to you.

Create an altar space and devote it to Odin. If you are a practitioner of Wicca or tarot, place the Hanged Man card on that altar, as well as runes, raven feathers, horseshoes, a representation of a wolf, and beer/mead.

When offering food, place foods that look like spears onto the altar. Garlic, leeks, cucumbers, asparagus, and so forth. You can also place beef, meat, pork roast, and steak as a food offering.

In terms of drink, Odin loves to drink. So red wine, mead, dark-colored alcohol like whiskey—anything along those lines would be a well-suited offering.

Odin loves poetry. You can write some of your poetry, venerating him, and ask for his help in your daily life. If you learn runes, praying to him will be easier, as he is also the god of runes.

In life, if you want Odin's favor, you must also pursue knowledge with the same relentlessness and fervor that Odin displayed in his life. As Odin once slayed monsters, so should you strive to slay metaphorical monsters that plague our world. Things like racism, homophobia, and sexism are some of the metaphorical monsters that you can fight to venerate Odin.

Thor — the God Of Thunder

The almighty god of thunder, Odinson, one of the most powerful of the Norse gods, ally to humans, Thor ruled over strength, lightning, thunder, oak trees, and bravery. He was considered extremely strong—arguably the strongest. However, he was not extremely wise or clever, unlike Loki or Freya, or Odin. To that effect, some of the giants teased him for his brawn-over-brains disposition.

Oh, yes, the giants loved to make fun of Thor because Thor was, let's put it mildly, quick to anger, allowing his rage to take control of him. And when Thor became furious, lightning issued from him, thunderclouds gathered over him, and he swung his hammer, hitting the giants in their heads. The sound of thunder drove fear into the hearts of the giants. Some would even go so far as to say Thor welcomed it when the giants teased him because it allowed him to go toe to toe with them.

Unlike what Marvel tells us, Thor did not marry Dr. Jane Foster. Instead, he married another goddess named Sif, and together they had Trud and Modi. Thor's house Thrúdheim was the biggest in all of Asgard. Thor also adopted a stepson named Ullr. Thor sired a son with the giantess Jarnsaxa. This son's name was Magni.

Particularly famous in Norse lore and modern adaptations are Thor's goats who drew his chariot. As Thor flew across the sky, the sound of the wheels and the sparks emitting from his chariot made people aware that Thor was flying over them. The funny thing about the goats, whenever Thor visited some far-off land, he used to slay the goats to eat them. Then, when he reached home, he revived them with his hammer.

Speaking of his hammer, the dwarves Eitri and Brokkr made a weapon one of its kind, a frightening armament capable of throwing out lightning bolts and holding enough power and magic within itself to tear down entire mountains. It also had auto-aim, allowing it to hit any target from any distance. This hammer was called Mjölnir.

Once Thor hit someone with Mjölnir, the hammer would return itself to Thor's hand. Mjölnir was not only capable of destruction but of bringing life to the dead as well. It could revive animals and humans alike. Also, it could make itself small enough to fit inside Thor's clothes.

Combined with his magical belt and gauntlets, the hammer made him extremely strong.

A famous tale regarding Thor is about him losing his beloved hammer. A giant Thrym stole his hammer and hid it within the recesses of the earth. Thor was quite a temperamental god; without his hammer, he was furious. So, Loki, normally very mischievous and sly, decided to help Thor out. Thrym told him that he would return the hammer in exchange for Freya's hand in marriage.

Freya, of course, said no. In her anger at this boisterous appeal, she became so furious that the entire Asgard shook to its core.

The gods decided to think up an alternate solution. Heimdall proposed that they should deceive the giant, but how? He suggested Thor wear a wedding dress, wear Freya's necklace, and go instead of her. Thor became extremely angry over this, but somehow the gods managed to convince him, and Loki joined in, deciding to accompany Thor as his bridesmaid.

When they arrived in Jötunheimr, the giant Thrym was surprised when he saw that "Freya" devoured an entire ox, eight salmon, and a complete barrel of mead during the feast. Loki explained, saying that "Freya" had not eaten in eight days in anticipation of her marriage, thus the hunger.

When Thrym decided to kiss "Freya," he recoiled in shock at her manly features. Loki said this was because she had been starving for eight nights.

Mjölnir was taken out from its hidden place and placed on the bride's lap as a customary gift. And that's when Thor decided to get rid of his drag persona and reveal himself. He crushed the skulls of all the giants present there with Mjölnir and returned with his hammer back to Asgard.

Thor was quite fond of humans and spent much time on Midgard. You could say that he was the god of the common man. This makes him less specific in terms of offerings than other gods, especially Odin.

In terms of food, whatever you offer, make sure it is in large quantities. Salmon, pork, beef, lamb, pickled herring, whatever you can think of. As I said, he's not very particular about what it is as much as he is about how much of it there is.

Dark beers, ales, meads, and stout should be offered as drinks.

You should consider offering him tools and hammers when offering him an item. Blacksmithing tools, any tools that come under the jurisdiction of manual labor, and even ornamental weaponry. If you can find something that's been struck by lightning, such as tree bark, you can offer that to him as well.

Remember that he was the god of common folk. He was very concerned with how humans lived their lives and if they were well or not. If you devote your time to the community and help out those in need, you will be venerating Thor in your everyday life.

Tyr — The Warrior God

The actual god of war in Norse mythology was not Kratos, despite what the PlayStation game might have you believe. Instead, it was Tyr, the lawgiver, the warrior, the bravest of the gods, and the binder of Fenrir. Once, he was even the leader of the gods of the Norse pantheon but was replaced by Odin.

Tyr was concerned with justice, especially justice in the field of battle. He was extremely fair and just in all the treaties he made.

A particularly well-known tale of his bravery included his binding Fenrir. All the gods were too afraid to approach Fenrir, but Tyr bravely decided to pacify the great wolf by putting his hand in the wolf's mouth while the gods bound him to a rock. When Fenrir noticed that this was a trick, he became angry and tore off Tyr's right hand.

As brave as this sacrifice was, this served as Tyr's downfall. His role became less important in the eyes of the gods as he was not at full strength. Once, when Tyr tried to defend Frey from Loki's insults, Loki snidely said that Tyr couldn't be the right hand of justice. Other gods, while they were not as cruel as Loki, also saw him as weakened and less worthy of overseeing his role as a god of war, law, and justice.

And his final fall will come at Ragnarök, when he will fight—ironically enough—another giant creature, a dog named Garm, who is the guardian of Hel. Tyr will defeat him singlehandedly but will also perish in this fight.

When considering offering something to Tyr, remember that he, like Odin, was a god familiar with sacrifice, as he gave away his right hand in the name of bravery. He was brave and honorable, despite the lack of his right hand. You can offer beef, pork, strong wine, and dark ale as foods to Tyr, and in terms of general offerings, you can choose the path of righteousness, honor, and bravery in your daily life. When you make a promise, make sure to keep it.

Followers of Ásatrú, who use altars as an extension of their veneration and offerings, can place an ornamental sword on the altar, decorate the altar with red and grey colors, and inscribe Tyr's rune on the altar items.

Bragi — The God of Poetry

Son of Odin, the god of poetry and music, Bragi was known for his wisdom, creativity, and knowledge of songs and poetry. The word Bragi means poet/poetry.

Bragi had runes carved on his tongue, presumably to enhance his eloquence. He was the husband of Iðunn, the goddess of youth and immortality. Bragi was depicted with a harp, which was a testament to his musical prowess and melodic nature.

His beautiful singing voice was second to none, and when he played the harp, the sound was nothing short of holy. Gods tried to keep him around so that he would delight and charm them.

Bragi had a central role in Asgard. He would welcome the fallen warriors into Valhalla and greet them with poetry and music.

In our modern life, it is important to remember that without entertainment in the form of music, songs, and arts, life would be extremely monotonous. Almost everyone listens to music. The gift of music and poetry makes the world much more alive. We should all be thankful to Bragi for it. In terms of food and drink, you can offer him anything that you would offer a welcomed guest in your house. As music and drinking go hand in hand (as do drinking and poetry), why not offer him a nice wine, whiskey, or beer? But it is not in food or drink that you should look for offerings to Bragi.

It is in music.

If you make an altar, place musical instruments on top of it, books of classical poetry, scores of music, runes specific to Bragi, and anything related to music or poetry.

If you want to offer your services to Bragi, think of all the indie musicians out there, the starving artists trying to survive in a world filled with record labels and corporatized music. You can support a musician by donating to them or buying their album, taking an eager person to a concert, visiting a musical show, contributing to a charity for musicians and performing arts, and giving money to street musicians when you come across them. That's how you honor Bragi.

If you are well-versed in poetry and are a bit of a poet yourself, you can write some poetry and offer it to Bragi, venerating him and his essence. Make sure it's a good poem, though. You're presenting your work to the god of poetry. It kind of sets the bar high. This should also be kept in mind when offering Bragi any story or song.

We have covered several of the notable gods in this chapter, and as we progress in our understanding of Norse mythology and Norse Paganism, we will also uncover other gods. We will also learn how to make offerings to the gods when we learn about modern pagan practices and belief systems such as Ásatrú.

The world of Norse mythology was rich in beings and creatures other than gods, goddesses, giants, and elves. In the next chapter, we'll take a deep dive into the various mystical, fantastical creatures that dwelled in the nine realms.

CHAPTER 6
THE CREATURES OF NORSE MYTHOLOGY

In today's age of skepticism, it has become hard to find wonderment when one looks around. The minute a kid turns into an adolescent, it's been brought to their knowledge that it was mommy and daddy who left the cookies and presents out on Christmas night and that Santa never existed. As their imagination suffers a severe blow, children have to come to terms with the fact that the Tooth Fairy, the Easter Bunny, and likewise so many other characters featured on the roster of their daydreams, and unbridled imagination start coming out as less-than-real. They come to terms with a reality where mystical creatures and fantastical figures do not exist outside the confines of entertainment.

Back in the age of wonder, this was not the case. Put yourself in the leather shoes of a Viking sailing in their longship and imagine what the world would have appeared from his perspective. Below him, in the sea, the great world serpent lay sleeping. Were this Viking to dive deep enough, he might come face-to-face with Jörmungandr himself. When he looked to the mountains, he knew as certain as day that those were the vestiges of Ymir. Those two crows flying across the sky could be Odin's ravens, Huginn and Muninn. Perhaps the All-Father favored this Viking and was keeping an eye on him. Fear took the Viking's heart as his ship lurched and bobbed against the waves. Was it possible that the infernal Kraken was below him, twisting its tentacles, waiting to attack?

"All-Father, protect me," He would supplicate.

And then, the dark sky would light up with lightning. Thunder would roar, and blue streaks would etch across the canopy of clouds, bolstering the spirit of this Viking and his fellow seamen. For as long as the ally of the people of Midgard, Thor, was on their side, no Kraken nor sea serpent could harm them.

At nightfall, the Viking would look to the skies, looking at the stars, wondering about the fiery depths of Muspelheim from where these embers came. Upon hearing the howl of a wolf at full moon's night, he would wonder if Ragnarök was near and if Fenrir had broken free from his chains.

By every definition, this old world was a magical world populated with mythical creatures. Almost all high fantasy novels, games, and movies have taken inspiration from the creatures mentioned in Norse mythology, from the elves, dwarves, and dragons in Lord of the Rings to the gargantuan Kraken in Pirates of the Caribbean, the influence of Norse mythology is still there.

We could all reignite that magic in our lives and find joy in believing again, just as the Norse did once and just as we did when we were little, and the world was still a place of wonder.

Let's look at Norse mythology's diverse ecosystem and populate our bestiaries with the creatures who thrived in the Nine Realms.

Elves

Long before Legolas, Elrond, and Galadriel existed in Tolkien's legendarium, the elves of Alfheim drove awe in the hearts of the Norse people. Described as more vibrant in their beauty than the sun itself, the elves were known to have an ethereal appearance.

While they were not considered as omnipotent in terms of godhood as the Vanir and Æsir, it was largely believed that the elves were powerful nonetheless, capable of making humans fall ill, controlling nature, holding sway over fertility, and using their divine magical knowledge for curing ailments.

In the Poetic Edda, Snorri Sturluson divided the elves into two categories: the light elves and the dark elves, the former residing in Alfheim while the latter, thought to be dwarves, living underground in Svartalfheim.

Before and during the Viking Age, people worshipped the elves and even hosted ceremonies in their honor, including one called Álfablót, which many modern-day Ásatrú communities still hold today.

According to lore, humans and elves could marry each other and produce offspring that resembled humans but had the magical abilities of elves. It might also be possible that humans could transcend and become elves after their death.

Huldra

Scandinavian folklore tells us a tale that would put the fear of Odin in the hearts of young single men everywhere. The Huldra was a gorgeous, elf-like female creature with flowing locks of long blonde hair. Donning a floral crown, this spirit lurked in the forest, looking for young men to marry.

You might be thinking that this creature doesn't sound half-bad. She's pretty, she's a maiden, and all she wants is to get married. Well, the tip-off might be the cow tail that she had. Most men fled in terror when they saw her, identifying her from that strange tail jutting out of her rear.

But what would happen if she caught up with you? She would trap you in the mountains until you finally gave in and agreed to marry her. If you refused to marry her, she would kill you. But you would be doomed regardless, for if you married her in a church or a temple in the name of the gods, her tail would disappear, and she would morph into the most hideous looking woman ever, gaining the strength of ten men. She'd then proceed to kill you, anyway.

Fenrir

It makes poetic sense that the harbinger of Ragnarök happens to be the child of Loki. Loki mated with Angrboða to produce three particularly quintessential offspring: the goddess of the underworld, Hel; the great serpent, Jörmungandr; and the humongous wolf, Fenrir. You might sympathize with him for a bit. As he grew older, the wolf kept growing in size, unable to control his stature. He grew so large that his gaping mouth was large enough to extend across the skies. Only Tyr was brave enough to approach and be friendly with the wolf. In time, he grew to the size of the apocalyptic beast that was prophesied to kill Odin.

Odin knew this and knew that there was no way to prevent this. But through his wisdom, he knew that he could delay the inevitable with extreme preparedness.

The first two times that the gods tried to tie down Fenrir, they failed. He'd break free from the fetters without breaking a sweat. But in their desperation, the gods went to the dwarves. The dwarves knew that this was an impossible task. So they crafted the constraints out of impossible things such as the spit of birds, beards of women, roots of mountains, the breath of fishes, stomping of cats, and the nervousness of bear. From this amalgam was created Gleipnir, a fetter that Tyr used to bind Fenrir. Then, for good measure, they pried his mouth open with a sword. Fenrir howled in pain and agony, his saliva dripping down and creating a river called "Anticipation/Expectation."

During Ragnarök, he will break free and kill Odin, devouring his body.

The Kraken

A great horror haunted the depths of the seas. This oceanic beast was larger than life. Large enough to be misperceived as an island. Were anyone to step foot on this "island," they would perish into the gaping maw of the fearsome Kraken.

When it would rise to the surface of the sea to devour ships, the Kraken would cause maelstroms and whirlpools. Sometimes, though, the Kraken opted for a pescatarian diet. It lured fish towards itself by secreting thick excrement that attracted fish from all over the area.

With large tentacles and a cephalopodic face that was huge enough to devour entire ships, could this mythical beast have been the ancestor of squids and octopuses? Or was it the other way around? Were squids and octopuses the inspiration for this creature?

In either case, the Kraken lives on in myth, whether in the form of Lovecraft's Cthulhu or in its original form in Pirates of the Caribbean.

The Mare

A wicked creature crawled atop people's chests as they slept, imbuing their dreams with horrors and paralyzing them in a state of fearful slumber. This is indeed where the word nightmare originates from.

While some believe that the mare was the embodiment of the souls of living people that left their bodies at night, others thought the mares to be malicious witches who could shape-shift into the form of animals when they were astral projecting.

A mare would touch a tree and cause its branches to entangle. It would touch a person and cause their hair to tie into knots.

The origins of this oppressive demonic spirit come from a saga written by Snorri Sturluson, in which he describes how King Vanlandi of Uppsala died at the hands of a mare.

It was said that when the king abandoned his wife, she became scorned and approached the Finnish sorceress Huld, asking her to exact vengeance. A bewitched king Vanlandi wanted to go to Finland, where his wife was. But the people around him insisted that he had fallen prey to witchcraft. Then the king suddenly became very sleepy and excused himself to his sleeping chambers. As he slept, he started moaning that the mare was upon him.

When his men broke into the room, they found the hideous creature sitting on him. She stood atop his legs when they tried to get her off his head. When they went to the legs, she raced back to the head. Through all this, the king was in utter agony. At long last, unable to take the suffering any longer, he died a painful death. This story accomplishes two things: It introduces us to a mythical creature while imparting the moral that one should never scorn their wife to the point of desperation.

Jörmungandr

The only thing preventing Ragnarök from happening is the Jörmungandr holding his tail in his mouth. The moment he releases his tail, Ragnarök will start. As he thrashes, he will cause the earth to shake. These earthquakes will also allow Fenrir to break free from his chains. Loki will also be set free as a result of this commotion. But what would prompt him to release his tail and come to the surface, causing earthquakes?

It is said that Ragnarök will be preceded by winters so cold that they will turn the seas cold. This icy water will make Jörmungandr extremely uncomfortable, beckoning him to thrash and cause chaos.

And then, as we read in the section about Thor, there will be a legendary fight between the Midgard serpent and the god of thunder. Thor will kill the serpent, but not before getting imbued with venom. Then, Thor will look around the battlefield and see that Odin is having trouble in his battle with Fenrir. He will go try to approach his father to help him but will only take nine steps before falling and dying because of the venom.

Auðumbla

If Odin, Vili, and Ve could be considered the patriarchal figures who took it upon themselves to create the world, Auðumbla, the primeval cow, could be viewed as the original matriarch. Her maternal nature allowed her to feed Ymir and the rest of Ymir's children from her milk. She did not want for much, only the salty rime on the surface of the ice.

If she had not licked away at the ice, Búri, the first of the Æsir gods, would have never been freed from the ice. In that way, she can be considered the primordial matriarch to the gods.

Níðhöggr

A dragon-like creature with deadly claws, a huge wingspan covered in scales, and rearing a horned head, this beast stayed at the root of the World Tree, gnawing away at its roots. He would chew on the bodies of the adulterers, murderers, thieves, and oath-breakers after they'd been banished to the shore of corpses, a location in the underworld reserved for criminals.

Níðhöggr hated the eagle who sat atop Yggdrasil and exchanged insults with it with the help of a squirrel. It is said that one day, one of these messages from the eagle will offend him so much that he'll shake himself free from the roots that have trapped him in the underworld, causing quakes across all Nine Realms. Once freed, the dragon will assist the giants in their fight with the gods.

To put this creature's size into perspective, think about how big the World Tree is. It nestles all Nine Realms on it. The World Tree is the cosmos itself. Níðhöggr is literally devouring the cosmos by gnawing the roots of Yggdrasil.

Ratatoskr

According to one particular account, this tiny, mythical squirrel might as well have been the cause of Ragnarök. So vile and filled with maliciousness, this squirrel wanted to bring about the death of the tree of life. But he wasn't strong enough or big enough to do that. But he looked to the top of the tree and saw the eagle. Then, he looked below to the roots and saw Níðhöggr.

A scheme formed in his mind. He decided to fuel spite between these two creatures by passing on insults from one to the other, sometimes making up even worse insults and adding embellishments for maximum emotional damage. One day, he will insult Níðhöggr to such an extent that Níðhöggr will break free from the roots, disrupting the tree, and will join the giants in the fight against the gods. Some accounts go so far as to claim that Níðhöggr will cause the tree to collapse and will even kill the eagle sitting atop it, all because he was so offended by what Ratatoskr had said to him.

Huginn and Muninn

The messengers of Odin, these two ravens acted as his eyes and ears. They would fly around the world and then return to their master to bring him vital information. They would sit on his shoulder whenever they'd return from their trips and caw everything they'd seen.

Odin held both these ravens in the highest of regards, paying more attention to what they had to say than his court subjects. In modern interpretations, the ravens symbolize Odin's knowledge and omniscience.

The Ravens were worshipped by the Nordic people and were depicted alongside Odin on numerous artifacts.

Norns

The three Norns controlled the fate of all gods, mortals, and living things. They decided what would happen, when, and how. Wyrd, one of the Norns, represented the past. Verdandi represented the present. Skuld represented the future.

The Norns had one more important role; they were caretakers of Yggdrasil. To keep it from dying, the Norns fed it water from the well of Urd and poured it over its branches.

The Norns appear at a child's birth and decide how long he'll live, what he'll be fated to do, and whether he'll live a good or bad life. They then weave a thread of life and designate it to the child.

Sleipnir

Despite the dubious circumstances in which this eight-legged steed was born, he became a figure of myth as Odin took a liking to it and deemed it worthy of being his steed. This horse was deemed the best horse among gods and men.

Svaldifari was an abnormally fast belonging to a giant who claimed that with Svaldifari's aid, he could build the borders around Asgard in less than a year. In exchange, the giant wanted to marry Freya. However, after taking Loki's word for it, the gods accepted the challenge. But as the giant progressed, it soon became clear that the wall would be built in less than a year.

So, Loki took one for the team, seducing Svaldifari by turning into a mare. The two horses raced around all night, putting a stop to the giant's work. Thus, the giant lost his wager. Loki had successfully seduced Svaldifari, but at what cost?

Well, Loki, in his mare form, became pregnant and gave birth months later to a foal with eight legs. Thus Sleipnir was the only creature in Norse myth born from two fathers.

Sleipnir was extremely beautiful, and Odin was so fond of him that he always took great care of him. Whenever Odin rode to war, he chose Sleipnir as his steed.

Trolls

Two kinds of trolls populated the Nordic land and mythology. One was the giant, ugly troll that dwelled in mountains, forests, and dark places such as under bridges. And then there were the smaller trolls who looked like garden gnomes or sprites. These lived underground.

Regardless of their hideous appearance, they were creatures of fantasy, possessing magical powers that included prophecy. They weren't the brightest of creatures, often seen as quite hostile towards humans who crossed their paths.

Trolls were not able to come into sunlight. Whenever they came into contact with sunlight, they turned into stone. Some suggest that the Scandinavian countryside, which is so rocky and littered with large boulders, is a testament to the existence of trolls who got caught in sunlight.

As far as their appetites are concerned, they can eat almost anything, ranging from rocks in caves to small humans. Sometimes, they'd devour live goats in one gulp, as these were their favorite cuisine.

Valkyrie

These brave, beautiful, fierce women, riding winged steeds, were chosen by Odin to serve a glorious purpose. They were chosen to escort fallen warriors who had died honorably in a battle to their eternal abode, Valhalla.

They were described as hypnotizingly beautiful, delicate maidens with flaxen hair and porcelain skin. But their traits did not just extend to their beauty or their role on the battlefield as escorts. They were also tasked with choosing who would live or die in a battle. They could even use their powers to ascertain who would live and die.

No alive human is allowed to see them or be intimate with them. Sometimes, when the Valkyries are not overseeing battlegrounds, they are allowed to travel to different realms in the guise of a swan. If someone were to see them without their guise, the Valkyries would turn into a mortal and would be unable to return to Valhalla.

But in Valhalla, they do spend time with the fallen warriors, freely serving them food and drinks. They'd fill horns full of mead from a cauldron in Valhalla that kept being filled with endless mead from an enchanted goat named Heiðrún.

Draugr

The term draugr means "someone who walks after death." The singular term is draugr, while the plural term is draugar. They're the Nordic equivalent of ghosts and zombies. They are, without a doubt, horrible creatures, carrying the unmistakable smell of decay wherever they go. Draugars are undead corpses that can not only move through rocks, thus explaining how they were able to escape their tombs and graves but also possess superhuman strength and can grow larger.

They serve many different purposes, including guarding their treasures, haunting living human beings, or torturing those who had tormented them in their life.

If they wished to kill a human, the draugars would crush them through their enlarged bodies, eat them whole, rip apart their bodies, and drink their blood. But this was not the worst thing they did. The most terrible ability a draugr possessed was the power to turn any sane person mad. They would drive living people insane, causing them to die out of hysteria or suicide.

How does one kill something already dead? The draugar could be killed if their bodies were dismembered or burned.

Some lore suggests that people believed that if someone was evil, malicious, unpopular, or simply vile, they would turn into a draugr after they died.

Have you picked up on a pattern in this chapter? Did you understand how several of the creatures mentioned were intricately linked to life and death? From the Norns that controlled the fates of all beings to the Valkyries that welcomed fallen warriors into Valhalla, many creatures played a significant role in the life of an average Nordic person. Some were seen as cautionary tales as well. If you were a bad person in life, there were chances that you could either get reincarnated as a draugr or get sent to the depths of the underworld where Níðhöggr would devour your body.

More importantly, several of these creatures highlight the inevitability of death, teaching us that it is wise to come to terms with the reality of passing from one world to the other. If a being like Fenrir can devour the greatest god of all time, Odin, and if Jörmungandr's venom can kill someone as brave as Thor, we are but mere mortals. Rather than fear death or cower from it, we should aspire to experience a life well-lived, and when it's our time to die, we will have accepted that death is just as much a part of life as birth, adolescence, youth, and old age.

This gives us a perfect opportunity to understand the nature of death and the afterlife in Norse Paganism.

CHAPTER 7
THE AFTERLIFE

What happens to a person after they die? Is there such a thing as a soul, and if so, where does it go after the mortal vessel has perished? Is death something to be feared and delayed, or is it something akin to a long-lost friend to be greeted at the end of one's life?

Why do we talk of death in the first place? Is it because it's a philosophical black hole in the face of which all logic, planning, thinking, and preparing fail? Is it because beyond death lies complete uncertainty and unknowing that we're so afraid of it? Are we afraid of not existing any longer? Or worse, if we still exist after death, are we afraid of existing in polarized states—that of reward or punishment? Does it seem cruel and arbitrary to us that we'd be separated from people we knew in our lives based on our actions?

Or is it simply the human condition that beckons us to take a scrying look into the great abyss of the unknown and divine some profound wisdom?

Humanity has struggled to understand and deal with death for as long as humans have been alive. All over the world, there are special funeral arrangements, services, and rituals that adherents to different religions follow to honor the departed's life and ensure that they find safe passage into the afterlife. The Greeks used to put coins on the eyes of a corpse as payment to the boatman Charon who would ferry the dead across the river Styx. The Hindus believe that cremation is the quickest way to release the soul of the dead to aid them in reincarnation.

This created a polarized worldview where on one end, those who believed in science completely denied the existence of an afterlife and refuted the existence of spirit, claiming that once you were dead, that was it. On the other end, you had adherents so afraid of going to hell that they bartered with clerics, trying to buy their way into heaven and avoiding hell by way of donation, confession, abstinence, and penance.

An over-reliance on any dogma can be considered extremist, even for those who look through the world with a scientific mindset. Science has yet to have all the answers, with many of its disciplines still in their infancy. To look to just science for answers is in itself a dogmatic practice known as scientism.

At the same time, abstaining from abstract activities deemed as sins just so you can avoid hell and get into heaven can, ironically, make a person miss out on living life. It also creates an opportunity for morally corrupt clergymen to abuse the faith of the vulnerable and the gullible. Televangelist pastors beckon you to curry God's favor by donating money to their megachurches.

And to think that all of that stems from a person's desire to fathom the afterlife.

Norse Paganism offers a comprehensive guide to the afterlife without being entirely factually didactic or by being admonishing. Unlike the Judeo-Christian worldview, one is not simply cursed to punishment in hell or rewarded eternally in heaven in Norse Paganism. A soul may travel to many different places if it wishes and may even choose to stay where it was buried. The Hel of Norse mythology was not like the Hell of Christianity. It was simply a place, not necessarily one of punishment.

But to understand the afterlife and the journey of the soul clearly, we must first understand how the Nordic people viewed the soul.

The Self

The concept of a singular soul—such as the life force of a human being—is a Christian concept. According to the Norse worldview, the human self was a far more complex entity. You could say it was modular, with several different autonomous parts that could detach from one another, capable of existing independently. The Nordic concept of the self saw the body as an axiom upon which a person's spirit, perception, and will existed.

The self had four parts: The Hamr, the Hugr, the Fylgja, and the Hamingja.

The Hamr

The Hamr meant the skin or shape of a person. The Hamr was the physical manifestation of one's self. It was the form that others could perceive in the real world. In other words, the Hamr was your outward body. In the Norse lore, your Hamr could change throughout your life, sometimes in evident ways such as through growing old from a kid into an adult and then into an aged person, and sometimes in abstract ways, such as how the color of a dead person changes from white to blue. The Hamr was not considered an absolute trait. It was alterable. Those who could shape-shift were gifted with the ability of Hamrhamr in which they could change their shape. One of the most prominent examples of this was Loki, who could alter his form at will.

The Hugr

The Hugr was an embodiment of your thoughts. Your personality, you're thinking, your manner of speaking, and all the quintessential things that made you unique in terms of character traits were all part of your Hugr. You may think of it as your consciousness. While the Hugr was considered an innate part of a person, it could cause changes far away. Those who possessed a strong Hugr could think about something and make it happen, much like having a strong sixth sense or possessing telekinesis.

The Fylgja

The Fylgja means follower. But what does that mean? Everyone has a Fylgja, an animal form related to a person's character. In European folklore, witches were symbolized as being surrounded by cats, owls, ravens, snakes, and toads—all of which were their familiar spirits, or Fylgja. The Fylgja can only be perceived by those who have a special sight. It is your familiar, whose well-being is tied to your well-being because if you die, your Fylgja will die as well, and if your Fylgja dies, you shall also die.

The Fylgja was also specific to the nature of a person. Someone who had a brave nature would have a lion as their Fylgja. A loyal person would have a dog or a horse as their Fylgja. A savage person could have a wolf as their familiar. Similarly, someone born in a noble house would have a bear as their Fylgja.

In life, if you feel drawn to a certain animal and feel as if there's some connection between you and them, or if some animal approaches you in a very magnetic way (a crow might caw at you and perch on your shoulder, a dog might wag its tail at you and lick your hands, a cat might purr and slide against your legs), there are chances that you possess the special sight that lets you see your familiar.

The Hamingja

The Hamingja is the fourth part of the self, according to Norse lore. This part equates to your luck. Luck was seen as a quality that was inherent to a person and their familial lineage. It was considered just as much a trait of a person as their intelligence, strength, wisdom, or dexterity with a weapon. Luck was a tangible thing, a personal entity that both caused and expressed itself in a person's wealth, success, power, and fame.

When a person dies, their Hamingja is reincarnated in one of their descendants, especially if the child bears the name of their ancestor. The Hamingja could also be lent to others who direly needed it, such as someone suffering from poverty or a warrior going on an inquest.

The poem Hávamál attests to the modular belief in the self.

It says,

> "Wealth will pass,
> Men will pass,
> You too, likewise, will pass.
> One thing alone Will never pass:
> The fame of one who has earned it."

It emphasizes that while your body may perish and your wealth will disappear, your legacy will live on, and through it, you shall live on. The belief that one's legacy and posthumous fame could practically ensure immortality through a life of hallowed remembrance was one of the reasons the Viking raiders were so fearless.

With such a complex concept of one's self, it is important to understand that there were several beliefs tied to these parts. For example, the Norse people believed in reincarnation. They held the belief that the Hugr of a person could transfer to the body of a newborn and that the Hamingja was something that kept passing down to your family at large.

A person, along with the components of their selves, could go to one of several places in the afterlife. Except for some cases (such as the death of brave warriors), the gods and goddesses did not pass judgment regarding reward or punishment for the departed.

The Realms of the Afterlife

It was customary to give a funeral filled with traditions to the departed. Upon their death, a person's corpse was bestowed with specific personal belongings that represented what kind of person they were and what sort of profession they practiced in their lives.

For example, a nobleman was buried with gold and jewels. A craftsman was buried with the tools of his craft. A warrior was buried with their weapons. Whatever items were placed beside a dead person were believed to aid them in their afterlife.

Another tradition was sailing the dead away on top of a burning ship, which was believed to provide them with a safe passage into the next realm. If someone was buried underground, burial mounds made of stone were placed in such a way that they resembled the shape of a ship.

Regardless of the type of burial, some mandatory rituals had to be performed at every funeral. It was mandatory to dress up the dead in new clothes so that they'd have beautiful clothes to wear in the afterlife. The deceased's life was celebrated through drinking, eating, chanting, and singing.

The five places in the afterlife that the dead could go to include:

- Valhalla
- Fólkvangr
- Hel
- The Realm of Rán
- The Burial Mound

But this list only refers to the main afterlife realms. The scope of the Norse afterlife is not just limited to these alone. There are other realms, such as Gimle and Vingólf, where the dead can go. In some cases, the dead can reincarnate as their descendants or even reincarnate as elves. If someone lived a life of evil, they could even reincarnate in their corpse as a draugr.

Valhalla

Also known as the Hall of the Fallen, this splendid place had a roof made of golden shields with spears for rafters. The seats surrounding the tables laden with food and drink were made of breastplates. Wolves guarded Valhalla. Eagles were said to fly above it. The dead who came here came to be known as einherjar. For someone to make it to Valhalla, they had to live a life of a brave warrior and then die a fitting death.

There were plentiful things to do in Valhalla besides just drinking and dining. The warriors would fight with each other, perform valiant acts, and take part in competitions. Each evening, their bodies would be restored to optimal health.

Ravenous from their daily effort, they'd take to the dining halls where they'd feed on the meat from the boar Sæhrímnir. This boar reincarnated itself every day after being slaughtered and butchered the day before, thus providing unending meat for the einherjar. The mead came from the udder of Heiðrún, a goat that provided endless supplies of mead. The einherjar dined with the Valkyries serving as their waitresses.

But lore tells us that this abode was not perceived as eternal. Upon the arrival of Ragnarök, Odin, the Valkyries, and the einherjar would leave Valhalla and take part in the final battle.

Fólkvangr

The goddess Freya got the first pick from the crop of dead fallen warriors, taking them to a land that reflected her personality in terms of being kind, beautiful, peaceful, and elegant. Here, they could rest in the meadow and enjoy their time in the hall known as Sessrumnir, where Freya herself dwelled. This hall was described as beautiful, fair, and containing many seats to accommodate the dead.

According to some accounts, this place was not just reserved for warriors. One particular woman swore never to eat anything until she had a chance to dine with Freya. When she died of starvation, she was taken to Fólkvangr and rewarded for her belief in the goddess. Here, she got to dine with Freya again.

Hel

The majority of people who die of old age or natural causes such as diseases go to Hel, which, unlike the Christian hell, is not a place of punishment but a place of existence where the dead rest. However, one particular place within Hel was reserved for the vilest of people, a place known as Nastrond, where Níðhöggr dwells. He fed on the bodies of these people as punishment for their inhumane actions.

The Realm of Rán

Those who died at sea were said to go to the realm of Rán, a giantess who married Aegir, the lord of the sea. In Rán's realm, there were treasures that she had taken from the sailors that had died at sea. Both the sailors and their treasures rested in this realm with Rán.

The Burial Mound

Sometimes, by choice, the dead could remain where they were buried and morph into a ghostly form known as haugbui. The haugbui was not considered a harmful entity like the draugr unless someone went out of their way to stomp on their burial mound. One can wonder why the haugbui chose to stay where they were buried. It was said that these people were so attached to the place where they had spent their lives that they were perfectly content staying here after passing, even in the form of ghosts.

However, if a person had been a terrible human being in their life, they did not get the chance to become a haugbui. Instead, they turned into a draugr, a malevolent being that could cause harm to others.

Gimle

Have you wondered where the righteous souls who will fall in Ragnarök will go? There's a special place for them known as Gimle, a hall brighter than the sun, where there's eternal happiness for its residents.

Vingólf

This enigmatic afterlife realm has quite contradictory origins. In some places, it is described as a hall where the gods and goddesses have assembled at times to drink ale and wine. In another mention, it was said to be a place just like Valhalla, where Odin sent the spirits of the brave fallen warriors. In a third instance, the name Vingólf is used interchangeably with Gimle. Regardless of its origins, this much is clear: It is an abode for those who were slain in battle.

From the account of the realms, we can gather that for everyone, whether they die of old age, drowning at sea, or falling in battle, there's a place in the next life. Those who wish to stay where they were in life can stay around their burial mounds as haugbui, content with where they are.

As opposed to the afterlives of other religions, there's more agency provided in the afterlife belief of Norse mythology, a belief that does not entirely have to root itself in the concept of reward and punishment.

But there's also a stern reminder that in case of living a dishonorable life, a life filled with evil and malice and crime, there's punishment awaiting in the form of Nastrond or by distorting into a draugr, just as there's a warm promise for those who die bravely that there awaits a hall with a roaring fire, hot food, and cold mead.

However, those are the exceptions rather than the rule itself, meant to signify that while the gods are not particular in doling out unfair sentences upon the spirits of the dead, they're not disaffected or indifferent to the actions either. If someone has gone out of their way to live an immoral life filled with evil acts and has caused significant harm to others through murder and thievery, they're not going to get away with it. Similarly, if someone has been brave enough to earn Odin or Freya's favor, they will be redeemed in Valhalla or Fólkvangr.

Pre-Christian Norse Afterlife

Some elements of Norse Paganism were influenced by the advent of Christianity, including the knowledge of a person's affair after death, making it extremely difficult to understand the original folklore about the afterlife. But through archaeological research, we know some things of the pre-Christian Norse beliefs about the afterlife, especially:

- You could be reunited with your ancestors and relatives after death, such as on the Holy

Mountain known as Helgafjell, where people reunited with their friends, family, and ancestors after dying.
- You could spend your afterlife doing something that you enjoyed doing in your life.
- You could call upon your deceased ancestors to aid you in times of need, especially in times of strife. This was so because the line between death and life was blurry, and if the dead wished to intercede in affairs, they could reappear from the afterlife momentarily to help their living relatives.

CHAPTER 8
DIVINING RUNE WISDOM

Similar to how Aramaic, Arabic, and Sanskrit came to be formed as evolutionary tools of written communication by the world's Semitic, Arabic, and Indian populations, the runic alphabets were the first writing system to be used by the Germanic and Norse people.

But there was more to these runes than met the eye. Yes, they functioned on a primary level as letters with which words could be formed, but there was an ideographic and pictographic symbolism behind each rune. To use a rune in writing was more than just to note something down; it was to invoke the secret meaning and the hidden magical power of the rune itself. And that is the meaning of the word rune. It means "whisper," "secret," or "magic."

Every rune possessed a name that gave insight into its significance both in terms of its magical abilities and philosophical depiction of the visual appearance and the sound it made when you pronounced it. For instance, the Tiwaz rune was called the T-rune. It stood for Tiwaz, also known as Tyr. Tyr was thought to dwell in the sky, and thus, the T-rune was shaped like an arrow pointing up. This arrow also hints at Tyr's adroitness and prominence in warfare. Besides being used to form longer words, the T-rune was used solitarily as well as an ideograph as part of a magical spell that would grant victory in a battle.

The collective name for the runic alphabet is the futhark, named after the first six runes Fehu, Uruz, Thurisaz, Ansuz, Raidho, and Kaunan. There are three main futharks, namely the Elder Futhark, the Younger Futhark, and the Anglo-Saxon Futhorc.

Elder Futhark

The Elder Futhark was the first to appear as a completely formed runic alphabet. Their development began in the first century CE and was said to be completed by the year 400. These had twenty-four characters, often divided into three families (Norse "ættir") of eight runes each, like so:

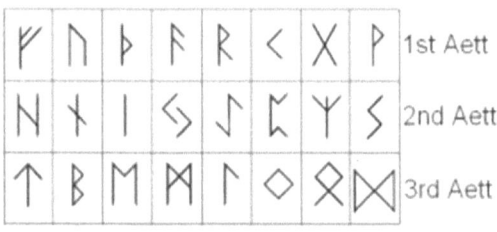

The Elder Futhark

The Younger Futhark

A simplified version of the Elder Futhark, these were used during the Viking Age at around 750 CE and soon replaced the older alphabet in common use in Scandinavia. The Younger Futhark had sixteen characters.

The Anglo-Saxon Futhorc

This thirty-three-character variant was adapted by the Anglo-Saxons to be used in England until the 9th and 10th centuries.

Runes were not commonly drawn on paper with pen and ink. Rather, they were etched onto wood, bone, metal, stone, and other hard surfaces. That's why they are so jagged, sharp, and angular.

Our present understanding of the futhark runes comes from the three rune poems documented in Iceland, England, and Norway, providing explanatory stanzas about each futhark.

Where Did They Come From?

There are two accounts, one a chronological account tracked through history, detailing how the runes might have been derived from Italic alphabets, the other a mystical one telling the tale of Odin as he hung from Yggdrasil, pierced with a spear, and waiting for nine days until the meaning and shapes of the runes were revealed to him.

The first account tells us that the Mediterranean people who lived south of the Germanic population in the first century used Old Italic alphabets. With time, the Germanic tribes took to the Old Italic alphabet and derived their letters.

Tracing the runes through history tells us that the first runic inscription that archeologists found was on the Meldorf brooch in the north of Germany. It was dated back to 50 CE. The next appearance of runes is on the Vimose comb in Demark and the Øvre Stabu spearhead from Norway. Both these items date back to 150 CE. Keeping in chronological order, the earliest carving of the entire futhark appeared on the Kylver stone from Gotland, Sweden, dating back to 400 CE.

Now how did the runes in their primitive form travel from Germany to Northern Europe? The Germanic warbands were the most dominant military power of that time, and it is hypothesized that they carried the runes from one place to the other, taking inspiration from the Old Italic alphabets. During the Proto-Germanic period, Nordic people's ancestors worshiped Odin under his original name Woðanaz and associated runes with him.

For the Proto-Germanic people, Odin, or Woðanaz, was the epitome of divinity, wisdom, magic, and mystery. From their point of view, the runes did not come into existence from a source as drab as the Old Italic alphabet. They believed that the runes were not crafted or invented but were rather preternatural and preexisting, deciphered by Odin after he underwent a great sacrifice. According to the poem Hávamál, Odin hung himself from Yggdrasil, pierced by his spear, and sacrificed himself to himself, after which:

"No aid I received,

Not even a sip from the horn.

Peering down,

I took up the runes –

Screaming I grasped them –

Then I fell back from there."

The runes seem to come from the waters of the Well of Urd, one of the wells that watered the Yggdrasil. This well was known to be a well of immense wisdom. This is corroborated by another poem called Völuspá:

"There stands an ash called Yggdrasil,

A mighty tree showered in white hail.

From there come the dews that fall in the valleys.

It stands evergreen above Urd's Well.

From there come maidens, very wise,

Three from the lake that stands beneath the pole.

One is called Urd, another Verdandi,

Skuld the third; they carve into the tree

The lives and fates of children."

The maidens mentioned in the poem are the Norns. The carvings in question are runes. From here, we can understand that the Well of Urd, the runes, magic, fate, and the Norns were all tied together.

As the lore continues, Odin presumably—after nine days of fasting and hanging—divined the runes by looking in the waters of the Well of Urd. Once he had understood the meaning and mysticism behind the runes, he imparted this wisdom to the humans, allowing rune masters to write down the significance of each rune and what it symbolized.

What Do The Runes Symbolize?

Plainly put, magic.

Cultures all over the world have attested to the existence of magic in some form or the other. Archaic languages, including Latin, Aramaic, Old Arabic, Sanskrit, and Persian, were all considered powerful enough for their words to serve as vessels of magic. In the pre-Christian Germanic worldview, the same belief was held. People believed in the power of words, believing that the correct pronunciation and the right utterance of a proper word could create an effect that would be difficult to describe in terms other than magical. The ancient Nordic people held the belief that words shaped reality. Words spoken and woven into sentences could create a powerful impact, sending forth energy into the world that could never be taken back.

The philosophy and symbolism of runes were intricately linked to the understanding that language structured one's perception. That thinking outside of language was virtually impossible because all thoughts took shape within the confines of one's language. In Proto-Germanic society, if one were to utter something out loud and make their thoughts public by way of speaking, it was considered to be made a part of the fabric of reality itself, going so far as to alter reality to make room for this new vocalization.

Coming back to runes, each rune represented a phoneme. A phoneme is the smallest unit of sound in linguistics. Letters such as a, b, s, t, and r are all considered phonemes. Each rune was considered the depiction of its phoneme in a visual form. Each phoneme also carries an innate meaning, which can be used collectively in the form of a word to give characteristics to the item or action being described by that word. This theory is known as phonosemantics, stating that there's an intricate connection between the sounds that comprise a word and the meaning of the word itself.

In simpler terms, there was a deep connection between the runes used to form a particular word, and this connection alluded to the mystery of the runes that Odin deciphered in the first place. Each of these connections was not an arbitrary connection but a meaningful one, extending not just to the relationship between the word and its phonemes but also to the word and its visual representation in the form of runes.

This sophisticated approach to language meant that runes weren't just a means for two people to communicate with each other but also a mode of communication between humans and the invisible powers and entities that surrounded them, such as magic, spirits, and gods.

The Eddas and sagas provide a testament to the fact that the runes possess magical attributes that work in a particular way. One example of that comes from Egil's Saga, in which Egil stops by a farmer's house to eat a meal. The farmer's daughter is severely ill. The farmer asks Egil for help. Egil investigates and discovers a whalebone with runes carved into it. Egil, a rune master, understands that the runes on the whalebone are causing the girl's illness. He scratches away the runes and burns the whalebone, then writes a different set of runes meant to counteract the effects of the previous runes. In time, the farmer's daughter recovers from her illness.

Even the Norns used runes to inscribe the fates of all living beings, suggesting that the runes were inherently magical.

Furthermore, the Rune Poems also attested to the existence of both phonological representation and inherent meaning of each rune.

What Do The Runes Mean?

Based on the meanings provided by the Rune Poems, here are the definitions of the twenty-four Elder Futhark runes.

Name: Fehu. **Phoneme:** F. **Represents:** Cattle. **Meaning:** Wealth, Success, Fertility, Abundance, Security.

The f-rune denotes money and material gain. It also symbolizes coming into wealth as well as accumulating wealth. A deeper meaning of this rune is destruction and sorrow if you choose to be stingy with your money and don't share it with those in dire need. It harkens you to follow a balanced path where you both spend your money and save it for future use. Another meaning of the f-rune is cattle, connoting the features of livestock such as sustenance and creation (Auðumbla being the primeval cow).

Name: Uruz. **Phoneme:** U. **Represents:** Bull. **Meaning:** Strength, Force, Wild, Freedom, Courage, Sagacity.

The u-rune symbolizes an extinct species of ox known as the aurochs. This animal used to inhabit Europe once upon a time and was considered an elemental force of nature. Much like the animal, the u-rune is a symbol of strength and equates to a human being's ability to defend themselves against danger and bring about positive change in their lives through courage.

Name: Thurisaz. **Phoneme:** Th. **Represents:** Thorn. **Meaning:** Danger, Conflict, Suffering, Sudden Reaction, Defense.

This rune is about brute strength, such as that wielded by Thor. You may use this strength to remove objects hindering your path or vanquish your foes. Another meaning of this rune is that of thorn, representing danger that lies hidden much like a thorn, only to pierce you suddenly. But this is a forewarning rather than a threat. You may prepare yourself for whatever challenges lay ahead by being stronger and more aware of your surroundings.

Name: Ansuz. **Phoneme:** A. **Represents:** Estuary or the Æsir god. **Meaning:** Communication, Talking, Mouth, Understanding, Inspiration, Prosperity.

This is a meta-rune, symbolizing the discovery of runes by Odin himself. As Odin once perceived the runes and conveyed their meaning to mortals, you too can communicate with others. This rune is also associated with Loki's intelligence, wisdom, and unusual insight. Combing both meanings, this rune equates to speech and the ability to convince others through your words.

Name: Raidho. **Phoneme:** R. **Represents:** Wagon or Horseback Journey. **Meaning:** Traveling, Journeying, Evolution, Rhythm, Movement, Growth.

The r-rune symbolizes a horseback journey or a wagon, signifying a journey. It may be a physical journey that takes you to different lands for better job opportunities or leisure or a spiritual journey that allows you to know more about yourself and the world around you. Raidho represents the evolution one undergoes after journeying from one place to another.

Name: Kaunan. **Phoneme:** K. **Represents:** Torch or Ulcer. **Meaning:** Pain, Mortality, Life.

With two apparent meanings, the k-rune is associated with ulcers/sores and fire/torch. As a symbol of an ulcer, this rune foreshadows pain and suffering. As a torch, it represents the enlightenment that one gets after lighting a controlled fire.

Name: Gebo. **Phoneme:** G. **Represents:** Gift. **Meaning:** Generosity, Exchange, Partnership, Relationship, Friendliness.

The g-rune is all about gift-giving and appreciating someone who gives you gifts. Giving someone gifts was considered a noble act in Norse culture, and it was a reciprocated act, meaning if someone gave you a gift, you had to give them one as well, which resulted in strengthening friendships and relationships. Gebo is also symbolic of the sexual union between two people through the act of gift-giving.

Name: Wunjo. **Phoneme:** W. **Represents:** Joy. **Meaning:** Pleasure, Prosperity, Happiness, Success, Comfort.

The w-rune means pleasure, upcoming happiness, and prosperous living. If you see this rune during meditation or divination, know that it's a good omen, telling you to be grateful for what you have and to be appreciative of what you will achieve soon.

Name: Hagalaz. **Phoneme:** H. **Represents:** Hail. **Meaning:** Nature, Challenges, Anger, Adversity.

The h-rune symbolizes hail, a destructive force of nature, foretelling the advent of calamity. Rather than cower from misfortune, one must seek to rise to the challenge and evolve into a better person as a result of adversity.

Name: Naudhiz. **Phoneme:** N. **Represents:** Need. **Meaning:** Conflict, Endurance, Independence, Self-Actualization, Willpower.

The n-rune represents need. It also represents the necessity of pain in this life. As the h-rune symbolizes adversity, the n-rune leads you to the realization that sometimes adversity and pain are necessary catalysts for personal growth.

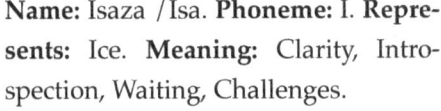
Name: Isaza / Isa. **Phoneme:** I. **Represents:** Ice. **Meaning:** Clarity, Introspection, Waiting, Challenges.

The i-rune is symbolic of ice. It equates to two particular things. First, the clarity of clear ice, such as on the surface of a lake in the winter, alludes to one becoming wiser and seeing things as they are. The second meaning of this rune refers to the barren nature of winter where frost hinders the growth of crops and subdues even the strongest of people into the confines of their homes.

Name: Jera. **Phoneme:** J. **Represents:** Year. **Meaning:** Cyclical Nature, Completion of Things, Changes in Things, Harvesting Time.

The j-rune stands for a year, especially a year that had a good harvest. This rune signifies the cyclical nature of time. For people who have spent a long time trying to accomplish something, this rune can bring the good news of expecting a great result.

Name: Eihwaz. **Phoneme:** Y. **Represents:** Yew Tree. **Meaning:** The World Tree, Enlightenment, Knowledge, Finding Balance, Death.

The i-rune stands for the yew tree, and as such, it represents the wisdom of Yggdrasil, the strength that is associated with trees, and finding balance in life. A yew tree, with its branches extending into the sky and its roots running deep into the ground, is the epitome of stability and balance.

Name: Perthro. **Phoneme:** P. **Represents:** Dice Cup. **Meaning:** Chance, Fate, Destiny, Luck.

The p-rune symbolizes the dice cup, and it can mean anything from taking chances, putting your faith in your luck, and accepting your destiny. Casting a dice cup and letting the dice fall as they may is innately a very fate-affirming activity where you make peace with the fact that whatever number the dice show is tied to your luck.

Name: Algiz. **Phoneme:** Z. **Represents:** Elk. **Meaning:** Guarding Something, Protection, Defensiveness.

The z-rune represents the majestic elk. Just as elks represent grandeur, strength, and power, this rune represents protection, defensiveness, and the strength required to guard those close to you.

Name: Sowilo. **Phoneme:** S. **Represents:** Sun. **Meaning:** Nurturing, Cleansing, Health, Resources.

The s-rune denotes the sun and symbolizes the nurturing elements of sunlight, such as providing energy, bringing warm light, and making the crops grow. The sun is an infinite resource; its light is considered one of the most vital necessities for all life on this planet. It encompasses the entire biosphere. In this regard, the s-rune is considered a benevolent rune.

Name: Tiwaz. **Phoneme:** T. **Represents:** Tyr. **Meaning:** Justice, Logic, Masculinity, Self-Sacrifice,

Self-Discipline. The t-rune is associated with the brave god Tyr, who, above all, chose self-sacrifice when he placed his hand inside Fenrir's mouth to subdue the wolf. Tyr was wise, logical, and quite strong. He was also a champion of justice. All of those traits are embodied in this rune.

Name: Berkanan. **Phoneme:** B. **Represents:** Birch Tree. **Meaning:** Femininity, Healing, Birth, Fertility.

The b-rune stands for the birch tree, a symbol of fertility, growth, and nurturing. This rune is associated with Nerthus, a goddess of fertility. This rune is said to preside over the four domains of life—birth, coming of age, marriage, and death.

Name: Ehwaz. **Phoneme:** E. **Represents:** Horse. **Meaning:** Journey, Transportation, Movement, Progress.

The e-rune attests to the relationship between a man and his horse. This bond was a strong one, tethered with loyalty, cooperation, and teamwork. A horse was symbolic of journeying, progressing through life, and being man's steadfast companion through thick and thin. In that regard, the e-rune is a benevolent rune.

Name: Mannaz. **Phoneme:** M. **Represents:** Humanity. **Meaning:** Cooperativeness, Society, Helping, Individuality.

The m-rune represents humanity in general and what sets humanity apart from other creatures. It symbolizes intelligence, wisdom, the ability to communicate, individuality, personality, societal relations, and culture.

Name: Laguz. **Phoneme:** L. **Represents:** Water. **Meaning:** Formlessness, Flow, Potentiality, Emotions, Depth, Hopes, Fears, Dreams, Rejuvenation.

The l-rune symbolizes water bodies such as lakes and seas. In its formlessness, water is filled with potentiality. It can be used to nourish fields and quench one's thirst, but just as easily, it can be an agent of chaos in the form of torrential rain and floods. But here, within the context of this rune, the nature of water is seen as beneficial. Water is the source of life and growth. The l-rune also implies fluidity of thoughts, emotions, and the depth of one's subconscious mind, where dreams, hopes, and fears dwell.

Name: Ingwaz / Ingaz. **Phoneme:** Ng. **Represents:** Seed. **Meaning:** Growth, Wisdom, Change, New Beginnings.

Ingwaz is associated with Frey. This rune signifies male fertility, peace, resting, attunement to nature, wisdom, and the evolution of one's psyche. This rune is also symbolic of completion, whether of a journey or a project.

Name: Dagaz. **Phoneme:** D. **Represents:** Dawn. **Meaning:** Awakening, Illumination, Completion, Hope, Certainty.

The d-rune represents the day. With daylight comes a new beginning. People deep in their slumbers wake up and head out to meet the day. With daylight, the shadow of the night passes, allowing illumination to light up all the fields, mountains, forests, rivers, and seas. To the travelers stuck in the dark, daylight comes bearing hope, telling them it is safe to travel again. Unlike the uncertainty that comes with the darkness of the night, this benign daylight establishes certainty.

Name: Othalan. **Phoneme:** O. **Represents:** Inheritance. **Meaning:** Heritage, Possessions, Experience, Value, Ancestry.

The o-rune represents your heritage and inheritance. This can be taken in a tangible meaning, such as the estate your ancestors left you or it can be understood metaphorically, such as your genetics and the tradition you carry on. You can also use this as the monogram for Odin.

odern Rune Usage

Followers of Norse Paganism use runes in their practices in three main ways:

Carving

The intent behind carving particular runes on rock, stone, bone, or any other surface is to open a channel of communication between the carver and the invisible world of gods, magic, and fate. In terms of invocation, rune-carving is the easiest and simplest form of veneration, invoking and hallowing a deity. One must understand that the runes have both an intrinsic and extrinsic representation, the latter being that of the cosmos, gods, fate, and magic, while the former being the representation of the human subconscious or psyche.

Traditionally, practitioners would carve the rune's outline into a surface, then coat it with blood, red dye, or crimson paint.

It should be noted that runic carving did not originate from a single source, so its usage had and continues to have variations from practitioner to practitioner.

The inherent intention, however, is the same. When carved onto a surface, the runes serve as a device that allows you to communicate with the primeval forces of nature, with the spirits of your ancestors, and most importantly, with the gods and goddesses whose favor you are trying to seek.

Divination

Divination using runes allows you to tap into your intuition, communicate with forces greater than you, and understand the significance of certain events. You may even foretell something that'll happen in the future.

Of the several types of runic divination, the simplest form is using a single rune for yes or no answers. The runemaster should ask a question, then proceed to take out a rune from the bag. Based on its symbol and meaning and the intuitive feeling the runemaster gets, the answer may incline towards a yes or a no.

Then there's the three-rune casting method, in which the runes were cast in multiples of three, representing the past, present, and future or situation, action, and outcome.

The most traditional way of runic divination is to cast or throw runes on a piece of white fabric while looking to the heavens and then reading only the runes that landed in the upright position.

Additionally, more experienced runemasters can use different layouts, such as the five-rune layout, the seven-rune layout, and the twenty-four-rune layout.

In the five-rune layout, the runes are laid out in the form of a cross with a question in mind. The runes at the bottom connote the basic elements that influence the question. The runes on the left highlight the problems surrounding the question. The runes on the top show the positives about the question. The runes on the right show the immediate answer to the question. Lastly, the rune in the middle shows the impact of the future on the question.

Meditation/Hallowing

Runes have inherent magical qualities that you can use to meditate. But because this is an open-ended practice with numerous interpretations and manifestations, this form of rune usage is considered very elusive and difficult. The principle behind meditation and hallowing using runes is to use carved/drawn runes for contemplation. One can contemplate the runes consciously in an attempt to uncover their mysticism so that one can better understand the universe and the events that take place within it, especially events that are going to take place in the future. One may even meditate upon the runes to tap into their powers.

For any three of these practices, you can build a dedicated altar where you can decorate the space with runes, symbols related to the runes, and whatever offerings you want to present to the gods. Additionally, you can carve your own runes or buy pre-carved ones from a store that sells paganism and heathenry supplies.

Runic magic takes quite some time to learn. Disciplines like runic divination and meditation require a lot of patience and effort before they can bear fruit. If you are just getting into runes, my advice to you would be to keep at it. The answers you seek are just within your reach. Remember Odin and how he suffered for nine days, hanging upside down from the tree. It was only after he had gone through a great ordeal that the runes became known to him.

Once the mystery of the runes manifests itself to you, you will thank yourself for sticking with this elusive, arcane, and powerful discipline. The mysticism behind the runes is not static. It's a dynamic discipline, with the meaning of the runes changing with context, deepening with wisdom, and becoming clearer with age.

CHAPTER 9
RITES OF PASSAGE

The Norse people had managed to not only survive but thrive in the face of harsh environmental challenges. As a people, they braved frosty winters and defended their towns from attacks by wild animals and rival warring tribes alike. They suffered through the severest spells of harsh weather when food and water were scarce, and primitive medicine was all they had to treat illnesses. They did not have access to advanced medicine such as vaccination nor had created intricate surgical procedures to save the lives of injured people or patients suffering from terminal diseases.

As a result, the mortality rate was quite high, not just in children but in adults as well. Upon the birth of a child, their life expectancy was merely twenty-years-old. Half of the infants who survived their births would just live till seven years. Half the population of their communities was made up of children less than the age of fifteen. Of the people who reached the age of twenty, only half would live to see the age of fifty. A mere one to three percent of the population has ever reached over the age of sixty. All of this was attributed to the high rate of mortality.

In those times, the birth process was precarious for both the mother and the child. The mother was susceptible, and there was a good chance that she could die during childbirth. As a result of the high infant mortality rate, it was not uncommon for Norse women to give birth to up to seven children in their lifetime. This mortality rate meant that most parents did not grow old enough to watch their children marry. Fewer grew old enough to see their grandchildren.

What do you think comes out of this much suffering? When at long last the Nordic people got a break, what was their reaction? They would celebrate wholeheartedly, reveling in their many ways by drinking, dancing, feasting, and venerating the gods. The harsher their conditions, the fiercer they celebrated whenever they appeared victorious, giving birth to many rites of passage and rituals that signify the importance of events such as childbirth and marriage.

Marriage

Norse weddings marked an occasion of celebration where two families came together as one. Marriage represented more than just the unification of man and woman. Norse people, particularly Vikings, built their families around the concept of alliances. In this way, a marriage between a man and woman was just as much an alliance of both families.

Before two people could marry each other, many negotiatory talks took place between both families. People from both sides of the family would come together and discuss different terms and conditions, including the price paid for the bride. This was known as mundr.

During these talks, they would also discuss peace treaties between the families and their allies and put forth terms to share their riches and wealth, such as their inheritances.

Norse weddings always took place on Frigg's day, given that Frigg was considered the goddess of love, familiar harmony, fertility, and childbirth, thus being the embodiment of a rite as fundamental as a wedding.

As this was an event that called for much preparation in the form of ceremony, drinking, and feasting, the people had to choose the most opportune date based on what the weather would be like on that day. This was to ensure that the ceremony could take place outdoors. Many guests would arrive from out of town, and preparations would have to be made for their lodging.

It was a mandatory—one could even say legal—requirement for the groom and bride to drink the honeyed mead during their wedding and for the remainder of the first month of their marriage, which lasted a moon cycle. And yes, this is where the concept of honeymoon comes from. One apparent reason for this obligatory month-long drinking rite was to facilitate conception. The other, less apparent, was to make the newlyweds comfortable with each other, letting relaxation and uninhibited time take hold of them so they could become better acquainted with each other in every sense of the word. We'll get to the why of it in a second.

Wedding celebrations were a matter of extreme mirth to both families and their extended relatives as well as their friends. The celebrations were spread over an entire week. The week-long length of the celebrations made the timing very critical, as it had to be arranged during a time when the harvest was readily available, and it wasn't snowing outdoors.

The bride and groom had special activities to perform preceding the wedding. First, the woman had to find a gift to give her husband on the morning after their first night together. Next, the bride would go to a bathhouse with the married members of her family. There, the women would remove a kransen (a circlet that symbolizes virginity) and place it in a box for the bride to give to her future daughter. The bride-to-be would then cleanse herself with steaming water, switch herself with twigs, and jump into cool water to completely clean her body.

While all this transpired on the women's front, the men took the groom for graverobbing. Yes, they would take the groom to the grave of his ancestor, from where he would have to take out a sword. This represented the man coming into his own and stepping into a new life.

Dirty from graverobbing, the groom would also head to the bathhouse and clean himself thoroughly.

Once they'd both cleaned themselves, they would dress festively for their ceremony. Nordic traditions paid more importance to hair than they did to dresses, as a woman's hair was a symbol of her femininity and sexuality. The longer and more decorative her hair, the more feminine and sexual she was considered. The bride was also adorned with a bridal crown that was passed down from mother to daughter through the ages. The groom would also oil and wax his hair, mustache, and beard. He would also wear the symbol of Thor, the hammer, as it was considered vital to fertility. Thor had a considerable role in the wedding ceremony. The bride would invoke Thor to bless her and the ceremony. Then she'd place a hammer upon her lap to ask for stronger children.

The legalities of the wedding—such as the exchange of goods, discussion of the estate, and finalization of mundr—took place before the main ceremony.

The main ceremony would also contain religious rituals such as blood sacrifice. The person who arranged the wedding, also known as the Gothi, would sacrifice a cow to Freya to bless the marriage.

The bride and groom would exchange swords and rings. The groom would give her the sword he got from his ancestor's grave, while the bride would give him a sword that was passed down to her family. Her giving him the sword would symbolize the passing of the role of her protection from her father to her husband. Through the exchange of swords, the two families became connected. From this moment onwards, both families would be responsible for each other, including protecting each other and interceding on each other's behalf.

While the swords interlinked the families together, the rings joined the groom and bride with each other.

Then there would be a foot race between the two families. Whichever family reached the feast hall first would win and get beer and mead served to them for the rest of the ceremony by the losing family. It was customary to let the bride and her family win the race so that the groom would approach her and carry her into his arms into the hall.

After a copious amount of drinking on the part of the bride, groom, and guests, they would feast on delicious dishes.

Since more often than not Norse marriages were arranged, meaning the two didn't know a lot about each other before, the honeymoon concept came about. The bride and groom were expected to acquaint themselves with each other during this time.

Childbirth and the Naming Ceremony

The arrival of a newborn was a highly anticipated event in Nordic culture. People would gather around the expecting wife and sing songs imbued with magic and invocation to the goddesses to ensure that the woman would give birth properly and the child would come into the world healthy.

The Norse women gave birth in their homes. This was an absolute necessity, both culturally and also because the women preferred to give birth in the comfort of their homes. Once a woman was eight months pregnant, she never left the confines of her home. Her husband also stayed with her. He was obligated to stay in the house with the expecting mother, regardless of his designation. He'd delegate someone else to perform his job and duties. When his child was born, the father has to perform a ceremony that would dub the child a person. He also had to be present during the birth, in the same room. This was legally enforced.

After the mother gave birth to the child (which, unlike modern methods of birth, was done upright), both of them were cleaned thoroughly. The child was wiped clean, and it was made sure that they were breathing properly. Then the mother accepted her child as hers by nursing it for the first time. During the first nursing, other witnesses, such as the midwife and the husband, had to be present.

During the first nine days, the child and the mother were taken care of, and more witnesses gathered for the upcoming ritual. During this time, the name was also finalized between relatives.

After nine days, the father took the baby and placed them on his knee. There, he saw the child and acknowledged that this was indeed his child. Then he sprinkled the baby with water and proceeded to name them.

The naming was not an arbitrary ritual. Norse people paid special significance to names, believing that names could give the child a certain trait. The names could also invoke the blessing of a god. They were also used as ancestor worship, as many Norse people named their children after their ancestors. Once chosen and given, the name was known to carry religious, spiritual, mystical, and ancestral significance.

Once the baby was named, they were considered a complete person, a fully-formed human being. After this, the mother went back to her daily duties in a matter of three days. If she were sick, she'd take a bit longer to recover, and then return to her regular routine.

Some accounts suggest that mothers fed their babies for up to two to four years, depending upon the availability of food and climate conditions. If other provisions were plentiful, she would wean the child earlier than four years, believing that the earlier the child was weaned and given proper food, the better their chances of survival. As a rule of thumb, most children were weaned at the age of two years. Regardless of how long the mother nursed the child, she kept the child by her side for one year after their birth, meaning she would literally strap the child to her side and carry it around everywhere she went.

Once the child was old enough to sleep on their own, they'd get a crib or a cradle.

When a child grew up, they would follow in their parent's footsteps. Let's say someone's father was a swordsmith; then the child would learn the principles of the craft from their father and assist them at the forge with their daily chores.

Children were expected to help around the house, including herding cattle, working the crops, and gathering firewood and fruits from the forest.

But life was not all work and chores for the kids. They were allowed to socialize with other kids their age and even play with toys. The boys were given wooden swords, shields, and smaller bows at an early age to learn the art of battle. Their elder brothers or father would teach them how to swing swords, raise their shields, and perfect their bow aim.

CHAPTER 10
PRACTICING MODERN PAGANISM

You can declare yourself a pagan by affirming the existence of the Norse gods and goddesses and making them an integral part of your life. If you already believe in them, feel their presence, and are influenced by their traits, then you are well on your way to becoming a practicing pagan.

While the old Norse religion does not exist in its original form, several branches of Neo-Paganism have emerged over the years, such as Ásatrú, Vanatru, Rökkatru, Heathenry, Odinism, and Thursatru, all of which serve to venerate the Norse gods and goddesses and recreate the old Norse religion that was followed more than a thousand years ago.

You may choose which form of Norse Paganism you most resonate with. There are as many forms today that are just as diverse in their practices and beliefs as the old Norse religion was. If you are more of an introvert and prefer worship and meditation in solitude, there are options for you, and if you're an extrovert who gets a kick out of community-based rituals and worship, there are avenues for you as well. While some branches have chosen to remain as authentic as possible, sticking closely to the original Norse religion in terms of practices, others have taken a dynamic turn and have adapted with the times, embodying the beliefs in evolved practices that are suitable to the modern era.

If the diminishing of the original old Norse religion upon the advent of Christianity can be likened to Ragnarök, then the resurgence of modern neo-paganism in the form of various branches of paganism and heathenry can be considered a rebirth of the world. A world that's getting populated by more and more pagans every day. Ásatrú, one of the forms of paganism practiced today, is now considered to be the fastest-growing religion in Iceland. Since 2007, the religion has seen a growth of more than 200%

Before you formally begin your journey into paganism, some things are expected from you:

- Growth. You will undergo both spiritual and mental growth as a result of walking along the pagan path.
- Individuality. As you walk further along this path, you will become your own person and will break free from conformity.
- Devotion. The best way to become a pagan is to do your fair share of research by reading the relevant literature and understanding the philosophies and mysticism of Norse Mythology. This is a feat that requires devotion.

Paganism does not demand you to be some prophesied chosen one who has registered with Mensa. Paganism accepts you as you are. You don't have to be special to venerate the gods and bring them into your life. You are completely fine as you are. In fact, this is one of the principles of paganism in general; accepting yourself for who you are and making peace with it. Embodying the principles of paganism in your daily life will allow you to live a more grateful, enjoyable, fulfilling, and wholesome life. So, without further ado, let's look at the different forms of Norse Paganism available today. Know that there's no wrong answer, and then go from there.

Ásatrú

Ásatrú is a neo-pagan revivalist religion that seeks to venerate the Æsir gods. Ásatrú's main focus is the gods Odin, Thor, Frigg, Tyr, Baldur, and other Æsir deities. The revival of Ásatrú took place relatively recently in 1973.

It came into existence after Sveinbjörn Beinteinsson, who was originally a farmer but later became the first high priest of his organization. He petitioned the Icelandic government, asking them to acknowledge the Icelandic Ásatrú Fellowship as a real religion. His appeal became successful and later on the religion was even acknowledged in Denmark and Norway. Today, there are more than twenty-thousand followers of Ásatrú all over the world.

Ásatrú's teachings come from the Eddas written by Snorri Sturluson. While there is no one set scripture, the adherents of Ásatrú do follow a collected medieval Icelandic book known as the Codex Regis which is based on Snorri's writings.

The priests in Ásatrú are known as Goði. They are responsible for performing ceremonies such as marriages, funerals, and blót.

The essence of Ásatrú is peace and tolerance. To that effect, Ásatrú disowns militarism and the glorification of battle, bloodshed, and military heroism.

Vanatru

Just as Ásatrú serves to venerate the Æsir gods, Vanatru is the denomination of Paganism wherein worship and veneration are focused on the Vanir such as Njord, Freya, and Frey.

While there are followers of Vanatru out there, Vanatru does not have a particular creed, a sacred book, rituals, or details about how Vanatru was created and who was behind it. Among this obscurity, there are a few depictions of Frey and Freya, as well as a couple of stories from the Eddas in which the three Vanir are mentioned.

This much is clear, though: this was a religion followed by people in the past, but as Christianity came to Scandinavia, it seemed to vanish.

Yet, the adherents to Vanatru still devotedly worship Freya and Frey and Njord, believing that the Vanir are still just as alive today as they were more than a thousand years ago, and so, even without a lot to go on, people have managed to reconnect with the Vanir gods and have created a beautiful religion centered around the Vanir.

This ambiguity has allowed followers of Vanatru to intuitively connect with the gods through meditation, divination, veneration, and runes.

Vanatru sets itself apart from Ásatrú by focusing on folk magic, divination, witchcraft, and rituals that serve to communicate directly with the Vanir gods and goddesses.

Rökkatru

It is completely natural if you don't feel as drawn to the Æsir and Vanir as you thought. Maybe, you are more in tune with the Rökkr, and perhaps the Rökkr beckon you toward them. While the Ásatrú and Vanatru followers venerate the Æsir and Vanir, respectively, the followers of Rökkatru venerate Loki, Hel, Fenrir, Jörmungandr, and Angrboða.

In short, the agents of Ragnarök. The name Rökkr itself refers to Ragnarök. Rökkatru also venerates the Jötnar.

This denomination seeks to liberate its followers from the polarity of good and evil, black and white. The Rökkr are not enemies and are not considered evil by those who follow Rökkatru. They are as fundamental to the existence of the Nine Realms as the Æsir and Vanir. The Rökkatru followers hold the belief that the actions of the Rökkr are a dire necessity so that the universe can be born anew again. Otherwise, without Ragnarök, what would be the point?

Followers of Rökkatru perform heathen magical practices such as seiðr. They also venerate the deities using altars, communicate with them through meditation, and even perform astral projection methods, including path walking and journeying. Rökkatru rituals also utilize runes and invocations.

Thursatru

Rökkatru and Thursatru resemble the left-hand path in terms of embracing the darker aspect of Norse mythology. Thursatru, similarly, embraces the chaotic nature of Norse myth, not shying away from it. Rather, it venerates the anti-cosmic forces known as Thurses (Jötunns), including beings such as Ymir, Loki, Hel, Jörmungandr, Níðhöggr, and Gullveig—all of which are beings that resonate with chaos.

If you want to put it into terms of traditional religions, Thursatru is the Satanism to Ásatrú and Vanatru's Christianity. It embraces the anti-Æsir, and the anti-Vanir, and looks forward to the coming of Ragnarök, not within an evil capacity but in an anticipatory capacity.

The rebellious nature of Thursatru has allowed its followers to be very individualistic in terms of their practices.

Whereas Ásatrú, Odinism, and other forms of Heathenry employ the Nine Noble Virtues in their belief system, the Thursatru followers do not adhere to these principles.

The Nine Noble Virtues include:

1. Courage
2. Truth
3. Honor
4. Fidelity
5. Discipline
6. Hospitality
7. Self-Reliance
8. Industriousness
9. Perseverance

While heathens and pagans use these virtues as a guide in their daily lives, those who adhere to Rökkatru and Thursatru tend to live life on their own terms, dismissing the notion of the virtues.

In regards to worship, Thursatru followers make offerings to the Jötunn, build altars, venerate, meditate, and even perform rune magic meant to appease the Jötunn.

If all the main branches of paganism are like different genres of heavy metal, Thursatru revels in considering itself the death metal of paganism.

Odinism

Odinism contains many of the same beliefs as Ásatrú, and both denominations are quite similar to each other. At one point, in 1997, Odinism and Ásatrú joined as one, but later on, because of a reason, the union was dissolved in 2002.

Some far-right, racist groups decided to make Odinism their banner for white supremacy, which gave Odinism a bad name, going so far as to make other branches of heathenry and paganism disassociate with it completely. This is not true of all branches but it is important to be aware of.

But racism and white supremacy is not what Odinism is about. In its purest form, Odinism venerates Odin and his Æsir kin. The majority of the beliefs come from the Eddas and poems, with an emphasis on Odin and his character.

Odinism has its own values quite similar to the nine noble virtues, all of which are inspired by Odin's tales and his characteristics. They are:

1. Strength is better than weakness
2. Courage is better than cowardice
3. Joy is better than guilt
4. Honor is better than dishonor
5. Freedom is better than slavery
6. Kinship is better than alienation
7. Realism is better than dogmatism
8. Vigor is better than lifelessness
9. Ancestry is better than rootlessness.

The mode of worship and veneration in Odinism resembles Ásatrú and Vanatru, as the basic idea behind veneration is the remembrance of gods, honoring their lives, and attempting to become like them. Odinists also observe the blóts that followers of Ásatrú observe.

By definition, such as seen in the Odinistic values, Odinism is a proactive religion. The Odin brotherhood goes so far as to distinguish itself, stating that while others hug trees, we cut them down and build fires from them. While others hold hands, we make fists. While others pet animals, we hunt them as prey.

Unfortunately, the fixation of the white nationalist and far-right movements on Odinism as a symbol of white supremacy has marred the name of an otherwise pure and sincere branch of Paganism.

Lokeans

Lokeans, much like those who follow Rökkatru, observe that Loki is not a force of evil or a devilish figure but an instigator of change, a patron of those who think outside of the box and don't fit into societal structures and traditional norms, and can transcend into a higher form using his shapeshifting powers.

Lokeans worship and venerate Loki as their primary deity, making offerings to him, seeking his counsel, and performing rituals that attract his attention.

Lokeans believe in finding Loki's energy and incorporating it into their daily lives.

They pray to him and share their thoughts with him, sometimes in a one-sided conversation, but other times, they get insight and whispers from Loki.

They make offerings such as mead and ale to him and even hold a Blót for him in a formal sense. Lokeans also set up a shrine in honor of Loki and worship him at an altar.

Lokeans stand by the principle that Norse mythology does not have distinct good and evil. They believe that Loki, while, yes, sometimes caused chaos, that chaos was necessary and meaningful.

Lokeans are still polytheistic, acknowledging the existence and importance of other deities within the Norse pantheon.

Other aspects that attract Lokeans to Loki include his sexual and gender fluidity, the extreme lengths he goes to achieve his goals (remember when he got Balder killed?), and how he is the harbinger of change. Loki faced change with a brave face and embraced it rather than cowering from it. Lokeans try to embody this principle.

Heathenry

Those who adhere to heathenry state that our ancestors were collectively heathens before the Christianization of the world. This statement does not limit itself to Scandinavia. In pre-Islamic Arabia, there was an entire pantheon of Arabic deities, such as Laat, Uzza, and Manat, that the Arabs used to worship and venerate before the arrival of Islam. In South Asia, the predominant population was Hindu and worshipped hundreds of thousands of different deities before missionaries from Europe and Arabia came and converted many of the people to Islam and Christianity.

Heathenry takes this belief and offers its followers to go back to the religion of their ancestors. The diverse belief system of heathenry encompasses beliefs from the old Norse religion, with influences from other heathen practices from other parts of the world as well, creating further denominations such as Frankish Heathenry, Gothic Heathenry, Saxon Heathenry, Frisian Heathenry, and Anglo-Saxon Heathenry.

Modern Heathenry takes the fundamental beliefs of Frith, Honor, Luck, Gifting Cycle, and Wyrd and Orlæg as its foundation.

Frith —A sense of peace, security, and inviolability that comes from making covenants not to harm each other.

Honor — Honor in ancient Germanic represented a person's usefulness to the community. An honorable person benefited their society, while someone with no honor caused the community a lot of harm.

Luck — Similar to the fate described in Norse Paganism, the heathen variant of luck includes one's character, strength of their frith, physical strength, fate, individual will, one's abilities, and the socioeconomic conditions in which one was born.

Wyrd and Orlæg — The Well and the Tree (Yggdrasil and the Well of Urd) represent the cyclical nature of time and the power entombed within the cosmos. One's Orlæg was considered to be the conditions that were chosen for them before they were born, including their sexuality, gender, economic class, social class, religion, parents, country of birth, and so on. Orlæg is the stats that you start with. Wyrd, on the other hand, is the connection that you form with others, the tapestry that you weave as you interact with the world and leave your mark on it. A heathen accepts the Wyrd and Orlæg as cosmic forces and affirms the cosmological concepts they represent.

Shamanism

Shamanism was and is still followed all over the world today. A shaman interacts with the spirit world directly via altered states of consciousness, such as vision quests and trances. The purpose of the shaman is to manipulate, guide, and utilize spiritual energy and spiritual entities in such a way that they can heal someone's illnesses, provide help to those who need it, and offer divinatory wisdom.

This ancient practice comes from the indigenous people of northern Europe and Siberia. The Proto-Germanic people considered Odin to be a master of many different disciplines, including shamanism. Shamanism has many commonalities with Norse mythology, particularly when working with spirits from the Norse pantheon.

Shamans believe that spirits exist and play a very critical role in the lives of humans. A shaman can communicate with these spirits. For example, a Nordic shaman would possess the ability to make contact with Odin's spirit and ask for aid. But not all spirits are beneficial. Some spirits can cause some serious harm, such as the djinns in Arabic lore and the draugrs in Norse mythology.

Shamanism teaches its practitioner to treat diseases caused by evil spirits.

Besides healing and working with spirits, a shaman can use trance techniques to visit other realms and enter different dimensions in search of answers. This may be done either through meditation or by consuming substances such as mushrooms.

Shamans can use familiars in the form of animals as spirit guides and message bearers. They can also perform different forms of divination, such as scrying, using runes, and throwing bones.

As a whole, this particular denomination of paganism is centered around divination and healing.

Wicca

Heathenry and paganism had many different forms in the pre-Christian world. Witchcraft, unlike how it is painted as an evil practice today, was a form of paganism in which the practitioners held beliefs that centered around nature, conducted naturalistic rituals, and practices that attune one to the world around them and allow them to communicate with the forces of magic that exist outside of the realm of the common folk.

Although Wicca is a revivalist, modern religion formed in the twentieth century, its roots go back in time, deriving from the wisdom of the ancient witches and warlocks who practiced the arcane art of magic. Wiccans are polytheists and can venerate any number of deities, including but not limited to gods and goddesses from the Norse pantheon.

Wiccans meet in the form of groups called covens. They don't exactly worship or venerate the biblical Satan, rather, they consider him a symbol of rebellion against the traditions put in place by Judaism and Christianity.

Wiccans channel the universal energy and perform magic with it to achieve desired effects.

The moral code of Wiccans tells them: "If it harms none, do what thy wilt."

There is no singular source from which Wiccans get their knowledge. It can be an individualistic or community-based practice based on one's preference. Like other forms of paganism, Wiccans also use rune magic, divination, scrying, and astral projection.

They also celebrate sabbaths and festivals, including Ostara and Yule.

Wiccans can choose one particular patron deity and work with them through meditation, veneration, and performing rituals.

Wicca finds its roots in Celtic paganism, but those roots are not exclusive to the Celtic. There is Germanic influence present as well, as seen in the immanent, animistic, and transcendental nature of the beliefs.

How Do I Become a Pagan?

Those were some of the modern versions of paganism. As a budding pagan, it is now your responsibility to treat this knowledge with the care it deserves. Throughout this book, I have given you the fundamentals of Norse Paganism and Mythology, introducing you to the various beliefs, gods, goddesses, rituals, customs, rites of passage, and stories that comprise the beliefs of Pagans the world over.

- Now, I want you to get some first-hand information by studying the Eddas and the historical accounts that are available online, reading will allow you to learn about the history, culture, mythology, folklore, and legends of Norse mythology, while giving you the freedom to decide for yourself what is true.
- Once you have perfected your theory, it is time to put it into practice. I recommend choosing a patron deity—there can be more than one—if you feel drawn to a particular one. Allow this connection to strengthen through meditation, veneration, and divination.
- You can follow the rites I've mentioned in the book or you can do your research and come across new ones. Then, if you feel inclined, you can create your rituals from the outline of pre-existing ones.
- It's best to join a community for the sake of celebrating different ceremonies, becoming a part of something larger than yourself, and performing communal rituals. But if you are more introverted, you can continue along the pagan path by yourself.

- Throughout this journey, if you come across a familiar spirit in the form of an animal, get the feeling that an ancestor is trying to get in touch with you, or simply feel the presence of an allied spirit, you should let them guide you.
- A word of warning: Some factions masquerade as Norse Pagans but are actually white supremacists and racists. You should steer clear of them at all costs. There's no connection between Norse traditions and white supremacy whatsoever.
- You should perform the rites and observe the festivals at their respective time of the year to foster a better relationship with the respective deities.
- Lastly, live your life bravely, follow the virtues embodied by the gods and goddesses, and be authentic in your everyday life. Align yourself with the beliefs that are shared in this book and Norse Paganism, and soon enough, you will become an experienced Pagan, guiding other newcomers to the light.

Sjáumst!

LEAVE A REVIEW!

Thank you for letting me be your guide through the fascinating history and mythology of the Norse.
Now, I'm sure you're wondering how you can help others experience the same joy and fulfillment that you have gained from reading this book.
Leaving a review can be a great way to help others learn about Norse Paganism. Your review can help people discover the book, and it provides an opportunity to share your own experience and what you've learned on your journey. OR type this URL into your device: http://amazon.com/review/create-review?&asin=B0BP1CVBQG

CONCLUSION

It was no coincidence that you came here. Old roots run deep. Together, you and I embarked on a journey. I as your guide, you as my disciple. Whether it was the call of a god or goddess that drew you here or curiosity, you were welcome.

I wanted to share the knowledge of the old Norse religion, Norse mythology, and Norse Paganism with you to better equip you with the information you need to take a step towards being a practicing modern pagan yourself.

- I introduced you to the concept of Norse Paganism and provided you with the framework for being a Norse Pagan.
- We learned who the Norse Gods were and about the worlds that they dwelled in.
- We took a deep dive into history, uncovering the Norse timeline through the ages, including the Viking age's advent and end. But this was only the beginning.

- From there, we delved into the creation of the cosmos, learning about how the universe came into existence according to the Norse worldview. From Yggdrasil to each of the Nine Realms, we traveled through the cosmos, marveling at the grandeur of Norse cosmology.
- As it was vital for becoming a Pagan that you understood the Pagan holidays, rituals, and festivals, I shared the details of the lunar calendar with you and described the Norse holidays. We learned how the days of the week came to be known as Monday, Tuesday, Wednesday, and so on.
- In the fifth chapter, we took a deep look at the Norse Pantheon of Gods, reading their stories and learning how to venerate them.
- I showed you how rich and diverse the Norse world was, with its many creatures such as the elves, trolls, Valkyrie, and draugrs.
- We took a pensive turn and deliberated over the Norse concept of the afterlife and how the soul was divided into different pieces. We found out where the deceased went after death.
- And then our learning took a magical turn, allowing us to divine the wisdom of runes, from their origin to their meanings. We even discussed how we can use runes in our daily lives.
- I interspersed Norse mythology, Norse Paganism, and Norse history in this book in such a way that would allow you to learn both the practices and the historical significance of the practices. Similarly, we looked at the two main rites of passage— marriage, and childbirth.

- And lastly, we reviewed the various denominations of Norse Paganism that are being followed today, equipping you with the right data you need to choose the branch that suits you best.

In my eyes, you are a Pagan already. All that's left to do is put what you have learned into practice.

I sincerely wish you the best of luck on your Norse journey.

If you want to help me spread this information to more people, please leave a review on Amazon.

Thank you for reading!

FREE GIFT JUST FOR YOU!!!
BEGINNERS KIT

Just starting out on your Journey learning about the magic of Norse Paganism.

Click here https://norsepaganwisdom.info/optin-page2bxjr47c or use the QR code below to get all the resources at your fingertips

What it includes:

- A copy of the Elder & Younger Eddas
- The Die Germania by Cornelius Tacitus
- The Hávamál
- The Heimskringla
- The Codex Regius

CITATIONS AND REFERENCES

INTRODUCTION

1. Knightly, Z. H. (2022, March 09). Introduction to Norse Heathenry. Retrieved October 15, 2022, from https://skaldskeep.com/norse/intro/

2. McCoy, D. (2019, February 08). The Ultimate Online Guide to Norse Mythology and Religion. Retrieved October 15, 2022, from https://norse-mythology.org/

3. Scott, J., Joachim, & Wright, K. (2022, November 02). A beginner's guide to norse mythology. Retrieved October 15, 2022, from https://www.lifeinnorway.net/norse-mythology/

4. Gaiman, N. (2019). *Norse mythology*. S.l.: Bloomsbury Publishing.

5. Nomads, T. (2022, March 21). Norse paganism for beginners: Quick introduction + resources. Retrieved

October 15, 2022, from https://www.timenomads.com/norse-paganism-for-beginners/

6. Routes North. (2022, June 20). Norse paganism: What is it, and what do its followers believe? Retrieved October 15, 2022, from https://www.routesnorth.com/language-and-culture/norse-paganism/

7. Smith, R. (2019). *The way of fire and ice: The living tradition of Norse paganism*. Woodbury, MN: Llewellyn Publications.

8. The Old Nordic Religion Today. (n.d.). Retrieved October 15, 2022, from https://en.natmus.dk/historical-knowledge/denmark/prehistoric-period-until-1050-ad/the-viking-age/religion-magic-death-and-rituals/the-old-nordic-religion-today/

9. McCoy, D. (2016). *The Viking spirit: An introduction to norse mythology and religion*. North Charleston, SC: CreateSpace Independent Publishing Platform.

Crawford, J. (2015). *The poetic edda: Stories of the Norse gods and heroes*. Indianapolis: Hackett Publishing Company.

THE FRAMEWORK FOR BEING A NORSE PAGAN

1. A guide to norse gods and goddesses. (1970, October 29). Retrieved October 15, 2022, from https://www.centreofexcellence.com/norse-gods-goddesses/

2. Knightly, Z. H. (2021, December 29). The Norse deities. Retrieved October 15, 2022, from https://skaldskeep.com/norse/deities/

3. Heritage Daily. (2021, August 26). Yggdrasil and the 9 Norse worlds. Retrieved October 15, 2022, from https://www.heritagedaily.com/2018/08/yggdrasil-and-the-9-norse-worlds/121244

4. The nine realms in Norse mythology. (2022, July 18). Retrieved October 15, 2022, from https://skjalden.com/nine-realms-in-norse-mythology

5. Mark, J. (2022, November 01). Ten norse mythology facts you need to know. Retrieved October 15, 2022, from https://www.worldhistory.org/article/1836/ten-norse-mythology-facts-you-need-to-know/

6. Knightly, Z. H. (n.d.). Yggdrasil. Retrieved October 15, 2022, from https://skaldskeep.com/norse/yggdrasil/

7. McCoy, D. (2018, July 05). Sources. Retrieved October 15, 2022, from https://norse-mythology.org/sources/

8. Paxson, D. L. (2021). *Essential ásatrú: A modern guide to norse paganism*. New York, NY: Citadel Press Books are published by Kensington Publishing.

9. Gefnsdottir. (2013, March 19). Vanatru: Clearing up some misconceptions. Retrieved October 15, 2022, from https://adventuresinvanaheim.wordpress.com/2013/03/19/vanatru-clearing-up-some-misconceptions/

Northern tradition paganism: Northern-tradition paganism & heathenry. (n.d.). Retrieved October 15, 2022, from https://www.northernpaganism.org/general/northern-tradition-paganism-heathenry.html

THE ORIGINS AND HISTORY OF NORSE PAGANISM

1. Nikel, D. (2022, February 03). The Viking timeline - what happened and when? Retrieved October 15, 2022, from https://www.lifeinnorway.net/viking-timeline/

2. Brownworth, L. (2014). *The sea wolves: A history of the Vikings*. United Kingdom: Crux Publishing.

3. The Viking Network. (n.d.). The Viking Timeline. Retrieved November 2, 2022, from http://www.viking.no/e/etimeline.htm

4. The National Museum Of Denmark. (n.d.). The Viking age. Retrieved October 15, 2022, from https://en.natmus.dk/historical-knowledge/denmark/prehistoric-period-until-1050-ad/the-viking-age/

5. Short, W. R. (n.d.). What happened to the Vikings? Retrieved October 15, 2022, from https://www.hurstwic.org/history/articles/society/text/what_happened.htm

6. History.com. (2009, November 04). Vikings. Retrieved October 15, 2022, from https://www.history.com/topics/exploration/vikings-history

7. Routes North. (2022, June 20). Norse paganism: What is it, and what do its followers believe? Retrieved October 15, 2022, from https://www.routesnorth.com/language-and-culture/norse-paganism

8. Nikel, D. (2020, December 03). Viking religion: From the Norse gods to Christianity. Retrieved October 15, 2022, from https://www.lifeinnorway.net/viking-religion/

9. Napoli, D. J., & Balit, C. (2017). *Treasury of Norse mythology: Stories of intrigue, trickery, love, and revenge*. Washington, D.C: National Geographic Kids.

10. Colum, P., & Pogány, W. (2019). *The children of Odin: The book of northern myths*. New York, NY: Aladdin.

THE CREATION OF THE COSMOS

1. Creation of the world in Norse mythology. (2022, July 18). Retrieved October 15, 2022, from https://skjalden.com/creation-of-the-world-in-norse-mythology

2. Campbell-Dagnall, H. (2020, February 05). The 9 realms explained - norse cosmology. Retrieved October 15, 2022, from https://viking-styles.com/blogs/history/the-9-realms-explained-norse-cosmology

3. Ashliman, D. L. (2010, February 17). The Norse Creation Myth. Retrieved October 15, 2022, from https://sites.pitt.edu/~dash/creation.html

4. McCoy, D. (2018, July 24). The creation of the cosmos. Retrieved October 15, 2022, from https://norse-mytholo-

gy.org/tales/norse-creation-myth/

5. Greenberg, B. (2022, January 04). The Norse creation myth. Retrieved October 15, 2022, from https://mythologysource.com/norse-creation-myth/

6. Gill, N. (2018, March 03). Creation of the world in Norse mythology. Retrieved October 16, 2022, from https://www.learnreligions.com/creation-in-norse-mythology-117868

7. McCoy, D. (2018, July 28). Yggdrasil. Retrieved October 16, 2022, from https://norse-mythology.org/cosmology/yggdrasil-and-the-well-of-urd/

8. Liam. (2022, October 02). Nine realms of norse mythology (all the worlds explained). Retrieved October 16, 2022, from https://vikingr.org/norse-cosmology/nine-realms-of-norse-mythology

9. Norse cosmology. (2021, November 20). Retrieved October 16, 2022, from https://mythopedia.com/topics/norse-cosmology

10. McCoy, D. (2018, July 14). The nine worlds. Retrieved October 16, 2022, from https://norse-mythology.org/cosmology/the-nine-worlds/

THE NORSE CALENDAR AND PAGAN HOLIDAYS

1. The Viking Calendar. (n.d.). Retrieved October 16, 2022, from http://www.vikingsofbjornstad.com/Viking_Calen-

dar.shtm

2. The Norse Wheel of the year: The Norse calendar & holidays. (2021, October 08). Retrieved October 15, 2022, from https://www.timenomads.com/the-norse-wheel-of-the-year-viking-calendar-holidays/

3. Ásatrú holidays. (n.d.). Retrieved October 16, 2022, from https://thetroth.org/resources/norse-pagan-holidays

4. The Viking Lunar Calendar: The names of months and days. (2022, July 18). Retrieved October 16, 2022, from https://skjalden.com/the-viking-lunar-calendar-the-names-of-months-and-days/

5. Norse holidays and festivals. (n.d.). Retrieved October 16, 2022, from http://thepaganjourney.weebly.com/norse-holidays-and-festivals.html

6. The Vikings days of the week. (n.d.). Retrieved October 16, 2022, from https://vikings.mrdonn.org/daysoftheweek.html

7. Viking festivals: A list of Scandinavian and Celtic related events. (n.d.). Retrieved October 16, 2022, from https://sonsofvikings.com/pages/viking-festivals

8. Norse Festivals. (n.d.). Retrieved October 16, 2022, from http://www.wizardrealm.com/norse/holidays.html

9. Knightly, Z. H. (2022, February 12). Norse holidays. Retrieved October 16, 2022, from https://skaldskeep.com/norse/holidays/

10. Valkyrja - The Old Icelandic calendar. (n.d.). Retrieved October 16, 2022, from http://valkyrja.com/220915.html

THE NORSE PANTHEON OF GODS AND GODDESSES

1. McCoy, D. (2018, September 04). The aesir gods and goddesses. Retrieved October 16, 2022, from https://norse-mythology.org/gods-and-creatures/the-aesir-gods-and-goddesses/

2. Greenberg, M., Dr. (2022, January 04). The Vanir gods and goddesses. Retrieved October 16, 2022, from https://mythologysource.com/vanir-gods-and-goddesses/

3. Friscia, M. (2021, March 29). Bragi: History and worship of the Norse god of music. Retrieved October 16, 2022, from https://www.uncoveringsound.com/bragi-history-worship-of-the-norse-god-of-music/

4. Greenberg, M., Dr. (2021, July 06). Who was Baldur in Norse mythology? Retrieved October 16, 2022, from https://mythologysource.com/baldur-norse-god/

5. Greenberg, M., Dr. (2022, January 04). Who was Frey in Norse mythology? Retrieved October 16, 2022, from https://mythologysource.com/freyr-norse-god/

6. Greenberg, M., Dr. (2021, January 18). Freya: The Norse Goddess of Beauty and Magic. Retrieved October 16, 2022, from https://mythologysource.com/freya-norse-goddess/

7. McCoy, D. (2018, July 06). Heimdall. Retrieved October 16, 2022, from https://norse-mythology.org/gods-and-creatures/the-aesir-gods-and-goddesses/heimdall/

8. Frigg – the goddess of marriage. (n.d.). Retrieved October 16, 2022, from https://historiska.se/norse-mythology/frigg-en/

9. McCoy, D. (2017, July 09). Hel (goddess). Retrieved October 16, 2022, from https://norse-mythology.org/gods-and-creatures/giants/hel/

10. Scott, J., Lagana, N., Mary, Aj, Schexnayder, S., & Crystal. (2021, October 08). Loki: The story of the trickster god. Retrieved October 17, 2022, from https://www.lifeinnorway.net/loki-norse-mythology/

11. Apel, T. (2021, November 18). Njord. Retrieved October 17, 2022, from https://mythopedia.com/topics/njord

12. McCoy, D. (2018, June 30). Odin. Retrieved October 17, 2022, from https://norse-mythology.org/gods-and-creatures/the-aesir-gods-and-goddesses/odin/

13. Thor: The god of thunder: Norse mythology. (2022, July 20). Retrieved October 17, 2022, from https://skjalden.com/thor/

14. Norman. (2022, May 10). Tyr. Retrieved October 17, 2022, from https://thenorsegods.com/tyr/

15. Bragi: History and worship of the Norse god of music. (2021, March 29). Retrieved October 17, 2022, from

https://www.uncoveringsound.com/bragi-history-worship-of-the-norse-god-of-music/

THE CREATURES OF NORSE MYTHOLOGY

1. McKay, A., Ivan, Vanoy, S., Minseo, O'Coileain, D., Draconian, . . . Bakken, T. (2021, October 08). Creatures in Norse mythology. Retrieved October 17, 2022, from https://www.lifeinnorway.net/creatures-in-norse-mythology/

2. Rhys, D. (2022, September 21). 15 unique creatures of Norse mythology. Retrieved October 17, 2022, from https://symbolsage.com/norse-mythology-creatures-list/

THE AFTERLIFE

1. Mark, J. (2022, November 01). Norse ghosts & the afterlife. Retrieved October 17, 2022, from https://www.worldhistory.org/article/1290/norse-ghosts--the-afterlife/

2. The multi-part soul. (n.d.). Retrieved October 18, 2022, from https://skaldskeep.com/norse/soul/

3. McCoy, D. (2017, July 09). Death and the afterlife. Retrieved October 18, 2022, from https://norse-mythology.org/concepts/death-and-the-afterlife/

4. S., J. (2022, October 14). Norse mythology afterlife: Afterlife in norse mythology: Norse afterlife realms. Retrieved October 18, 2022, from https://blog.vkngjewelry.com/en/norse-afterlife/

5. The afterlife of norse mythology compared to the afterlife of Greek mythology. (2021, May 05). Retrieved October 18, 2022, from https://www.grin.com/document/1025978

DIVINING RUNE WISDOM

1. McCoy, D. (2018, July 04). Runes. Retrieved October 18, 2022, from https://norse-mythology.org/runes/

2. Talisa + Sam | Two Wander. (2022, September 27). Rune meanings and how to use rune stones for divination. Retrieved October 18, 2022, from https://www.twowander.com/blog/rune-meanings-how-to-use-runestones-for-divination

3. Chamberlain, L. (2018). *Runes for beginners: A guide to reading runes in divination, rune magic, and the meaning of the elder futhark runes.* Santa Barbara, CA: Chamberlain Publications.

4. Bernott, K. (2021, March 22). The elder futhark runes and their meanings. Retrieved October 18, 2022, from http://www.shieldmaidenssanctum.com/blog/2019/3/12/the-elder-futhark-runes-and-their-meanings

5. The Pagan Grimoire. (2022, August 13). Your guide to the 24 elder futhark runes and their meanings. Retrieved October 18, 2022, from https://www.pagangrimoire.com/elder-futhark-rune-meanings/

RITES OF PASSAGE

1. Silver, A. (1970, January 01). Rites of passage: Birth. Retrieved October 18, 2022, from http://nordicwiccan.blogspot.com/2012/12/rites-of-passage-birth.html

2. Rite of birth: The-Ásatrú-community. (n.d.). Retrieved October 18, 2022, from https://www.theÁsatrúcommunity.org/rite-of-birth

3. Ruth Morales, V. (2021, August 20). A guide to Viking wedding rituals & traditions. Retrieved October 18, 2022, from https://www.yeahweddings.com/viking-wedding-traditions/

4. Harvey, S. (2021, November 08). An insight into Viking wedding and Norse wedding traditions. Retrieved October 18, 2022, from https://scandification.com/viking-wedding-and-norse-wedding-traditions/

5. Tomlin, A. (2022, October 01). All you need to know about Viking weddings. Retrieved October 18, 2022, from https://www.routesnorth.com/language-and-culture/all-you-need-to-know-about-viking-weddings/

PRACTICING MODERN PAGANISM

1. Staff, Sigurþórsdóttir, S., Gunnarsson, O., & Helgason, M. (n.d.). 11 things to know about the present day practice of ásatrú, the ancient religion of the Vikings. Retrieved October 18, 2022, from https://icelandmag.is/article/11-things-know-about-present-day-practice-Ásatrú-ancient-religion-vikings

2. Lafayllve, P. M. (2013). *Practical heathens guide to Ásatrú*. Llewellyn.

3. Ember, C. (2015, October 29). What is Vanatru? who are the Vanir? Retrieved October 18, 2022, from https://embervoices.wordpress.com/2013/10/02/what-is-vanatru-who-are-the-vanir/

4. Rokkatru for dummies - magic forums. (2015, August 11). Retrieved October 18, 2022, from https://www.spellsofmagic.com/read_post.html?post=767428

5. What is Thursatru? (n.d.). Retrieved October 19, 2022, from https://thursatru.squarespace.com/whatisthursatru

6. Odinism. (n.d.). Retrieved October 19, 2022, from https://www.compellingtruth.org/Odinism.html

7. Lokeans for dummies. (2012, October 23). Retrieved October 19, 2022, from https://www.spellsofmagic.com/coven_ritual.html?ritual=2288&coven=628

8. What is Heathenry? (n.d.). Retrieved October 19, 2022, from http://heathengods.com/what/

9. Secunda, B. (2020, May 08). What is shamanism? Retrieved October 19, 2022, from https://www.shamanism.com/what-is-shamanism

10. Berger, H. (n.d.). What is Wicca? an expert on modern witchcraft explains. Retrieved October 18, 2022, from https://www.brandeis.edu/now/2021/september/wicca-berger-conversation.html

FREE GIFT JUST FOR YOU

FREE NORSE GOD & GODDESSES CALENDAR
Use this link https://norsepaganwisdom.info/squeeze-page1679502439646
OR
Scan the QR code below for your FREE Calendar NOW!

INTRODUCTION

I have always been a big believer in magic. I think that we take a lot of things for granted that are no less magical than they were a thousand years ago. Take memory, for instance. How amazing is it that we can recall something and have it play in front of our mind's eye while we're living in a completely different moment? Dreams—where do they come from? How is it that sometimes we can foresee the future in them?

And for those of us who do not have dreams and memories of the days of yore, we have these compact little dimensions of magic that line millions of shelves in libraries all over the world, these volumes of pages that can instantly make us hallucinate another time, another people, another tale. As Stephen King said, books are a uniquely portable magic.

Ever since I learned how to read, I've been portal-hopping into different times, learning about the legends of yesteryear and long-lost cultures.

I hoped to write such books one day and write two of them, I did. Both were about a subject that has long been near and dear to my heart. Ever since I was a little girl, I was fascinated by the stories of the Norse gods and goddesses, likening myself to Freya, she of the cats. I even had a makeshift chariot that I used to tether my cats to, hoping that they'd somehow transport me from my home in Kungsträdgården all the way to the past when gods like Odin and Thor oversaw the affairs of the Vikings when goddesses like Freya and Idunn blessed others with fertility and immortality.

Becoming a Norse Pagan and practicing paganism allowed me to bring that magic into my life by understanding Old Norse history, learning more about the gods, finding ways to venerate them, putting runes to work in my daily life, and understanding the mysticism of Norse magic.

And that is what it all comes back to—magic. Raw, unbridled magic.

In this book, I hope to help you unlock the ancient magic of Norse holidays, festivals, and celebrations, creating a splice in the space-time continuum to help you travel to a past of roaring fires over which boars were roasted, flagons filled with ales being drunk by hearty men with braided beards, brawny Vikings brandishing their battle-axes and calling for the All-Father's aid before diving headfirst into the ranks of their enemies, and practitioners of holy but dangerous magic performing rituals like seidr and spa to lift the veil from the future and peer into the possibilities of tomorrow.

Close your eyes. Imagine yourself standing at the cusp of a jet blue fjord, deep green hills all around you, the sky lumbering with heavy gray rainclouds, lightning flashing from behind those clouds, thunder rumbling deep in the vastness of the firmament, and those longships sailing down the fjord, carrying dozens of Norse warriors returning from a brave battle.

This is not just a vision. This is the memory of the world trying to make its way to you through these words. More than a thousand years ago, when myth was material, and the fibers of fables wove the fabric of reality, the Norse people lived fully actualized lives, had their daily routines, their customs passed through to them by their forefathers, and their celebrations to mark special occasions where mirth and merriment were called for.

That is where I'm taking you. Perhaps you shall see behind a tree the shapeshifter god of mischief, Loki, lurking, conspiring, thinking about how to take down Baldur. Maybe that grim bearded figure with the long cane is more than an old man in a busy marketplace. Notice his eyepatch and his intensity? Those ravens perched nearby? This could be the god of gods, Odin.

You are nearly there.

Step past the threshold and join the old gods and the old Norse people. Peer into their lives, learn how they used to brave hardships and celebrate their victories with flamboyant feasts while regaling each other with verses of skaldic poetry, and finally, become a part of them in spirit by celebrating those sacred days with a community of like-minded modern-day paganists who have revived the ancient magic, the same magic that shall now course through you.

Over the course of this book, we shall go over the Norse calendar, understand their division of the year into months, and see which celebrations and traditions they observed in which month. We shall take the pagan calendar and elucidate the festivals and sacred days within, starting with an overview and history of that particular holiday, the rituals followed in honor of that day, and related recipes and lore concerning that day.

Some prominent holidays observed by the Norse Pagans include Midsummer, Yule, and blóts which venerate Thor, Odin, Freya, the ancestors, and Valkyries. Different times of the year marked different celebrations depending upon occasions like harvesting, the heralding of summer, and to mark the end of the year.

After you've read this book, you will have an appreciation of the Norse culture and all it entails, including, in large part, the holidays, traditions, and various celebrations. You'll understand the importance of venerating the gods and goddesses through these rituals and festivals and learn how doing so can open a two-way communication channel that you can utilize to attain the gods' favor. Most importantly, you will be able to celebrate the Norse traditions like a true pagan.

A soft prerequisite for reading this book would be to understand the basics of Norse Paganism and Norse Mythology and know the lore of the gods and goddesses. Throughout this book, I will occasionally touch base with you and define words like blót, sumbel, seidr, and so on so that this book is inclusive for all readers. Wherever it is needed, I shall fill you in on the backstory of the Norse gods in context with the celebration.

So, without further ado, let us travel back in time to Scandinavia in the Viking Age.

Come, it's almost time for a feast and some good mead.

CHAPTER 1
THE NORSE CALENDAR

I f you asked someone their age back in ancient Norse times, they would tell you that they were a certain number of winters old. A child would say that he had lived through ten winters. This is just one of the characteristics of the Norse calendar, which was based on the seasons. The year was divided into months based on where the sun was in the sky, whether food was available or not, and the fertility of the land.

Scandinavia was home to some of the most extreme weather conditions, particularly in the winters. The year, reflecting that, was divided into summer and winter, both periods equally long.

Unlike how we celebrate New Year's, the Norse folk observed April 14th as the start of the new year, what with it being the first summer day as well.

The Norse calendar was considered lunisolar, utilizing both the sun's and moon's positions to mark days and months.

The modern Gregorian calendar follows an absolute chronology. For instance, this year is 2023 C.E. At any given time, a person can state absolutely that it's been x number of years, and the people would automatically understand their reference, making it easier to recall things in a uniform matter.

The Norse people, on the other hand, used relative chronology. They used to denote the number of years after certain important events. For instance, if there had been a great battle, they'd use that as a reference in time and say that it has been "two winters since that great Battle of Skellige."

It was not until the early 1100s that an Icelander named Ari "the Wise" Þorgilsson tried to get people to use absolute chronology.

Since it was a lunisolar calendar, the year was divided into phases of the moon, i.e. from full moon to full moon or new moon to new moon. Basing their division on moon sightings was not particularly accurate for the people, as nights in Scandinavia used to be quite bright, making it difficult to find the moon.

Picture it for a moment—the aurora borealis in all its cyano-green splendor dancing across the horizon, the rich tapestry of the Milky Way shining from on high, the lights from the stars shimmering in the sky. It's no wonder that the Norse Pagans held firmly to the belief that the sky was made from Ymir the giant's skull, and these stars were sparks captured from the fiery realm of Muspelheim, set into the dome-like jewels by the Gods Odin, Vili, and Ve.

THE DIVISION OF THE YEAR

The brightest period of the year, known also as the nightless time, was called Nóttleysa. Another interpretation of that word would be insomnia. These were the months we now know as May, June, July, August, September, and October. The time of the year these months coincide with was called sumar, as in summer. The sun was considered to be the bringer of warmth, light, and life. When it was high in the sky, that's when the Norse folk worked on their lands to grow crops.

The darkest period also called the period of short days, was known as Skammdegi. November, December, January, February, March, and April fall into the category of these vetur (winter) months.

The Old Icelandic calendar had its own names for the months and sometimes added a 13th month to make adjustments in the calendar. This month was called Silðemanuður, the Late Month. The Norse people also added four extra days in the middle of summer, calling them Sumarauki. As every month was 30 days long, these extra four days brought the day count of the year to 364, which is precisely 52 weeks. However, in leap years, instead of four days, seven extra days were added to Samarauki, making the year 53 weeks long.

The summer months were called Harpa, Skerpla, Sólmánuður, Heyannir, Tvímánuður, and Haustmánuður.

The winter months were called Gormánuður, Ýlir, Mörsugur, Þorri, Goa, and Einmánuður.

Each month in the Norse Calendar always started with the same day of the week.

SOLSTICES AND EQUINOXES

Solstices and equinoxes had a lot of importance in those days and affected the calendar, marked many of the celebrations, and were used as predictors for the arrival of different seasons as well. As Scandinavia was in the far north, these equinoxes and solstices were more noticeable there than anywhere else. For that reason, the equinoxes and solstices served as markers for significant celebrations such as blóts.

The Spring equinox served as a herald for Sumarmál, also known as the coming of summer. It marked the last days of the winter half of the year. Around this time, the food reserves of the people would have been running low, and they'd have desperately needed for summer to come. Sumarmál therefore served as a celebrative time to rejoice the end of hardship and for the arrival of ease. People used to move out from the confines of their homes, take in the daylight and the warmth of the sun, and schedule trading, travel, raiding, and feasting.

The Summer solstice marked Miðsumar (aka Midsummer). The Miðsumar blót has been noted in Snorri Sturlusson's sagas, stating that it lined with both the Norse religious beliefs and also with celebrating the bounties that summer brought.

The Autumn equinox served as the reminder that summer had ended and now winter had arrived. One of the most documented celebrations of this time of the year is

Vetrarnætr, Winter Nights. This time of the year coincided with the first winter month, which made it the ripe time to slaughter animals, salt and smoke them for the purpose of storing them for the winter ahead, and for stocking up their food reserves. This time of the year was also a popular time for weddings.

The Winter Solstice marked Miðvetr, Midwinter, which was a time for the Yule celebration. And yes, it's the same Yule that was later adopted by Christianity while still retaining many of its pagan rites. Originally, Yule was a celebration to mark the passing of winter. A blót was held to venerate the gods and ask for growth, good fortune, and bounties in the upcoming year. People would brew and drink Yule ale, gather around a roaring fire, and drink to their hearts' fill while cheering each other and venerating the gods.

THE CALENDAR MONTHS

Let us take a brief look at the Norse Calendar months before delving into them deeper in the upcoming chapters. The calendar was divided into two parts: Skammdegi, the winter months, and Nóttleysa, the summer months.

Skammdegi, also known as Vetur or Dark Days

Gormánuður (14th October to 13th November) Slaughtering Month

The first month of winter was called slaughtering month or butchering month. On the first day of this month, a winter blót was held to venerate Freyr and to thank him for his fertile bounties of the summer harvest. It's in this month that people start stocking up on animals and storing them for the upcoming months. That's how it got its name.

Ýlir (14th November to 13th December) Yule Month

This was the second winter month, also known as the Yule Month. The word Yule comes from one of Odin's names, Jólnir, which bore the word Jól. According to Norse Mythology, Odin traveled around Midgard and visited the locals. The kids used to fill their socks with hay for Odin's eight-legged steed, Sleipnir. In exchange, the white-bearded god would give them gifts in return. Sound familiar?

This month is also related to fertility and was a time that related to the cultivation of the earth.

Falling in winter, Ylir was also one of the darkest months. People spent most of their time indoors by the fire, eating the food they had harvested earlier that year.

Mörsugur (14th December to 12th January) Fat Sucking Month

During this month, the Norse folk provided nourishment to themselves by sucking on animal fat or bone marrow. Winter solstice is held this month, mostly on the 21st of December.

Some accounts differ, stating that the reason this month got its name was because the cold winters and short days literally sucked the light out of the people, making them resort to use candles made from tallows.

Þorri (13th January to 11th February) Frozen Snow Month

Þorri is the fourth winter month. It's when the Þorriablót is held. Women of the household invited Þorri, the winter spirit, into their house. This month was also a time when men were celebrated for their actions. They could choose a day for celebration, but warily. If the weather on that day was terrible, it was said to be a bad omen for the men.

Historically and traditionally, special dishes like sheep heads, rotten shark, meat jelly made from lamb's head, ram testicles, and other acquired taste delicacies were consumed during this time. Why? Because at this time of the year, the rations of the Norse people had run out of perishables. These hardier foods remained preserved for longer and provided the essential nutrients that the Norse folk needed to survive during this time.

Gói (12th February to 13th March) Sowing Month

The daughter of Þorri was known as Gói. The fifth month of winter was named after her and a blót was held in her honor. Additionally, this month was also considered women's month, just like the previous one was considered men's month. Men looked after their wives and celebrated women's achievements. It was also a time for planting the seeds for the incoming summer.

Einmánuður (14th March to 13th April) Lone Month

This month was dedicated to young boys. The month got its name because it was the last winter month. March 21st was considered to be the Vernal Equinox. On this day, a feast took place to celebrate fertility.

Nóttleysa, also known as Sumr or Nightless Days

Harpa (14th April to 13th May) Gaukmanadur

The first of the summer months, Harpa was dedicated to girls just like the three previous months were dedicated to men, women, and boys. The third biggest blót, also called the summer blót, was held this month to venerate Odin. This blót was meant to ensure victory in battles and wars, and happiness and tranquility in long travels.

Skerpla (14th May to 12th June)

Presumably named after a forgotten Norse deity, the second month of summer was considered the nesting season for birds. People in Iceland used to pick up those eggs for eating. It's interesting to note that it's considered illegal to do that nowadays in Iceland.

Another important facet of this month was the newborn lambs, who used to run free in the fields to suckle from their mothers. At night, the farmers used to milk the ewes in pens.

Sólmánuður (13th June to 12th July)

The summer solstice was observed in this month. It falls on the 21st of June these days. This month was named after the sun and was considered to be the lightest period in the entire year. Heads of households used to assemble and discuss political matters in this month, voting on different decisions. Given that it was the brightest time of the year, it was common for people to get married in this month.

Heyannir (13th July to 14th August) Hay Collecting Month

This month marked the midsummer. During this month, people used to gather hay, mow their grasses, water their plants, collect ferns, and stored fruit that couldn't bud.

Tvímánuður (15th August to 14th September) Corn Cutting Month

During this month, grain was harvested and corn was cut. Its name means the second to last month before winter. For the Norse people, harvesting was an important part of their designation, as this was dependent on the weather. They counted on the weather to be good so that they'd be able to harvest.

Haustmánuður (15th September to 13th October) Autumn Month

The last month of summer was also when the Autumnal Equinox was observed. Today, it falls on the 21st of September. This month was a reminder for people to be done with harvesting and get ready for the harsh winter months that lay ahead. Blóts for gods and goddesses like Sif, Thor, Gerdr, Freya, and Freyr were common during this month to thank them for the harvest and for providing people with the necessary means to survive the winter.

NORSE DAYS OF THE WEEK

The seven days of the week were named after different gods, except for Saturday, like so:

Monday — Manadagr (Moon Day)

The first day of the Norse week, Monday, was named after Mani, who had been punished to ride through the sky in his chariot forever. Mani had been named after a god who was considered way too brash. Mani was condemned to guide the course of the moon every night because of this. Mani is being pursued by a wolf who chases him across the horizon every night and ultimately catches him every night. And when that happens, the sun rises, and a new day begins.

Tuesday — Tysdagr (Tyr's Day)

Tyr, the OG god of war, patron of warriors, the lord of the sword, and the upholder of the law, was whom Tuesday was named after. It was agreed that if a war had to be started, the best day to do that was Tuesday.

Wednesday — Odinsdagr (Odin's Day)

Wednesday was named after the All-Father, the king of all the gods, the most powerful being in the Norse pantheon, the wisest of all deities, the diviner of mystical magic, and a patron of poetry.

Thursday — Þórsdagr (Thor's Day)

Thursday was named after Thor Odinson, the god of thunder and wielder of Mjolnir. When his chariot strode across the sky, thunder rumbled in the clouds, and lightning sparked from the wheels of the chariot.

Thursday was considered an excellent day for making decisions or holding meetings. This day, the day of the Midgard patron god, was also considered a very magical day.

Friday — Frjádagr (Freya or Frigg's Day)

Devoted to either Freya or Frigg, Friday was seen as a day to manifest the characteristics of the Norse goddesses—fertility, love, femininity, motherhood, and magic.

Saturday — Laugardagr (Laundry/Washing Day)

The Norse folk had set this day aside for taking baths and washing their clothes. It wasn't that they didn't take baths on other days of the week. It's just, Saturdays were sort of like their bath bomb, shower-gel, sit-back-in-the-tub-and-drink-wine kind of days.

The Norse folk, especially the Vikings, were famous for their hygiene. At one point, the English royalty, when they were being raided by the Vikings, became so afraid for their women, stating that the Vikings had such a rigorous hygiene routine—what with their braided and oiled hairs, their fresh smells, and their frequent bathing—that they were afraid their women would fall for them.

Sunday — Sunnudagr (Sun Day)

Sunday was named after Sol, Mani's sister, the goddess of the sun. Sol was also continuously being chased by a wolf who'd catch up with her at the end of every day, allowing her brother Mani to take to the skies and pull the moon.

Hopefully, by now, the Norse calendar, its associated days and months, and holidays are clear to you. Moving forward, we'll take a look at the major celebrations in each month and understand how they were celebrated, what sort of traditions were followed, and what each holiday signified.

CHAPTER 2
YULE

Yule remains one of the oldest pre-Christian Norse midwinter celebrations. The name is derived from the word hjol, which means wheel, serving to pinpoint the moment when the year's wheel is at the lowest point and is about to rise, as in the return of the sun from the wintery depths back into the sky. It's a harkening to summer, a time to wait for Baldur's return from the realm of Helheim. It is believed that upon his return, the winter grip on Midgard loosens, sending things back to their summer glory.

In 2023, it was celebrated on January 16-19. In 2024, it will begin on January 25 and will last three nights of the full moon.

The Icelandic sagas and other historical texts have given us descriptions of how Yule used to be celebrated. During this time, it was said that the veil between the living and the dead was at its thinnest.

Yule had 12 traditional days that began the festivities at the sunset of the winter solstice. And yes, you'd be right in connecting the dots. This, indeed, was a tradition stolen (alongside so many more others pertaining to Yule) in the name of Christmas and was distorted into what's now known as 12 days of Christmas.

The first night of Yule was a celebration for the Dísir and Frigga. It was called Mothernight. This night represented the rebirth of the world from this cavernous darkness back into the light. It was the shortest day of the year and the longest night. There was a vigil on this day, followed by a mothernight blót.

Odin, one of whose names is Jólnir (aka the Yule One), and all the other gods and goddesses were believed to be nearest to Earth at this time of the year. I almost feel forced to mention that the whole concept of Odin on Sleipnir descending upon Midgard and giving gifts and everything was also taken and morphed into the concept of Santa Claus.

Yule was also seen as the season during which the dead returned to earth and shared feasts with their beloved family members. Other creatures of fantasy, like elves, trolls, goblins, and fairies, also roamed around at this time of the year. They were either warded off for safety or had to be invited in for the sake of friendship and tranquility.

At this time of the year, Odin's horde of the dead rides most viciously. They can take you back to Hel if you cross their path. But it won't hurt if you put out food and drink for them, as the Wild Hunt isn't all evil. It can also come bearing gifts.

YULE CELEBRATIONS

Yule was celebrated by dancing, drinking, feasting, and hanging out with one's family. Some people used to burn sun wheels as part of the festivities going around. Some people used to swear oaths on holy boars. You read that right. There used to be boars that were hallowed for the sake of swearing oaths to. This particular thing survived in Swedish customs. They baked boar-shaped bread or carved blocks of wood shaped in the form of a boar and covered in pigskin for the purpose of Yule-oaths. Oh, and if that wasn't cute enough today, heathens bake boar-shaped cakes to make Yule-oaths to.

The more meaningful and promising of oaths and promises were taken during the feast or at the end of the sumbel. At the risk of sounding pedantic, here I'll note for the third time that the whole new year's resolution concept is a watered-down version of the Yule-oath.

As is the decoration of the house with fir or pine trees. That used to be a Germanic custom as well. The tree represented Yggdrasil. As is the Yule log, which was supposed to burn all night to symbolize the resilience of life and light in the face of cold and darkness. People used to use the ashes of the Yule log as amulets to wear for the rest of the year.

The 12 days of Yule were marked by making bread, cookies, cakes, and decorations. This is a custom that you can still put into practice during those twelve days. Each day was viewed as a miniature version of each month of the year.

Thor was also honored and venerated during Yule for driving back the frost giants. As was Frey, for giving us fertility and prosperity in the past year and the upcoming year. Odin was revered as the god of all and the leader of the Wild Hunt.

CELEBRATING YULE LIKE A PAGAN

You can get started with the simplest and most convenient tradition. Bring a fir or pine tree and decorate it. At its core, this remains a pagan tradition. The tree here represents the Yggdrasil—something that many religions have tried to emulate.

A Yule log is another great way to celebrate Yule. You can find a great oak log and set it ablaze in your fireplace or as a bonfire. You can use its ashes to use for lighting next year's log.

Next up, you can host two different Yule blóts if you're in the mood for festivities. One can be a Mothernight blót in honor of Frigg, and the other can be a Midwinter night blót in honor of Thor.

Any oath that you swear on Yule is considered unbreakable according to pagan law. So, whatever oaths you do make during the feast, sumbel, or drinking, you have to be very mindful of your words because the gods are watching.

Besides the Yule feasting, blóts, and offerings, one last important part of the celebrations was brewing ale and drinking it. If you're not particularly fond of making your own mead, there's always store-bought mead that you can drink to commemorate this special celebration.

Oh, and one last thing. Yule was a time for giving gifts. The Norse people were big on giving gifts to each other, and this was especially observed during Yule.

CHAPTER 3
YULE RECIPES

KRANSEKAKE

A TRADITIONAL SCANDINAVIAN YULE DESSERT IS KRANSEKAKE, A RING-SHAPED CAKE MADE OF SEVERAL CONCENTRIC RINGS OF ALMOND CAKE AND TOPPED WITH WHITE ICING AND SUGAR-COATED ALMONDS.

INGREDIENTS

Dough
- 8 ounces (2 cups) sliced blanched almonds
- 3 cups confectioners' sugar
- 1/2 teaspoon coarse salt
- 2 large egg whites
- Unsalted butter, softened, for molds

Icing
- 1 pound confectioners' sugar
- 3 large egg whites or five tablespoons meringue powder mixed with 1/2 cup water
- Paste or gel food coloring (optional)

DIRECTIONS

1. Grind almonds with a grinder or food processor
2. In a bowl, mix in almonds just ground with sugar. Once mixed well, add in the two egg whites and mix. (There will be a point when using your hands to mix makes sense because of the texture of the dough.) Once it gets like this, put a piece of plastic wrap on top and place it in the fridge for at least 3 hours
3. Now that it's cold, the dough will be easier to mold. Roll the dough until it becomes one finger thick, about a ½ inch.
4. Preheat the oven to 200C.
5. You use molds or draw rings out on a piece of parchment paper. Make 18 rings of the right size so they can rest on each other. Once you place the dough rings in molds or on parchment paper – put them in the fridge for 15 minutes to harden (8-10 min middle shelf)
6. Make icing:
   a. Combine confectioners' sugar and egg whites in the bowl or in an electric mixer fitted with the paddle attachment). Mix on medium-high speed until combined and thickened, about 8 minutes
   b. If decorating with more than one color, divide the icing into batches. Using the end of a toothpick, add food coloring until the desired shade is achieved
7. Assemble rings to make a tower. Use the icing to help them stick together
8. Serve and enjoy!

POLKAGRISKOLA
SWEDISH PEPPERMINT CARAMELS

INGREDIENTS

- •4ounces hard peppermint candies
- 1 ¼cups heavy cream
- 1cup superfine sugar
- 6tablespoons golden syrup (British) or 6 tablespoons dark corn syrup
- 3tablespoons honey
- 7tablespoons unsalted butter

DIRECTIONS

- Put the peppermint candies into a plastic bag and crush them coarsely with the flat side of a meat mallet. Using a large sieve, sift candy pieces, discarding fine powder; set candy pieces aside.
- Line the bottom of an 8"x8" baking pan with parchment paper; grease parchment paper with nonstick cooking spray and set aside.
- Heat cream, sugar, syrup, and honey in a 6-inch diameter 2-quart saucepan over medium heat; stir until sugar dissolves, about 5 minutes. Bring to a boil and attach a candy thermometer to the side of the pan; cook, without stirring, until mixture reaches 250 F, about 45 minutes. Remove pan from the heat and add butter. Using a wooden spoon, stir until smooth, about 3 minutes.
- Pour toffee mixture onto prepared baking pan and sprinkle evenly with peppermint candy peices, pressing them lightly into toffee with the back of a spatula. Let cool completely; cut into 64 squares to serve.

Enjoy!

CHAPTER 4
DISABLÓT

Disablót is a pagan festival that honors the Norse goddesses, spirits, and ancestors. Collectively, the latter two are called Dísir. The word itself is a concatenation of Dísir and blót.

As a festival, disablót was more associated with harvesting. Like Sígrblót, this was held in a very private manner within one's house as a way to honor one's female ancestors and the female goddesses and spirits that looked over one's family.

That being said, there was not exactly a specific day for this sacrificial holiday. It could have been held during winter nights. Some accounts state that it took place at the beginning of February.

HOW WAS DISABLÓT CELEBRATED

Historically, it was a day for venerating one's female ancestors and deities. The people did this by setting up alters and setting out offerings of their favorite drinks, food, and tokens. It was a time when female deities like Freya, Frigg, Skadi, and Sif were invoked so that they'd look over the people and grant their favor. It wasn't just reserved for the deities. The Norns, as in the sisters who shaped the fate of everything, were also venerated during this time, as were the Valkyries, spirits who took the fallen soldiers to Valhalla.

The blót was very family oriented, from what we can tell from the historical sagas. As it was family-focused, both old pagans and modern heathens today observe some part of this in the privacy of their homes.

The disablót was described in Olaf Hraldsson's saga as:

> *"In Sweden there was an age-old custom whilst they were still heathen that there should be a blood offering in Uppsala during Góa-month. Then they would sacrifice for peace and victory for their king. And thither would they come from all over Sweden. There also were all the Swedish things. There was besides a market and a fair, and it lasted a week. But when Christianity came to Sweden they still kept the law thing and the market there. And when Christianity prevailed throughout Sweden and the kings no longer sat in Uppsala, the market was shifted and held at Candlemas. It has always been held then ever since, but now it does not last more than three days."*

In the Ynglinga saga, it was said:

> *"King Adils was at a sacrifice to the goddesses (Dísir) and rode on his horse around the temple; the horse stumbled under him and fell; so the king also rolled over, and his head fell against a stone, so that his skull burst and his brains lay on the stone.*

> *That was his death; he died in Uppsala and there is now his howe. The Swedes called him a mighty king."*

The other traditional part of this blót was called charming the plow. It was when farming equipment, seeds, and the farming fields were blessed and charmed so that they'd grow plenty of harvest during the summer.

HOW YOU CAN CELEBRATE DISABLÓT

This is a day for all the women in your life, not just your wives and partners. It can serve as a day where you appreciate your mother, aunts, sisters, and daughters. There's a certain divinity in femininity, especially within Norse Paganism. From the magical rite of giving birth to the transcendental duty of bringing the brave dead to Valhalla, there have been various ethereal acts that women have done in Norse Mythology.

Frigg, the mother of Baldur, did everything she could to ensure that her son would be unharmed by every single being in the world. She took an oath from every single creature and unliving thing as well so that they would not harm her son. That is just one example from hundreds where deities of Norse Mythology have shown their quality.

You can venerate individual female deities today, such as:

- Freya for fertility
- Idun for her fruitful bounties
- Eir for growth, nurturing, and healing
- Frigg, for courage, hearth, and wisdom
- Sif for sustenance

You can light a candle at your altar for your female ancestors and the goddesses. If there's a feast or a gathering at your house for this blót, share stories of the women in your life, tell the remarkable tales of the goddesses and the dísir. Did your loved ones leave any recipes? Perhaps some special recipe for chicken pot pie by your grandmother or the perfect brisket by your nana? It can be an excellent time to cook such a meal and offer some of that food with some wine to your female forebears.

If you're in the mood, there's always a bonfire that you can light to sit around, drink, and share stories of your female ancestors.

Pray to the dísir. They're listening to you. You've held this blót in their honor. Now you have their ear. Ask for help. Seek their counsel for whatever troubles you're facing. You can pray for protection on your life's journey.

Lastly, you can keep the dísir in your mind and do something that would make the goddesses, the Dísir, and your ancestors proud.

CHAPTER 5
ÞORRABLÓT

This Norse festival used to take place in the month of Þorri, which, as we saw from the first chapter, took place between January and February. This year, in 2023, it was celebrated from January 20th to February 18th. If you'd put yourself in the shoes of the Norse folk, you can imagine how they must have felt by then, what with being smack in the middle of winter. It must have been tiring for them to brave through that harsh weather without many resources. And as we'll see in this chapter, the resources that they did have were very harsh in nature.

WHAT WAS ÞORRABLÓT?

Today, Þorrablót is still celebrated in Iceland as a cultural celebration. For Norse Pagans, this is a time to celebrate the winter spirit Þorri.

Þorrablót was seen as a midwinter sacrificial celebration wherein offerings were made to Þorri and the Norse gods.

After the Christianization of Scandinavia, it was abolished, with its traces just left in historical texts. But old roots run deep, and if given time, they resurface, just like Þorrablót resurfaced late in the 19th century, and it is still being celebrated by pagans all over the world.

Simply put, like other blóts, this blót was considered a sacramental feast. Þorri was seen as this personification of the Scandinavian winter, often depicted as being brute, merciless, and cold. In the Orkneyinga saga, Þorri (his name literally meaning "frost") was said to be a Finnish King to whom early offerings were made at midwinter.

Other sources state that this blót was in honor of Thor. But there's a disagreement between both theories. Some say that Thor and Þorri are one and the same and that Þorri is just the post-Christian version of Thor.

The celebration of Þorrablót comes at the start of Bóndadagur, a day reserved for celebrating husbands, and ends with Konudagur, a day for celebrating women or wives.

As for why it was celebrated, the historical consensus is that it was meant to be this reinforcing event where people would bolster their spirits with traditional food, give each other the encouragement they needed, and acknowledge and venerate Þorri, letting him know that the Norse folk's spirits had not died down in this winter and that they acknowledged the fact that he was a necessary force of nature, and not something vile. And if this celebration was meant for Thor, it was because he protected Midgard folk from the Rime-Thurses, aka the frost giants, in those vulnerable winter months.

Þorrablót was also celebrated to await the arrival of summer.

As with any blót, the celebration included copious amounts of alcohol and meats. But these meats and delicacies differed from the regular menu at other blóts.

Interestingly enough, the weird selection of food was one of the factors that caused this celebration to be revived in Reykjavik in the 1950s when a restaurant started offering food that was exclusive to the Icelandic countryside.

HOW WAS IT CELEBRATED?

With lots and lots of bizarre cuisine, that's how. And for good reason. With the blót taking place in the middle of winter, people used to come together in each other's houses for drinking, eating, roasting, toasting, and loads of merriment. Traditionally, this was a time not for plundering, pillaging, raiding, or hunting; this was a time to sit by the fire, be with one's family, and survive through the cold and dark days of winter.

Because of the timing of this blót, much in the way of food was not available, with the only available food being pickled and smoked produce left over from the previous year.

What kind of produce? Well, there was rotten shark's meat, congealed sheep's blood in a ram's stomach, boiled sheep's head, blood pudding, sour ram's testicles, liver-suet sausage, headcheese, and whale blubber.

After eating this food, it was washed down with strong alcohol. In modern times, Brennivin, also known as Icelandic schnapps, is drunk after all that food.

The reason for this peculiar assortment of food was because these parts of the animals were tough, didn't rot or decay or soften as much, and were hardy enough to survive through the winter, although they were preserved in fermented whey. This fermented whey is used to break down the proteins in the food, making it tender and more easily palatable.

Another reason for this strange buffet was that the Norse folk utilized all parts of an animal, especially in winter, wasting nothing. That's why body parts like the stomach, head, testicles, brain, and intestines were used.

HOW YOU CAN CELEBRATE IT

If you are a vegetarian or are averse to the strong aforementioned seafood, you can avoid the meats in favor of vegetables, bread, or other favorable food while remembering the spirit of this celebration.

It's about being close to your family in tough times. Back in those days, winter was no laughing matter. The Norse folk did not have the same luxuries that we do, which meant that the mortality rate was quite high. But they did not let their hardships deter them; rather, they found purpose in these hardships, celebrated the fact that they braved them, and became closer to one another.

You can host a dinner for your friends and family, followed by a round or two of drinks. After that, how about an intimate sumbel where you and your friends and family can venerate the gods and remember the ancestors? There can be singing, dancing, telling tales, playing group games, and whatever way of merriment suits you best.

Back in the old days, Þorrablót used to be a very lively affair with performances, singing, poetry reading, and dancing. If you're in the mood for something more festive than a home dinner, how about assembling with fellow neo-pagans to celebrate Þorrablót with a communal spirit?

More than any other celebration, Þorrablót was one where traditional cuisine came into play and continues to be an important part of the festival. It's an example of how history, culture, and creed can be preserved in forms other than written and spoken; it can also be stored in food.

CHAPTER 6
BÓNDADAGUR AND KONUDAGUR

The months of Þorri and Góa had celebrations for men and women respectively. The men's version —or husband's day—was called Bóndadagur and the women's version was called Konudagur.

In the modern calendar, Bóndadagur falls on the 21st of January and Konudagur falls on the 18th of February.

BÓNDADAGUR

On this day, the men of the house were treated, celebrated, and pampered.

On the morning of Bóndadagur, the man was supposed to go out of his house dressed in just a shirt, with one leg of his trouser dragging the other one behind. While hopping on one leg, the man would go and hop from house to house, rousing other men and greeting Þorri.

On this day, the man's wife was supposed to take more care of him than usual, offering him the delicacies of the season, spending time with him, and indulging him. For the women, it was a chance to show their appreciation for all that the men had done over the year. Women were also known to give their men presents or gifts, particularly something that related to their profession.

Because of their vicinity, Þorrablót and Bóndadagur have had similar themes in the past, especially when it comes to food. In the old days, the only cuisine available to the Norse folk during this time was hardy, fermented food like ram testicles, lamb's head, blood sausage, dried fish, and blubber.

The revival of this day has seen new traditions in Iceland, where instead of offering their men the aforementioned foods, women prepare more traditional dishes, take their men out on a date, and buy them presents. Still, some tradition has managed to seep into the modern version of man's day. Women in Iceland cook smoked lamb called hangikjot for their men.

This was often seen as a time for reciprocity. The men appreciated what their women did for them, and made sure to pay it back the next month on Women's Day or Konudagur.

Traditionally, this was a day when men flaunted themselves in feats of strength. After a feast, the men would get together and playfully fight with each other, participate in tug-of-war competitions, and race each other around the commune.

If you're wondering how you can celebrate this day (as a female), plan a special day for the special man in your life. It does not have to conform to something traditional. Most men are very individualistic when it comes to preferences. Perhaps your partner is an introvert who does not like going out and partying as much as he likes sitting by the fire, reading a book, or watching a movie with you.

A nice way to celebrate this day would be to make him a meal that he likes. If he likes hanging out with his friends, have him do that. Maybe invite all of his friends over to catch a game on the TV.

KONUDAGUR

Women's Day, or konudagur, was celebrated in Góa. Góa was the daughter of Þorri and the great-grandaughter of Frosti. Once upon a time, she took a fancy to a boy during Þorrablót and ran away with him. Her father was so worried about her that he sacrificed to the gods to find out where his daughter had gone. That sacrifice took on the name of Góublót.

In that spirit, konudagur used to be celebrated. It was a time when the women of the house were appreciated by the men. Their husbands used to bring them flowers, gifts, and trinkets. For the men, this was an opportunity to pay back the affection that they had received a month ago on Men's Day.

For the men, this was also a time to show appreciation towards the female goddesses, especially those who had to do with fertility and motherhood. They paid their respects to Frigg and Freya, who were considered goddesses of marriage, domesticity, motherhood, fertility, and love. As this was considered a blót, there was a traditional feast followed by drinking and toasting. The toasting, in this particular case, was for women and their feats throughout the year. Braving the winters was not just the man's business in the old days. The women had just as much responsibility during that time, from raising little children in the cold to providing hot meals to everyone in the house and so much more.

As a pagan, you can celebrate konudagur with your wife, girlfriend, or partner in the following ways:

- Learn about the history of the old Norse goddesses. It's a time for us to learn to be appreciative of the feminine side of divinity and how it manifests in the women around us.
- Treat your lady to a great night out, be there for her in ways that she wants, listen to her, and make her feel appreciated by giving her thoughtful presents.
- Become a part of the conversation about women's rights and gender equity and take the necessary steps to be an ally to those who are experiencing human rights hardships under the name of feminism.

If you're a woman, this can be a day:

- To treat yourself. Visiting a spa wouldn't exactly be out of tradition. Back in the olden days, women used to visit Icelandic hot water springs for a relaxing bath.
- To invite all your lady friends and host a gathering. Again, this is a very traditional thing that the women of yore used to do. They'd get

together for lunch, spill some Norse tea, and connect with each other as well as the goddesses. Getting together with other women can be a great way of harnessing female energy, reenergizing yourself, and reminding yourself of the resolve that you possess, that the legends of old such as the shieldmaidens and Valkyries possessed, and that the goddesses, benevolent and caring that they are, are looking over you.

CHAPTER 7
SÍGRBLÓT

Summer was now upon the Norse folk, and for them, this meant one thing—victory! They had braved through the sheer winter and had come out on the other side alive, jubilant, and their spirits undeterred. This holiday fell on the fourth full moon after the winter solstice. This year, it was held on April 6th.

WHAT IS SÍGRBLÓT?

In the Ynglinga saga, Odin proposed three holidays:

"There should be sacrifice towards winter for a good year, and in the middle of winter for a good crop, and a third in summer, that is the victory sacrifice."

The three holidays that Odin was referring to were Winter Nights, Yule, and Sígrblót.

This celebration was carried out in Odin's name and was dedicated to victory in war, good fortune on raids, and pleasant journeys. In his book about Norse Mythology,

John Lindow wrote that the summer ceremony was all about victory, not just in terms of post-winter victory, but a victory of every sort. Now that winter was over, the Vikings were getting ready to go on long journeys, prepare for battles, and make plans for raids. The departure of ships, the planning of attacks, and everything else came at a time when Sígrblót was being celebrated.

There's an interconnectedness between Sígrblót and the summer months. The last five days of the winter half of the year were called Sumarmál, which meant the summer portion. They were also known as Sumarnætr, meaning summer nights. Just like winter nights. Just as the Alfablót and Disablót were held during Vetrnætr, Sígrblót was celebrated during the Sumarnætr.

We cannot fully understand how important this time of the year was for our ancestors. Nature was being reborn, the trees got their leaves back, flowers started blossoming in the meadows, and the ice that had frozen over the lakes and bays started thawing, making it possible for the Vikings to move beyond their farmsteads.

If I may give a brief and relevant example, imagine the lockdown that we all had to collectively face during the COVID outbreak. We weren't able to get out of our houses, weren't able to socialize with friends and family members, and, more importantly, were kept from doing things that were important to us, such as our jobs. It was a time when we were all literally bound to our houses.

For the Norse folk, it was like that but worse. There was also the brutal cold, the lack of resources, and on top of that, no infrastructure of healthcare that could see them through their winter-borne diseases. It didn't last for a few weeks. It lasted for half the calendar year, this tempestuous time.

To come out of that, unscathed and alive, was cause enough for them to celebrate with each other. And that's why they celebrated Sígrblót with as much fervor as they did.

It was at this time of the year that the Norse folk saw the splendor of Freyr, Odin, and Baldur. Freyr blessed the people with summer bounties, made sure that the lands were fertile, and allowed the farmers to plant their crops so that they'd be ready for the upcoming months. Odin, by dint of his being a warrior god, saw over the affairs of the warriors and the fighters and bode them strength in their battles to come. The god of sunlight and splendor, Baldur, radiated his light everywhere, thawing the ice, nourishing the crops, and ensuring that the beauty of summer redeemed itself from the icy grip of winter.

HOW CAN I CELEBRATE IT?

One of the more profound ways in which we can get in touch with our ancestral roots is by putting ourselves in their shoes. Imagine yourself a Norse pagan in ancient Scandinavia. Now try to bring up the same feelings as a Norsemen would at the time of Sígrblót. They are happy that they can now see the sun in all its summer splendor. They want to greet the sun. So should you. Sígrblót is a three-day celebration that starts on the first Sun. Historically, people used to go and greet the sun by watching the first sunrise. They also happened to have warm drinks in hand.

You can do the same. Go with your friends or family, preferably after drinking an energizing warm beverage, and then go on a hike or a walk along the beach or in an open park. Here, you'll get your first sighting of the summer sun, and it should be a magnificent one. By Odin's beard, this is the same sun that your ancestors beheld all those thousands of years ago. And it is the same sun that you are witnessing.

A blót would not be complete without giving your offering to the gods. Remember Freyr, Freya, Odin, and Baldur during this particular blót. While traditionally, they used to offer animals and blood offerings, we understand that being a modern pagan means that some of the traditions have to be brought up to the times. Instead of meat or blood, think about making sacrifices at a makeshift altar, sacrifices containing wine, mead, or any special token that the aforementioned gods and goddesses loved.

Odin loved his ravens. Perhaps some raven feathers would be a good tribute for him?

Freyr loved his enchanted ship given to him by the dwarves. He also had a thing for boars. He'd certainly appreciate a maritime gift, perhaps one of those tiny ships in a bottle? You are allowed to be as creative as you desire.

Freya had a thing for cats (as don't we all?), and Baldur had a thing for beauty. Are you picking up what I'm laying down?

An offering was usually made by placing it at an altar and then verbally letting the god know that it was for them and for what purpose.

A blót would also not be considered complete without a blót feast. Your ancestors celebrated this particular day with a warm spirit. You can also enjoy a grand feast with your family. Heck, if the modern religions can have their Easters, Christmases, and Thanksgivings, we can have our Winter nights, Yule, and Sígrblót!

You can close off this blót with a round of sumbel. It's when everyone gathers around, passes a flagon or horn of mead, and toasts the gods, the ancestors, and the legends of yore. It's also the right time to share your stories with others and listen to their tales.

Lastly, Sígrblót is a wonderful time to set goals for the summer. It was a time when victory was sought from the gods. You can also seek victory for the goals that you set.

CHAPTER 8
MIDSUMMER

With its celebrations synonymous with Sweden, Norway, Finland, and Denmark, where it is observed as a national holiday, the festivities of Midsummer fall between the 19th of June to the 25th. It was a time to celebrate one's connectedness to the summer side of nature, the light, warmth, greenery, and fertility of the land. The pagans celebrated this occasion as a victory of light against dark, and thanked the gods and goddesses (namely Freyr, Freya, and Baldur) for the joys of summer. It was an occasion marked by bonfires, diverse foods, and rituals to ward off evil spirits. As this was the longest day in the year and the shortest night, this was the perfect time for such rituals.

They would light these huge bonfires to ward off darkness and all the bad forces that it contained. Plants were another magical aspect of this celebration. The utilization of green magic for attaining powers during the summer solstice was one of the reasons why women placed flowers and herbs under pillows on the eve of Midsummer.

It's a holiday that has retained its authenticity to this day and is celebrated wholeheartedly in Scandinavia. This year, in 2023, it's going to be celebrated on the 24th of June.

WHY WAS MIDSUMMER CELEBRATED?

Midsummer was a time to pray for abundance in the harvest. The harvest in question was not just that coming from crops and farming. Fertility, especially in women, was celebrated, and those who had been newlywed were honored and prayed for so that they'd have good offspring. It was a time to celebrate the serenity of nature, something that the Norse folk had very little of during the winters.

The Swedes, Finnish, and Danish all celebrate it in their unique ways.

The people of Sweden often moved to greener pastures during this holiday to celebrate in nature. For them, the Midsummer festivities began on Midsummer's Eve. During the day, they collected herbs, flowers, and greenery to make flower crowns and to decorate the maypole.

A maypole was a long pole that had been painted green or white, wrapped in several colorful ribbons, and then decorated with flowers. It was then raised in a very green and open area, such as a garden or a field, and then the people danced around it to commemorate midsummer.

The evening itself was a huge event with many people gathering together to party, feast, eat, drink, and dance. The evening had a special significance when it came to romance. If a woman put flowers under her pillows on this evening, she'd get visions and dreams of her future husband.

Swedes ate traditional Swedish dishes like herring, potatoes, and lutefisk on this holiday. Speaking more on this subject, there were also loads of aquavit (a distilled spirit native to Scandinavia), grilled fish and meat roasts. For dessert, people ate lots of strawberries with cream.

A dish made from fermenting herring called Surstromming has a very pungent flavor and smell, and midsummer is considered incomplete without it. During the celebrations, people gathered around the table with their family and friends and used Surstromming as the main dish for dinner. Of course, it came with sides of sour cream, chopped onions, boiled potatoes, and crisp bread.

HOW I CAN CELEBRATE MIDSUMMER

As a Norse Pagan, now is your time to make your festivities public and let it be known that you're going to uphold ancient traditions. Today, you can add your own dash of fun to things by making midsummer celebrations unique. Of course, you are expected to go outdoors and celebrate with traditional foods and drinks, do flower wreaths, and light bonfires, but you can do it all by adding your flair to things.

Go out!

The Swedes used to run to the hills and pastures during midsummer. So should you. Any green place would work, really, as long as you can be there and be festive. The subtler intent behind the meadow frolicking and pasture dancing is a deep appreciation for the bounties of summer.

Greenery, free-flowing water, blue skies, and the resplendent sun—these are all hallmarks of summer and a time when the Norse used to make the most out of this weather by harvesting, farming, and tilling the soil.

It doesn't just have to be some public green place; you can book a summer cottage, go out into the woods, or camp by a placid lake. Remember, it's all about leaving your unique footprint on the celebration.

Berries and Cream

While, okay, yes, for the more pedantic of my readers, I acknowledge the fact that strawberries technically belong to the banana family, but for the sake of the celebration, we're still going to count them as berries. Besides, there are also blueberries, mulberries, cherries, and all sorts of other fruits that exist in the legitimate berry family that you can include in your feasting.

And this is a day for traditional feasting. A day where pickled herring, salmon, vodka, schnapps, and healthy servings of potatoes and onions are supposed to entice you and then assuage your hunger.

Make use of the internet's rich reserves of recipes to make strawberry shakes, smoothies, cakes, and desserts. You can combine going out and feasting by taking some of your friends and family out for a picnic, complete with a checkered cloth and a big picnic basket.

Don't Forget the Flower Crowns

One of the more quintessential of midsummer celebrations are the flower crowns that are made from wildflowers found in summer fields. If you can, be very liberal with the flowers. Put 'em in vases, hang 'em in the maypole, make wreaths out of them, and of course, the flower crowns. And then dance with the scent of those flowers intoxicating you, giving you a natural high. Feel the nature all around you, on top of your head, and under your feet as you try to envision how the old Norse must have felt during this time. It's one of the ways you can be close to your ancestors during midsummer.

Mark the Occasion with a Bonfire

No midsummer would be complete without a bonfire, a bonfire specifically for the purpose of keeping the light going even at nighttime and for drawing away all the horrors, dark forces, and evil entities in the area.

If you're living in the American Midwest or Scandinavia, midsummer might be an excellent time for you to find a midsummer festival going on in your vicinity. They raise the midsummer pole, dance to traditional Scandinavian music, and make collective wreaths. Most modern-day festivals also offer meals, lodging, and plenty of activities throughout the entire day.

CHAPTER 9
FREYFAXI

Freyr was one of the most revered of the Norse gods. Originally a Vanir god, he was sent to Asgard after the Æsir-Vanir war and lived there with his sister and father. He later became the ruler of Alfheim, the home of the elves.

As the god of fertility and peace, he was linked to a good harvest, sunshine, the weather, favorable wind, prosperity, and male virility. Of his many responsibilities was to provide abundance, joy, good weather, great harvest, reward hard work, and give courage where courage was needed.

He could control the weather, especially the rain and the sun. He'd come to the help of those who needed his aid when it came to growing their crops.

But that did not mean that Freyr's expertise and godhood were limited to just agriculture. He was a major god, along the ranks of Odin and Frigg, and Thor.

THE CELEBRATION OF FREYFAXI

Also called Freysblót, the celebration behind this day is supposed to be an introspective one, calling to mind the fact that even though most of us do not practice farming ourselves, we still rely upon it just as our ancestors did thousands of years ago. We still eat the food that the farmers grow; it's just now we get it from farmer's markets, the grocery store, and supermarts. But we must not lose sight of who is responsible for these bounties.

It's Freyr, god of the sun and rain and harvests. The Norse folk thanked him for his gifts at Freyfaxi. And just as they did then, so should we now because without Freyr's light shining upon us, we wouldn't be able to get food.

Celebrated at the end of July or at the start of August, it falls in line with Lammas.

Historically, people used to celebrate this day by baking phallic-shaped bread to honor Freyr. It wasn't all phallic shaped, even though the phallus is one of Freyr's symbols, what with him being the god of male virility.

VENERATING FREYR

In terms of temperament, Freyr's more of a calm and cool god. He's easy to work with and venerate. It's almost second nature for him to come down and help those who direly need his aid in terms of farming, agriculture, and harvesting. But that is not the entire scope of his help.

Today, on Freyfaxi, you can venerate him for any number of reasons:

- If you're a parent, you can thank and venerate Freyr for making you a parent. As the god of male fertility, Freyr's responsible for ensuring that people get blessed with children. Well, it's a joint effort between him and Freya, his sister.
- If you're a landowner and use that land to grow crops.
- If you've particularly enjoyed the summer and spring seasons this year. Freyr's responsible for that in large part, as he controls the rain, the sunshine, and the wind.

When making an offering to him, you can place baked bread on the altar. The ingredients of this bread must be as natural and organic as possible, as Freyr's kind of a stickler for that. Any locally grown or organic food would be excellent as an offering to him. If it's a meal that you're offering as a sacrifice, make it a homely, nice meal that comes from humane and ethical sources.

Freyr loves his beer and cherries. Consider offering him a local craft beer and a bowl of cherries with a side of bread.

It doesn't just have to be food. You can offer him clothing. He's fond of linen—it being a plant fiber—and cotton. Freyr's favorite colors are gold, green, and yellow. He used to wear this special crown made from wheat, barley, and leaves. If you make that, you'll have his attention for sure.

He was not big on hostility, so offering him any weapons—even something as trivial as a belt knife—would not be wise. While other gods might appreciate weapons—Odin, Thor, Heimdall, to name a few—Freyr does not want any sort of weapons as offerings or in the vicinity of his blót.

One special sign that Freyr's going to send you, especially if you've called onto him and are in need of his help, is he's going to blow on your chest or forehead. You'll feel a gentle wind there. This, according to him, is called blowing his light into you. Afterward, if you concentrate, you'll feel a coolness coming off from where he blew into you.

A simple Freyfaxi ceremony can include the following:

1. A sacred space
2. Some attendees for the event
3. Venerating Freyr by reading Skaldic poetry
4. Filling a horn with mead and passing it around while toasting Freyr and asking for his blessings
5. Hailing Freyr and emptying the libation for the local spirits

Begin by setting up a space that you've consecrated for the blót. Welcome everyone who's attending and have them seated around a circle. Then, explain the purpose of the blót out loud.

"Today, we're here to honor and venerate the Norse god, Freyr, the lord of Alheim, a chief Vanir."

Pass around the horn of mead to everyone attending, and then have each of them toast him by saying, "Hail Freyr, god of sunshine, god of rain, god of the summer harvest. Bless us with your abundance, Lord of Alfheim. Bless us with your prosperity, O' wise and generous Freyr. Hail Freyr!"

If anyone has any offerings to make for Freyr, they can place them at the helm of the sacred space, where you can place a makeshift altar. Once the horn of mead has made a complete circle, hail Freyr one last time and then pour the libation out in the open.

In doing so, you'll have pleased Freyr and will have ensured that the god of fertility bestows his blessings on you and the attendees of the blót.

CHAPTER 10
HAUSTBLÓT

Around the 20th to 23rd of September, the Norse pagans used to celebrate the autumn equinox, also called the Haustblót. It was a time for them to anticipate the shortening of days as the winter neared. For the next six months, winter's hold would be long, fierce, and dark. At this time, the crops were coming to an end, and those in charge of harvesting them were starting to gather and preserve them for the long winter ahead.

At this time, in the autumnal season, the world became red and colorful, with various shades of red, orange, and yellow, everywhere as far as the eye could see. Some likened it to blood, others likened it to fire. At this time, the animals started to hibernate and birds migrated to warmer locations. Ravens would be seen flying across the horizon, seeking carrion.

For the Norse folk, this was a time to give thanks to the gods and goddesses of fertility for the bounties they had gifted in the summer. These bounties would see them through the winter. It was also a time to pray to the gods, the spirits of the land, nature, and the ancestors to look over the people, to give them courage, and to keep their hearts and hearths warm in the winter. The Norse folk believed in elves—as we've seen in Alfablót—and they considered these elves powerful beings who could turn the lands fertile if they wished. This was a time for the people to pray to the elves so that they'd maintain the lands during the winter so that they'd be fertile in the upcoming summer.

Haustblót was also known as the fall feast or Winter Finding. Remember the three sacrifices that Odin mentioned? One at the beginning of winter, one in the middle of winter, and the third in the summer? We've already covered the latter two. Haustblót was the one at the start of winter.

Besides the blót, people used to celebrate it with bonfires, singing, dancing, feasting, and bidding the summers goodbye. It was also time for the people to start gathering their livestock, such as their sheep, and round them up.

Every autumn task that had to be done was done around this time—gathering and storing wood for the fires, making sure that all the ships were tied and moored, ensuring that all the enclosures around the farmsteads were secure, checking on the food reserves to see if they'd last through the winter, doing necessary repairs around the house, making everything winter-proof, and preparing winter clothes for everyone in the house.

The two main deities who were venerated during this blót were Freyr—because he's the god of sunshine, prosperity, rain, and fertility—and Skadi—the goddess of winter, hunting, and frost.

HOW YOU CAN CELEBRATE

Bonfires, dancing, and feasting aside, this is a great time to start taking care of your pets. If you have dogs that are winter-sensitive, it's time to arrange indoor heating for them. The same goes for cats and parrots, especially if you're living in an area that gets affected by winter. Make sure that your animal family is in good health. It might be an excellent time to take them to a vet for their yearly checkup.

For some reason, it's just hard for me to picture barbequing in the summer. The heat of the grill and the whole hassle of having to maintain it in scorching temperatures is something that I'll never get. But come fall, especially on those crisp and cool nights, there's nothing better than a family barbeque. Just so we're on the same page, the family gets together for the barbeque, it's not the family that gets barbequed. And for Haustblót, I see no better reason than to take that grill out, light up the bonfire pit, and gather the family around for a nice barbecue.

If that's not your speed, then why not try your hand at a seasonal feast? Fall foods like squashes, nuts, root veggies, and apples can make one heck of a mean salad. It's a great time for foraging for wild edibles like pawpaws, walnuts, and crab apples. And since it's the fall, you can do with a plump pumpkin too.

While supermarkets and grocery stores have made the entire point of storing food redundant, there's still some traditional satisfaction to be had in going old-fashioned and canning your food, fermenting it, dehydrating it, and freezing it, especially if you want to keep true to the haust-blót theme.

The old Norse pagans used this celebration as a time to be introspective, thoughtful, and grateful. They thanked each other, the gods, and their ancestors for everything that they'd reaped during the summer. We can continue that tradition and be thankful for our prosperity, wealth, and happiness.

It's also a reminder to us that our ancestors, with sheer perseverance, hard work, and patience, harvested the land and reaped the rewards of their hard work. It's a testament to the fact that no effort goes wasted. If we can put this thought into daily practice, it can boost our morale and provide us with hope and courage. Hope and courage that we all need sometimes.

Now's your last chance to get in all the fall colors before the winter. A solitary or group hike might be an excellent opportunity to get all those fall sights in. Take a few hours out of your day today and indulge in all the colors that nature has to offer.

Lastly, as this is a blót, do not forget the chief gods and goddesses to venerate at an altar this time of the year. The ones at the top of your list should be Freyr, Gerðr, Freyja, Thor, Sif, Odin, Freya, and Skadi.

CHAPTER 11
VETRNÆTR

Cyclicality had been hardwired into the ethos of the Norse folk. It was a somewhat harsh concept that they had all come to terms with, whether it was in the form of Ragnarök (the destruction of the world and the death of the gods, followed by the rebirth of the world) or their daily lives (where they had to strive through the summers to be able to endure the winters), and in doing so had created a rich celebratory culture that propped it up.

End of the winter? That sounds like the best time for a feast and some merriment.

End of the summer? Oh well, we did as best as we could, and now it's time to reap the rewards of our hard work through some lively celebration.

WHAT IS VETRNÆTR?

It was in this similar vein that Winter Nights or Vetrnætr was celebrated. It held a significant position among their annual celebrations. Observed at the end of the summer and at the cusp of winter, Vetrnætr was one of the most mentioned celebrations in the old sagas. In fact, in the Ynlingsaga, it is mentioned alongside Jólablót—also known as Yule—and Sigrblót—which was the victory sacrifice at the start of each summer.

If you're wondering when Vetrnætr begins this year, it's on October 28th, 2023. It is said to occur on the first full moon of October. This was how the old Norse people kept track of time, by assigning it relativity to the moon. In this way, Vetrnætr was also said to be celebrated three full moons before Yule. Each new moon was the start of a new month for the Norse people, and some appearances of the moon were celebrated, such as Vetrnætr.

While Winter Nights were celebrated for many reasons, one of the main reasons for observing this celebration was the Wild Hunt. If you have read the Witcher books, played its games, or watched the TV show, you might have heard of the Wild Hunt. The Wild Hunt was this great, phantasmal nocturnal horde that stampeded across the night sky. It was also called Odin's Hunt or Terrifying Ride.

Some said that if the horde—that prowled through the wilderness—came across a person, or if a person was unlucky enough to look up to the night sky while the Hunt was on the prowl, they'd take that person's soul to Hel. It was said that the first frost of the year was left in the wake of the Hunt, letting people know that the horde has passed for the time being and also serving as a cause for celebration.

Other prominent reasons to celebrate this holiday included thanking the gods for a successful harvest and asking for their protection from the toils of winter. As hardy as the Norse folk were, they knew that they had to take the winters seriously. This celebration was done more in that vein than any other.

According to some sources, Winterfylleth, Haustblót, Disablót, and Winter Nights are just different names for Vetrnætr.

WHEN TO CELEBRATE IT?

Winter nights were celebrated in Gormánuður. It was a three-day affair that began on the first full moon after the first proper frost. Besides being a lunisolar calendar, the Norse calendar also relied upon weather patterns, which is why the exact timing of this celebration was not absolute. Later on, though, when the Viking Age arrived in 800-1000 CE, people began to celebrate Winter nights on a set date.

On modern calendars, the celebration lands between the 19th and 26th of October. According to historian Andreas Nordberg, major holidays, blóts, and sacrifices were held 28 days after an equinox or solstice, as we discussed in the previous chapter. This meant that the Winter nights took place roughly 28 days after the Autumnal equinox.

WAS IT JUST THE NORSE WHO CELEBRATED WINTER NIGHTS?

The Norse Sagas have clear and frequent mention of Winter nights. Therefore, it's safe to say that Winter nights fall within the Norse pagan branch of heathenism. Other celebrations that line up with Winter nights include Samhain, which is considered to be the origin of

Halloween. As Winter Nights is a Norse celebration, Samhain is a Gaelic one and is observed by modern-day Wiccans, Celts, Irish, and Scottish people.

Coming back to Winter nights, today, most Scandinavian organizations celebrate it and consider it a festival. All over the world, wherever there are Norse Pagans—such as in North America, Canada, United Kingdom, Winter nights are observed. Within Norse Paganism, communities like Ásatrú and Vanatru observe this celebration as it pertains to both the Æsir gods and the Vanir ones. Frey was honored during Winter nights as well as Odin, Skadi, and Ullr. Sometimes, even good old Thor was thrown into the mix.

For modern paganists, the Winter Nights have held the significance of being one of the primary festivals that also happens to be true to the lore, meaning it hasn't been reinvented or shaped in the past century. Even though our modern calendar has shifted so drastically, Vetrnætr still marks a pivoting point in the year when the sun and warmth finally retire and make way for the cold and dark.

As modern-day Norse Pagans, it falls on us to uphold the traditions of our ancestors, spiritual or otherwise.

HOW CAN I CELEBRATE VETRNÆTR?

Keep it simple

Unlike the bigger holidays like Yule, Vetrnætr does not require as much planning or preparation. This holiday comes at very short notice. More importantly, it's about spending time with your loved ones in the comfort of your warm home, gathered around a fireplace, welcoming the change in weather with songs, drinks, food, and laughter. It's a way to remind us that the coldest and darkest months can have the warmest and lightest moments.

Be generous

Speaking of which, one other purpose of Vetrnætr was to help people cope with the anticipatory anxiety of the upcoming challenges of winter. Nowadays, even though we have department stores, marts, and shops that have everything available year-round, this celebration can serve as a great reminder that the Norse folk found courage in each other's company despite the scarcity of resources. Perhaps that's what we need sometimes, too. It can also be a time when we become more mindful of those in the world who face shortages of food, water, and resources.

In that spirit, you can donate to your local shelter, soup kitchen, and charity organizations.

Feast with your family

You can invite your closest friends and family members for a dinner where you can perform a ritual blót and sumbel. Doing so can help you reconnect with your faith and assert the significance of the gods and goddesses, especially at this time of the year.

Welcome your forebears

Your ancestors are a part of you. This concept is seen in the Norse concept of soul. The Norse believed in a multi-faceted soul, with each part heading in different directions after a person's death. Our ancestors, through one of the facets of their souls, live within us.

When you gather around with your friends and family for the feast, invoke your ancestors, remember them, and welcome their spirit to the feast. You may remember them by sharing their life stories, discussing their acts of valor and honor, and talking about how they were in life.

Sumbel

A sumbel is a ritual wherein you make toasts to deities, your ancestors, and to the heroes of yore while drinking from a shared horn filled with an alcoholic drink, preferably mead or ale. Additionally, as is common during a sumbel, the last round of drinking comes with making oaths. As this is just the start of winter, now might be an excellent time to take some oaths.

Blót

You can honor the gods by symbolically offering food and drink to them. You can perform a blót by casting your offerings into a fire or by placing them at an altar.

The four gods that you should remember at this time, specifically for the blót and sumbel, are Freyr, Odin, Skadi, and Ullr.

Back in the old days, they used to offer meat as an offering to the gods, which made sense since a lot of the meat could not be stored for the winter. Meat, along with ale and mead, were the prominent offerings during the blóts historically.

Say a prayer

During these celebrations, the Norse folk used to say, "Til árs ok friðar!" which meant "to a good year and peace."

You can say this prayer with your friends and family, and add some more festivity to it, such as:

"To my friends and family,

May your bellies be full with warm food,

May your cups ever remain filled with good drinks,

May your kin and kith be safe from all harm and danger,

May your crops (businesses, endeavors, careers, etc.) grow,

May you prosper in every endeavor you partake in,

May your door be open to those less fortunate than you,

May your skills remain sharp and your senses agile,

May we all now feast as if we had Sæhrímnir in our hall and Heiðrun on our roofs!"

CHAPTER 12
ÁLFABLÓT

Álfablót, meaning ritual for the elves, was a sacrificial celebration that was shrouded in secrecy. Its significance has been attested in historical texts such as the Austrfararvísur. An excerpt from the text is as follows:

> "'Do not come any farther in, wretched fellow', said the woman; 'I fear the wrath of Óðinn; we are heathen.' The disagreeable female, who drove me away like a wolf without hesitation, said they were holding a sacrifice to the elves inside her farmhouse."

It is from this passage alone that it is clear that Álfablót was a secretive affair, unlike most communal Germanic celebrations.

The elves were thought to be these godly beings, possessing abilities like magic, grace, and splendor. They could interfere in the affairs of humans and make someone's health better or worse, depending upon that person's standing with the elves. The elves had their own realm called Alfheim, of whom the god Freyr was the ruler, along with his wife, Gerd.

This year, Álfablót will be celebrated on the 28th of October 2023 or the 27th of November during the full moon.

WHAT WAS ÁLFABLÓT?

Strangers were warded off at this time of celebration, and only those who belonged to the household could partake in this indoor ritual. Considering that most Norse rituals, in some way or other utilized the outdoors for their processions, the Álfablót was quite distinct in terms of this aloofness.

Even though there is not enough to go on, it's been gathered from resources and historians that animals were sacrificed, and their blood was poured on a cairn or a hilltop. The meat could have either been left for the elves as tribute or eaten by the people as part of a feast to honor the Alfheim residents.

One particular historical account from 14th-century Norway states that women used to bring food to caves and cairns and then consecrated it to the elves and then ate it later on. Just as offering food was considered important for this ritual, so was beer. Some men were designated as beer men, who had the role of providing beer as well as drinking copious amounts of it.

From here, we can infer that Álfablót involved sacrificing animals, followed by a feast and drinking. It is also suggested that since this was near the time of the Wild Hunt's appearance, there was an air of fear around this celebration. Perhaps that's why it was celebrated so furtively.

WHY WAS IT CELEBRATED?

This was a day to honor one's ancestors and other beings like elves and spirits of the land. In some accounts, it is believed that after a person died, in a specific case, they'd transcend into an elf. This was one of the many possibilities for those who had died. They could go to Valhalla, Folkvangr, Hel, linger as a spirit on earth, or, in this case, become an elf.

So, people had two causes to celebrate this day. Firstly, they could implore the elves to grant them favors. As mentioned before, the elves had almost godlike magical powers that they could use to bring about good health, luck, and prosperity to a person. Inversely, they could also bring bad luck and bad health to someone. Was it perhaps that the people were afraid of the elves' wrath that there was an air of fear around this celebration?

Other gods were worshipped and venerated during Álfablót, too, including Freyr.

The Norse folk believed that they were not alone in the world. Besides the gods, goddesses, animals, and plants, they believed that the world around them was filled with mystical creatures like sprites, supernatural entities, dwarves, trolls, huldras, and elves. Elves, the Norse people believed, could impart wisdom, guidance, and magical aid.

The people who celebrated Álfablót wanted to build a relationship with the spirits around them, particularly those of the elves, believing that these spirits were linked to the fertility of the land (a recurring theme for this time of the year) and their ancestors as well. It was a very exclusive time, one where strangers were not allowed near the farmsteads.

HOW WAS IT CELEBRATED?

You'd be surprised to know that this ceremony, quaint and secluded as it was, was initiated and administrated by the woman of the household.

Since this was a blót, like most blóts, it had three major parts—the consecration of the offering, the sharing of the offering, and the libation. In the past, the offering was an animal. For modern practice, you can either make do with food or meats that you sourced from a store strictly for the purpose of sacrificial offering. You can also make do with mead and beer and skip the meat entirely.

The first step was consecrating the offering, the leader of the ritual would offer the sacrifice to the elves, ancestors, and gods, and then sacrifice the animal. They'd then spill its blood on the ground. The remaining parts of the offering were served as a feast, the drinks as a libation, and then, after remembering the ancestors, elves, and gods, the ceremony would come to a close with a prayer.

HOW CAN I CELEBRATE IT?

Remember the intent behind Álfablót. It's to remember your ancestors and to get back in touch with the spirits of the land. You can take your cue from how Álfablót was celebrated by the old Norse people and choose to host a dinner just for your family. It's at this dinner that your family members can gather and drink toasts to the deceased members of your family and honor them by sharing their stories.

This can also be done after dinner, in your backyard, or around a bonfire.

Of course, if you have offerings, you can leave them by a makeshift mound, altar, or out in nature. Spirits and animals can come to find that offering easily.

AFTERWORD

While I have tried to present to you as many Norse Pagan holidays as I could, I will admit that this list is not exhaustive. Truth is, there's no list out there that's completely exhaustive. So much of our history has been lost. We have the sagas and the historical texts to guide us in the right direction, but even then, there's no telling how many other holidays and celebrations the Norsemen used to celebrate that have not made their way to us through history.

Some of them have been tarnished by Christianization, morphed, and disfigured from their original roots. Take Yule, Midsummer, and Freyfaxi for instance. It is because of the hard work of many pagans that we still have an understanding of the underlying real holidays and traditions that existed more than a thousand years ago.

But just as I have cautioned you right now, I must also give you good tidings. The good news is that the gods have not abandoned us. The mere fact that paganism and heathenry have been revived after all this time, its rituals, traditions, and celebrations being recreated by devoted pagans all over the world, is proof that the Norse gods are still there and they still care about people like you and me. Our efforts, our observance of the festivities, they're not wasted. Trust me. The gods and goddesses witness us, and when our need is dire, they come to aid us.

We must hold on to the hope that just as all of the current paganism has made its way back to us, so will more of it through the help of the gods. My effort to bring these celebrations to you and your efforts to read them and learn more about paganism can be likened to Odin's quest to unearth great mysteries. It was in search of these mysteries that he lost his eye. That he wedged his spear in his side and hung from the Yggdrasil for nine days and nine nights, bleeding out, he came out on the other side with the wisdom of runes, with the knowledge of fate and magic, and just like him, we're coming out on the other side with knowledge of ancient magical traditions.

I intended to share with you the Norse calendar and the major holidays through this book, and I feel like I have done that. Let's do a summary of everything we've learned in this book.

- In the beginning, we went over the Norse months of the year, the characteristics of the lunisolar Norse calendar, and what each month denoted. With an understanding of the agricultural and summer/winter polarized calendar of the Norse folk, we moved on to the major celebrations that they observed throughout the year.
- We began with Winter Nights and learned how the arrival of winter foretold a time of hardship for the Norse folk.

- In a similar spirit, we learned about Álfablót and how it was a time to venerate one's ancestors and the Alfheim elves.
- Next, we saw how the Norse people observed Þorrablót, a time when people bolstered each other's spirits to endure the rest of the winter.
- We also took a look at the Norse men's and women's day, Bóndadagur and Konudagur, and how both of them were celebrated.
- Moving on, we saw one of the important celebrations, Sígrblót, or the victory celebration that heralded the arrival of summer.
- Speaking of summer, we discussed the Nordic origins and celebrations of Midsummer, and what sort of cuisine was preferable at that time, along with the importance of flowers and green magic.
- We went over Yule and saw how this once Pagan celebration had been morphed into modern-day Christmas. In this critical chapter, I filtered out the original Pagan holiday, giving you the authentic experience of how Yule used to be celebrated.
- Then we learned about Disablót, a time to venerate the Dísir and female deities.
- The second last chapter was about Haustblót, a time to give thanks for the harvest and get ready for the winter by winding up one's autumnal tasks.
- Lastly, we saw how Freyfaxi or Freysblót was a time to venerate the god of sunshine, rain, harvest, and fertility.

And now, I am confident that you have the framework for the annual celebrations that the old Norse Pagans used to observe, that many modern-day neo-pagan organizations like Ásatrú observe to this day. Some of these are holidays and celebrations that are still being celebrated in Scandinavian countries, such as Midsummer.

The purpose of sharing insights about these celebrations was to instill a deeper appreciation for the old Norse culture that still lives on to this day in our hearts and in our practice. Equipped with this information, you can become the most authentic pagan version of yourself.

If you liked this book, I have two others that are all about Norse Mythology and Norse Magic. Please do check them out on my Amazon author's page to learn more about the Norse gods and goddesses, the Vikings, the history of the Norse folk, and how you can become a practitioner of Norse magic by utilizing runes—and so much more!

I'd love for you to share your feedback with me and rate this book on Amazon so that other readers who are looking for helpful stuff about Norse mythology can find their way to this book.

I am deeply grateful to you for reading and reviewing this book and for striving to become a better pagan.

Sjáumst sienna!

RESOURCES

1. Amajarl. (2022, January 20). Álfablót - The forgotten rite of ancestor worship. https://draugablikk.com/myth-mankind/alfablot-the-forgotten-rite-of-ancestor-worship/
2. Fornkunskap. (2014, October 1). Vetrnætr. https://fornkunskap.wordpress.com/2014/10/01/vetrnaetr/
3. Furstenau, S. O. (2022, January 1). The Old Norse calendar. https://www.icelandicroots.com/post/the-old-norse-calendar
4. Hartman, J. (2022, October 13). Vetrnætr for the family. https://www.pagankids.org/post/vetrn%C3%A6tr
5. Nomads, T. (2021, October 8). *The Norse Wheel of the year: The norse calendar & holidays*. Time Nomads | Your Pagan Store Online. https://www.timenomads.com/the-norse-wheel-of-the-year-viking-calendar-holidays/
6. Quickbutik. (n.d.). Álfablót - old norse Halloween - soldiser - norse jewelry & accessories. https://soldiser.com/pages/alfablot-old-norse-halloween
7. Rummel, R. (2018, September 6). *Iceland's Thorrablot Festival keeps Viking Cuisine alive*. Atlas Obscura. https://www.atlasobscura.com/foods/thorrablot-midwinter-festival-iceland
8. *Þorrablót*. Guide to Iceland. (n.d.). https://guidetoiceland.is/connect-with-locals/sigrunthormar/orrablot
9. Wikimedia Foundation. (2023, February 19). *Man's day and woman's day (Iceland)*. Wikipedia. https://en.wikipedia.org/wiki/Man%27s_Day_and_Woman%27s_Day_(Iceland)
10. Arithharger. (2017, March 21). *Sígrblót – the victory blessing*. Whispers of Yggdrasil. https://arithharger.wordpress.com/2017/03/21/sigrblot-the-victory-blessing/

11. Norman, R. T. (2023, May 21). *What are all of the Scandinavian midsummer traditions?*. Scandinavia Standard. https://www.scandinaviastandard.com/what-are-all-of-the-scandinavian-midsummer-traditions/
12. Viking Dragon / Jelling Dragon. (2021, December 13). *The origins of yule*. Viking Dragon / Jelling Dragon. https://thevikingdragon.com/blogs/news/the-origins-of-yule
13. Bernott, K. (2023, February 1). *What is Dísablót?*. SHIELDMAIDEN'S SANCTUM. http://www.shieldmaidenssanctum.com/blog/2023/2/1/what-is-disablot
14. Vanorio, A. (2022, September 5). *Haustblot: Norse Fall Feast*. Celebrate Pagan Holidays. https://www.celebratepaganholidays.com/fall/haustblot-norse-fall-feast
15. *Freyfaxi: The-Ásatrú-community*. the. (n.d.). https://www.theÁsatrúcommunity.org/freyfaxi

THANK YOU FOR LETTING ME BE YOUR GUIDE

I'm sure you're wondering how you can help others experience the same joy and fulfillment you have gained from reading all 3 of these books.

Leaving a review can be a great way. Your review can help people discover the book and provide an opportunity to share your experience and what you've learned on your journey.

To leave a review, scan the QR code above OR type http://amazon.com/review/create-review?&asin=B0CKJ7BBLL

www.ingramcontent.com/pod-product-compliance
Lightning Source LLC
LaVergne TN
LVHW041737060526
838201LV00046B/836